From
**Model Railroader**
M A G A Z I N E

# HO LINESIDE INDUSTRIES YOU CAN BUILD

KALMBACH **BOOKS**

The material in this book has previously appeared as articles in MODEL RAILROADER Magazine. They are reprinted in their entirety and include an occasional reference to an item elsewhere in the same issue or in a previous issue.

Publisher's Cataloging in Publication
(Prepared by Quality Books Inc.)

HO lineside industries you can build.
    p.  cm.
    "From Model railroader magazine."
    ISBN 0-89024-271-2

    1. Railroads—Models.  I. Model railroader.
TF197.H65 1996        625.1'9
                QBI95-20870

Cover Design: Kristi Ludwig

# CONTENTS

A tank car has been spotted at the Kehm Oil Co. by a Boston & Maine local freight, and it's time for the train to continue its daily run. The author photographed the scene outdoors on a small module; the locomotive is a Sunset Models HO scale B&M K-8 2-8-0.

# Bulk oil depots

In steam and early diesel days, these small facilities were found along sidings everywhere

### BY PAUL J. DOLKOS
### PHOTOS BY THE AUTHOR

BULK OIL DEPOTS, with their multiple tanks, catwalks, piping, and small sheds, offer an interesting contrast to the typically rectangular, generic structures of model railroad towns. The presence of tank cars is a nice contrast to the strings of boxcars parked at other industries on the layout. Since many dealers started in the coal business, you can even throw in a coal trestle for still more variety.

The concept of a bulk oil depot is simple. It receives large volumes of petroleum products (regular and premium gasoline, kerosene, diesel fuel, and heating oil), which are stored in the tanks. The products are then transferred to tank trucks, which deliver them to local customers. To accomplish the loading and unloading, there is an unloading pipe, where the product can be pumped into the selected tank. Then, on demand, the flow can be reversed through the pipe network to the truck-loading area.

Today petroleum products come to small bulk oil depots in highway tankers, not railroad tank cars. But that shouldn't get in our way. Even if we're modeling contemporary railroading, we can still have a bulk oil depot in our town scene. The only difference is that the rail siding — if it's still there — should be weedy and the tracks rusty.

#### TYPICAL DEPOT

The drawing accompanying this article shows a fairly typical facility arrangement. Once served by the Santa Fe, this bulk oil depot in Olathe, Kans., has since been dismantled. The photos of other facilities should help you with placing details and coloring and weathering the structure.

The typical number of storage tanks for a small-town depot is five or six. At some facilities all the tanks are identical; at others there are several different sizes. Most tanks hold at least a carload of 8,000 to 10,000 gallons or even more. These tanks are commonly 8 to 10 feet in diameter and anywhere from 15 to 30 feet long. A larger facility may have a couple of 50,000-gallon tanks.

During the 1950s there was a wide variety in tank installations because many tanks were built to order for the depot, others were purchased second hand, and even tank car bodies were sometimes used. You'll often see tanks

mounted horizontally on piers built up of steel, concrete, or brick, though tanks (usually higher-capacity units) are also found standing vertically on a gravel bed or concrete pad.

Tanks, generally painted white or silver to reflect the sun and minimize heat expansion of the liquid stored, were originally riveted together; in later years they were welded.

Ladders and catwalks provide easy access to the tank tops. There are relief vents on top of the tanks to release internal vapor pressure. On the side of the tanks a bolted access hatch permits cleaning. There is also a water-draw-off valve — a 1″ pipe located about 3″ above the tank bottom.

Many tank installations are surrounded by an earthen dike or concrete wall to contain the fuel in case of a leak. The containment capacity was supposed to equal that of the largest tank plus 10 percent. Generally bulk plants in small towns didn't have dikes, but this is a detail appropriate for an urban setting or a modern facility.

### UNLOADING DETAILS

There are two types of tank car unloading facilities. One is simply a hose that attaches to intake pipes low on the ground next to the siding. There are at least two unloading pipes, so a high-flash product like kerosene won't be pumped through the same pipe as gasoline, a low-flash fluid, and cause contamination. The other end of the hose is attached to the bottom valve underneath the tank car.

The more visible facility is a pipe stand that's about the height of a tank car. Part of the piping swivels so that it's at a 90-degree angle to the car. Another piece of pipe, which is loose and long enough to dip to the bottom of the car, is inserted into the car through the manhole in the dome and then coupled to the pipe, which swivels over the car. With either method, once the connection is made the petroleum is simply pumped out of the tank car.

**Above:** Depots had a variety of tank sizes. New tanks were added as additional types of fuels had to be stored and were placed wherever space permitted, resulting in a helter-skelter arrangement. This depot was in Bonner Springs, Kans. **Below:** This depot in Forest Jct., Wis., consists of four vertical tanks and a utility building with a platform for truck loading.

At the Purcell Oil Co. in White River Jct., Vt., tank cars were unloaded at ground-level pipes near the pump house shown in the center of the photo. Boxcars with packaged oil products were spotted at the large office/warehouse building farther down the siding.

# Typical small bulk oil depot

**1. COMBINATION OFFICE/WAREHOUSE.** Usually 12 to 18 feet wide and 18 feet long or longer. Drums of oil, grease, and other products are stored in warehouse prior to resale to service stations. Loading dock and doors could be located on rail siding so loads can be moved directly into warehouse.

**2. TRUCK LOADING RACK.** Company delivery trucks are filled here. Rack is built into dock in sketch. Rack may be an independent structure built with wooden posts and galvanized metal roof and walls. Various pipes lead to rack from tanks, through the pump house.

**3. STORAGE TANKS.** Their capacity is usually 8,000 to 10,000 gallons, but facilities in urban areas may hold as much as 50,000 gallons. Variety of shapes and sizes exist.

**4. TANK CAR UNLOADING.** Top unloading pipes shown. Alternate arrangement would be ground-level pipes with hoses that attach to bottom outlet valves of cars.

**5. PUMP HOUSE.** Small 5 x 6-foot to 8 x 12-foot building. 2 x 4 stud construction with galvanized metal roof and walls. May be built on a poured concrete slab.

**6. CATWALKS.** Wood or metal. Provide for easy access to tops of tanks for checking levels and safety valves.

**7. SHED.** Company delivery truck (or trucks) stored here.

**8. GAS PUMP.** For filling of company vehicles. Some larger depots may have their own garages as well.

**9. PORTABLE TANKS.** Loaned out to customers, such as farmers, who want bulk fuel storage at their own locations.

**Below:** Most elements of a bulk oil depot were at this Conoco depot in Olathe, Kans.: vertical unloading pipe stand, vertical and horizontal tanks, truck unloading pipes, and wooden walkways.

At a Texaco facility in Georgetown, Del., there are ground unloading pipes for the rail siding where the fuel is pumped into the tanks and then later into trucks for local delivery at the roofed loading rack.

When the Bolinger Oil Co. in Olathe, Kans., replaced its tanks with shorter ones, new piers had to be built. Note the containment dike, also the warehouse door for unloading packaged goods and drums.

### PIPING

All the tanks are tied together with a network of pipes varying from 1½" to 3" in diameter, depending on the volume of business. The pipes are supported 10" to 14" above the ground by small concrete piers. A pump ties the system together. Modern pumps are relatively small and found nestled in the piping network itself. Older facilities house the pump and the associated pipe manifold in a small pump house.

The pipes are painted either white or aluminum, and the line valves are painted to designate which petroleum product that particular pipe carries. In the Midwest at least, red designates regular gasoline, white premium, blue diesel fuel, and green kerosene.

At the truck loading end of the depot, the pipes emerge on a platform or loading dock. Here they swing over the top of the tank delivery trucks for loading.

### OTHER STRUCTURES

To complete the oil depot there will be an office, a warehouse, and possibly a garage, with none being very large. Sometimes the various functions are combined into a single structure. The warehouse would be used to store packaged petroleum products such as cans of motor oil, 55-gallon drums, and gasoline pumps and signs if the facility were an oil company distributor and served gas stations. One depot I observed had a warehouse door on the rail siding to receive packaged items from boxcars. This gives you a reason to drop off more than just tank cars at a bulk oil depot.

Some depots have a cluster of 50- or 100-gallon tanks on stilts stored on the property. These are loaned to customers, such as farmers who want to store fuel. Woodland Scenics offers 1:87 scale models of these semiportable tanks.

Another interesting detail found at many depots is a gasoline pump to fuel company vehicles.

### COMPACT COMPLEX

Even with all these components, not much real estate is required. A location that's just 60 x 150 scale feet is sufficient for a convincing model; even smaller spaces would work. Competing depots were often located next to each other on land leased to them by the railroad.

The simplest depiction of a depot would be to establish a car spot by placing unloading pipes on a town's public or team track. The petroleum would be pumped to an off-line location that may or may not be visible from the railroad.

### MODELING A FACILITY

So where do you start in organizing and duplicating these elements into a credible model? None of the elements of a bulk oil depot is difficult to build in model form. If you don't want to construct tanks out of an appropriately sized tube such as PVC pipe, you'll find many tank kits listed in the catalogs. I'd use the smaller ones, as large ones overpower the rest of the model. The wooden catwalks can be built up piece by piece with styrene or stripwood. Etched boxcar running-board material could be used for metal walkways. The pipe network can be made with styrene rod.

If your model will be in the foreground, you can incorporate pipe-joint and elbow detail into the piping maze. One source of this detail is the Williams Brothers fittings kit. Since my model is a couple of feet from the layout edge and the piping can't be seen clearly, it doesn't have such details.

The tanks offer large surfaces for the dealers' names, slogans, and oil company logos. When decorating the tanks of your model, consider whether the facility is locally owned. My model represents a local depot, using the owner's surname and selling a specific brand. I used logos from a tank car decal set and dry-transfer lettering for the signs.

There's something about an oil company sign, especially if it has the name and logo of a regional or long-gone brand, that attracts attention. Visitors to your layout will enjoy looking at a bulk oil depot, maybe as much as you do building one. ǭ

This truck-loading rack has steel I beams supporting the roof over a wooden dock. Details to model are the pipes, overhead light, covered pump, and "No Smoking" signs.

# Build a molding plant that

Varying rooflines, a variety of construction materials, and pastel storage tanks and piping add a lot of interest to this attractive modern plant.

# eceives plastic pellets by rail

Haines-Robinson Industrial Plastics could be a customer for your HO railroad

## BY JON GREGGS
### PHOTOS BY THE AUTHOR

THIS modern industrial plant started as a device to disguise a long empty stretch of basement wall with something more than an ordinary two-dimensional backdrop. A fellow railfan introduced me to the prototype during a casual afternoon of train photography. As soon as I saw it, I realized that this was *the* building to hide my wall.

The Haines-Robinson Industrial Plastics Co. is a manufacturer of foam insulation and plastic packaging. The general setup of the building is quite appropriate for any industry that uses plastic resin as raw material. Plastic granules are received from petrochemical companies in large covered hoppers. The number of inbound cars varies with business volume, so nearly any number of cars could be delivered on a model railroad. Normally, two cars sit beside the building, but a third isn't unusual. Granules are unloaded with a pneumatic pipe system that connects the silos and the plant.

Later, a second longer photo and notetaking session provided all of the information that I needed to develop the drawings and model. I couldn't get far enough away to take just one photo of the entire structure, so I wound up taking a number of overlapping side views to use in estimating dimensions. These estimated measurements turned out to be more accurate than you might expect, as the main structure is built entirely from 8″ x 16″ concrete block. I just counted the blocks to get the critical dimensions.

### GETTING STARTED

From the beginning, I planned to mount my HO scale plastics plant on a solid base made from 3/4″-thick plywood, 5′-2″ long and 8″ wide. Modelers in other scales will need to adjust these dimensions to suit. I used a piece of well-seasoned plywood (it had been inside for approximately a year) and reinforced it with two full-length stiffeners to prevent warping.

Lay out the inside wall locations and then glue 1/2″-square stripwood inside the lines on top of the base. Figure 1 shows this strip and the wall mounting method using small wood screws through the styrene feet. When the glue has

dried, seal all sides of the base with clear varnish to protect the wood from scenery materials.

To ease handling, I suggest splitting the project at the middle joint and working on the walls as north and south sections. Begin each portion by organizing and numbering the pieces of block material. The plans show the arrangement I used, which varies a few scale feet in length to match the cast block wall sections. There are five additional rows of blocks along the top of each wall piece. It's a good idea to cut and label the pieces and fit the detail parts prior to final assembly.

The uppermost wall sections are Evergreen metal siding or roofing, and the foundation is plain .040″ sheet styrene. Figure 2 shows my wall pieces with some completed details. I cut out the detail openings using a small saw, a sharp hobby knife, and a small flat file. Most of the ventilators, both exposed and covered, have louvers made of Evergreen 1 x 4 or 1 x 6 strip.

Pikestuff no. 1009 ventilators are fitted in two places for variety, but they're really too big to be used unaltered. Make the rounded covers by first

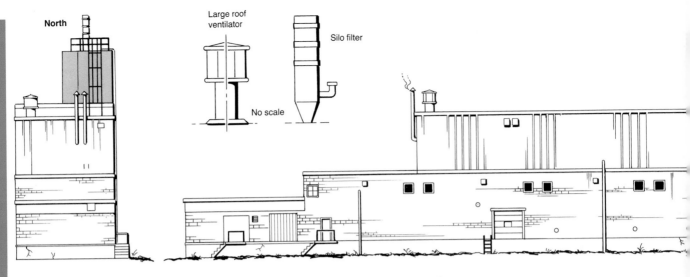

North

Large roof ventilator

Silo filter

No scale

## Bill of materials

**Detail Associates**
2504 .012″ brass wire
2507 .022″ brass wire
2509 .033″ brass wire

**Evergreen styrene**
4521 metal roofing, 1 pkg.
4529 metal siding, 2 pkgs.
8102 1 x 2 strip, 2 pkgs.
8104 1 x 4 strip, 1 pkg.
8106 1 x 6 strip, 1 pkg.
9010 .010″ plain sheet, 1 pkg.
9020 .020″ plain sheet, 2 pkgs.
9030 .030″ plain sheet, 2 pkgs.
9040 .040″ plain sheet, 1 pkg.

**Grandt Line**
5156 nut-bolt-washer castings

**Microscale decals**
87-002 freight car data
87-527 modern diesel

**Pikestuff**
1004 long block wall, 4
1005 intermediate block wall, 1
1006 short block wall, 2
1010 cement staircase, 2
1102 solid entry door, 1
1107 freight door, 1

**Tichy Train Group**
8002 safety cage ladder and staircase, 2

**Woodland Scenics**
ballast
field grasses
ground foam

**Miscellaneous**
ABS plastic pipe, 1½″ o.d.
brass tubing, assorted
corrugated aluminum
cyanoacrylate adhesive
Hydrocal or casting plaster
liquid plastic cement
matte medium
paints
plywood, ¾″ thick
styrene rod, assorted diameters
weathering chalks

attaching .020″ styrene quarter-circle sides to the wall, bending the curved front section (.010″ sheet) by hand, and then cementing it in place starting at the top wall joint. Next, line the window openings with 1 x 4 strip and add the Pikestuff doors. I compromised on the large vehicle door at the north end and used Pikestuff's no. 1107 door. However, I scratchbuilt the freight door at the south with a laminated styrene frame set into the surrounding blocks. See fig. 2.

The personnel doors are all Pikestuff no. 1102, with the doorknobs shaved off. Make the stairs from Pikestuff no. 1010 steps with the sides removed. For the platforms outside the doors, laminate thicknesses of .020″ sheet styrene and butt-join them to the stairs. It's a good idea to wait until you've finished painting the walls before installing the stairs and their .012″ brass wire railings. I didn't wait and found the steps were in the way. Two doorways at the far south end are filled in, one with concrete blocks and the other with siding that matches the upper walls.

## THE WALLS AND DETAILS

When you have all the wall pieces ready, start cementing them together. Figure 3 shows my method of bonding the wall sections by applying liquid cement from the back, using a steel rule and a ceramic tile to ensure straight and flat wall sections. Be sure to match the proper ends of the Pikestuff blocks, as it does make a difference.

Next, combine the completed walls to make a three-dimensional building. Check the corner alignment with a square as each joint is made. See fig. 4. Then add reinforcing gussets in the corners and strips of ¼″-square styrene inside the top edges of each wall as shown in fig. 5. Cement the roof panel of .030″ styrene to the underside of these strips, and allow the assembly to set hard. Finally, completely enclose the ¼″-square strip with additional styrene strip as shown in fig. 6. More gussets may now be added between the roof and walls.

I found that most of the small details are easier to install after painting. These items include the fire bell (made from a

**Fig. 1. ANCHORING WALLS, Above:** The author recommends using a few strips of ½″-square stripwood to back up all of the joints that are located between the walls and the base. He used wood screws driven through plastic feet to hold everything in place.
**Fig. 2. WALL FABRICATION, Right:** Each of the wall sections must be trimmed and have its openings cut and fitted before the different subassemblies are cemented together.

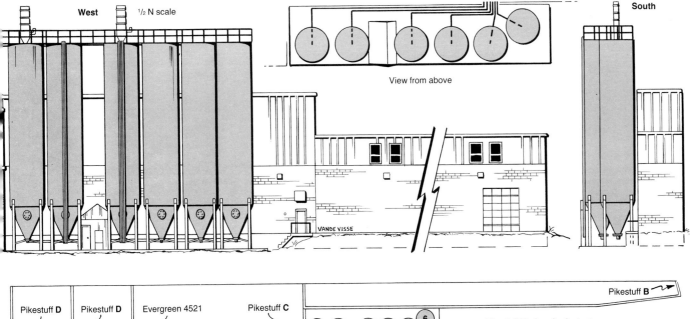

West    ½ N scale                                                    South

View from above

Pikestuff **D**   Pikestuff **D**   Evergreen 4521   Pikestuff **C**                                            Pikestuff **B**

① ② ③ ④ ⑤ ⑥        Pikestuff block    **A**: shortest
                                          selections        **B**: short
                                                            **C**: intermediate
                                                            **D**: long

West elevation showing        Scratchbuild          No scale              Pikestuff 1102              Pikestuff 1107
wall construction

Evergreen                       Evergreen 4521       **A**   Evergreen 4529        Evergreen    4529
4521

**B**  **C**    **D**    **D**    **D**   **D**    **D**    **D**    **D**   **D**  **B**  **D**  **B**  **D**    **C**

VANDE VISSE

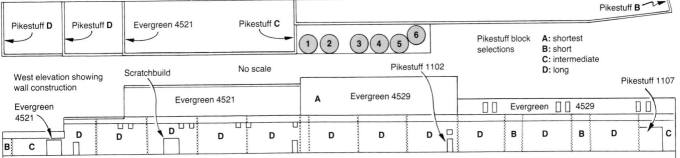

1:144 scale aircraft wheel), mercury-vapor lights (laminated styrene), Tichy Train Group safety cage ladder at the back of the main roof, discharge tubes (sprues from Tichy's ladder and .040″ wire), and window glazing. Add small sheet-styrene boxes, painted black, behind each of the windows to hide the empty interior.

Next, fabricate the large ventilator on the south end of the main roof from ³/₈″-diameter tube with a styrene base and a thumbtack top. Use pieces of ¹/₁₆″

aluminum tubing, cut a scale 14 feet long, to make a pair of gas stacks for the upper south end wall. Top them off with rain guards that are made from small brass roundhead screws with their slots filled.

## THE SILOS

Inexpensive ABS plastic plumbing parts make it easy to reproduce the plant's multiple silos. I found that sink waste pipes, or tailpieces, have an outside diameter of 1¹/₂″, which works out

to be about 11 scale feet. Saw off the end flange and use a miter box to cut two pieces 45 scale feet long. Make sure your cuts are square. Wet-sand each piece, first with 220-grit wet-and-dry sandpaper and then with 400-grit, to smooth the rough plumbing parts.

Through experimentation I invented a way to match the silo cylinder to the cone-shaped base. I cast each base with yellow dental plaster or Hydrocal, using a kitchen funnel as a mold. Either plaster works, and it's possible to cast

**Fig. 3. CEMENT APPLICATION.** A flat ceramic tile and a steel rule help align everything before liquid plastic cement is applied to the back of each wall joint.

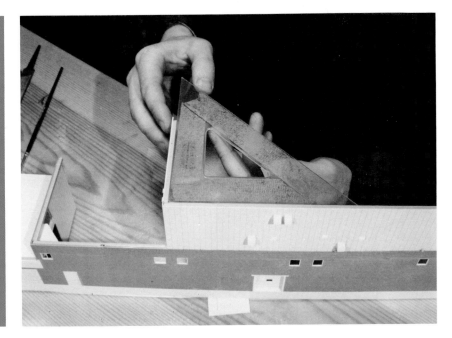

**Fig. 4. SQUARING CORNERS, Above:** A small Plexiglas drafting triangle is a handy lightweight tool that makes it easy to hold a joint square until the plastic cement sets.

**Fig. 5. REINFORCING CORNERS, Right:** Simple triangular gussets add strength to interior building corners and joints between the roof and side walls. Strips of 1/4"-square styrene are added along the tops of the walls to maintain alignment as well as to provide cementing surfaces for the inset roof installation.

**Fig. 6. COPING TRIM, Below:** Once the roof panels are in place, strip styrene trim is added along the edge to get a finished appearance.

**Fig. 7. CASTING SILOS.** The author uses a "third hand" device to clamp the plastic funnel and tubing in the proper positions to cast the tapered end of a silo with molding plaster.

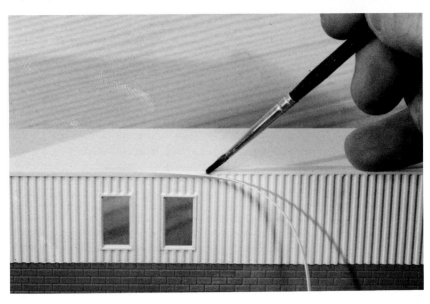

**Fig. 8. SILO SUPPORTS.** Square brass tubing is used for the supporting legs of each silo. Bits of brass wire serve as the cross bracing.

the cone right onto the cylinder as shown in fig. 7.

Alignment is critical as the pipe must be vertical, with the funnel squared up and centered beneath the cylinder. Plug the bottom of the funnel before pouring the plaster. Use enough plaster to fill the bottom 1″ of the pipe so it provides plenty of support. If the cone casting doesn't look right, break away the plaster while it's still damp and try again. I did find that once the plaster has fully hardened, it really sticks to the plastic.

Carefully scrape away any excess plaster with a knife. By being careful, I was usually able to get a short length of plaster out of the funnel neck with each cone to help simulate the discharge outlets. I let the plaster castings harden until they're completely dry, which usually takes several days. Then I paint them and fill any visible air bubbles.

My silo legs are $3/32$″-square brass tubing, $14^{1}/_{2}$ scale feet long. The prototype silos have round legs set into the edge of both the cone and the vertical cylinder, but this is one of the hardest joints to duplicate in the modeling world. Matching 1 or 2 joints in this manner wouldn't be too bad, but 24 is too much hassle. Lots of industrial silos have square legs, so that's what I used on mine.

Wrap a paper collar around the pipe, fold it into quarters, and use it to mark the leg spacing on each cylinder. I used cyanoacrylate adhesive (CA) to secure the brass tubing to the plastic pipe. See fig. 8. Next, make the small braces from .022″ brass wire and attach them to the base of the cone with more CA. I finished off the bottom of each cone with styrene shaped to match the actual piece and two small holes for the outlet piping.

Careful attention to small details like the pastel color-coding, safety railings, tank supports, and pneumatic piping is necessary to obtain maximum realism in any modern industrial model.

The silo tops are covered with rough-cut .020″ sheet styrene cemented in place with thickened CA. After the CA has set hard, shape the styrene to match the cylinder.

Cut the silo walkway base as a single piece made from .020″ styrene. My northernmost octagon was incorrect, so I chopped it off and made another. The sketch in fig. 9 shows the method I used to make the railings, though Plastruct molded railings could be used. A North-West Short Line Chopper makes short work of the 300 or so pieces of Evergreen 1 x 2 strip required. Be sure to let each step dry for a few minutes — and squint to check the alignment as the scale 1 x 2 is small.

When everything is attached, the railings are surprisingly strong. My walkway is connected to the building with another Tichy safety ladder with extra 1 x 2s inside the safety hoops. The ladder ends at the building edge with additional safety caging.

Rectangular mechanical control and filter boxes sit atop the first and third silos. I made mine from laminated styrene, shaped to match the photos and detailed with six Grandt Line nut-bolt-washer castings on the braces of the upper portions. Finish the silos by adding square lifting rings to the top edges in places where they don't interfere with the walkway.

My silos sit on a double thickness of

Very little model railroad real estate is required to add this major industry to an HO layout. Note the spillage beneath each unloading connection.

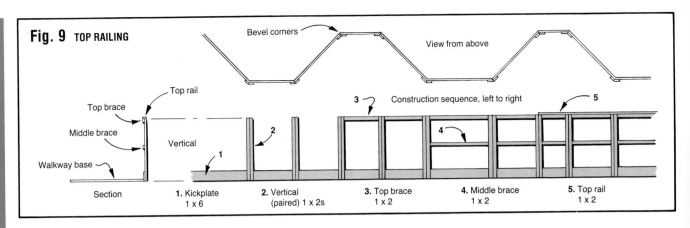

Fig. 9 TOP RAILING

Bevel corners — View from above

Top rail

Top brace

Middle brace

Vertical

Walkway base

Section

3 — Construction sequence, left to right — 5

4

1. Kickplate 1 x 6
2. Vertical (paired) 1 x 2s
3. Top brace 1 x 2
4. Middle brace 1 x 2
5. Top rail 1 x 2

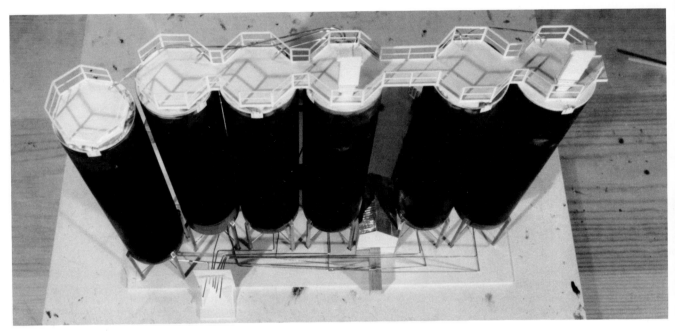

**Fig. 10. SILO DETAILS.** Scratchbuilt railings and pneumatic piping must be carefully fitted to keep everything straight during assembly.

.040″ sheet styrene that represents a concrete pad. It takes a while to get all six silos mounted in a straight line and vertical. Glue thin cardstock shims to the underside of individual silo legs. Small pegs of plastic rod may be used to hold the alignment. Once you've positioned the silos, build and install the pump shed between them. See fig. 10.

Make the rear vacuum tubes, which run from the bottom of the silos into the building, using .033″ brass wire. One set disappears behind the shed; the other leads into separate openings behind silo no. 5. It's impossible to test-fit these tubes with the silos against the building, so I glued a template to the back of the pad to align the tubes as shown in fig. 11.

### ELECTRICAL EQUIPMENT

After you've finished the tubes, move the concrete pad to its location beside the building and drill the holes for the tube ends using the jig. Use the same procedure to build and locate the six pneumatic tubes on top.

I put a lot of effort into scratchbuilding

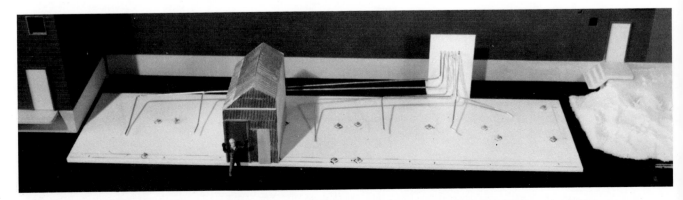

**Fig. 11. PIPE TEMPLATE.** Low-level pneumatic tubes are simulated with brass wire that's bent to fit into a template made of scrap styrene.

The template is used later to drill the mounting holes through the building wall and then it is discarded during the structure's final assembly.

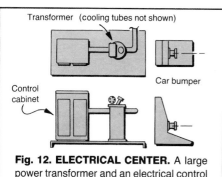

**Fig. 12. ELECTRICAL CENTER.** A large power transformer and an electrical control box are located adjacent to the building.

my transformer and control cabinet. Since then, Walthers has released an electric utility pole set that includes transformers that will serve just as well. My control cabinet is a simple styrene box with wire handles.

### FINISHING DETAILS

A fire standpipe and its protective post stand next to the transformer. Fabricate them from styrene rod and nut-bolt-washer castings for the hydrant valve and covers. The railcar vacuum pipe is .060″ styrene rod, a scale 80 feet long, with intakes near each end and every 15 feet or so (six altogether). The last intake is just beside the little shed.

### PAINTING

Painting the plastics plant and its parts takes almost as long as building them. I used Testor's Model Master paints, using an airbrush on most of the structure. Only the smallest detail parts are brush-painted. I mixed most of the colors to match the original building, but I had trouble getting certain hues as most hobby paints are already color mixtures.

I painted everything before doing the final installation on the base. It's best to paint both major building sections beginning with the foundation and working upwards with progressive tape and paper masks to protect previous colors. I used four different reds on the concrete block sections to reflect different paint jobs on the prototype.

The transformer control cabinet needs many warning and information stickers. See fig. 12. I found them on Microscale's nos. 87-527 modern diesel and 87-002 freight car data decal sheets. They're too small to read, so I just matched shapes and colors. The fire bell markings are from the same sets. I used a cutdown lube plate to simulate the prototype's black triangle which says, "Phone the fire department if bell is ringing."

### FINAL INSTALLATION

Installing the building sections is easy: Just run the mounting screws into the prepared holes in the mounting strip. Once the building sections are in place, add a tar roof with flat black enamel. After the paint has dried, flood the roof with matte medium and sprinkle on very fine ballast.

The concrete pad (without the jig) goes on next, then the silos with their individual lower vacuum pipes. Use thickened CA for this to provide enough setting time to get everything aligned properly. Don't forget the shed.

Attach the walkway across the top of the silos next. I had to add an extra small bridge between the fifth and sixth silos to replace the one I removed earlier. Add the top vacuum piping for each silo, the mechanical units on silos 1 and 3, the ladder and safety cage down to the roof, and the small lights between the piping to complete the structure.

Use Shinohara code 70 flextrack to simulate the prototype. The track should be almost invisible . . . about as neglected as track can get. To duplicate this appearance, pour a thin mix of casting plaster right over everything. You now have about 10 minutes to get the tops of the ties and the sides of the rails uncovered. Work on short sections at a time, and keep a damp brush and plastic scrapers ready to remove excess plaster. Use an eyedropper to apply plaster close to the building. After the plaster has set, paint it dark gray to match the local soil. The rails should also be painted a dark rusty color.

Apply fine ballast and turf-sized ground foam, using matte medium as an adhesive. Cover most of the scenery with the low materials, and add patches of tall weeds made with Woodland Scenics new field grasses. I used two different colors (Natural Straw and Harvest Gold) for more realism and trimmed them to a scale 12″ to 18″ high after the glue set.

Powdered chalk is an excellent weathering medium. Again, I use a dark gray to match the local soil, which is very fine and blows everywhere. Put gray chalk dust on everything, some for general blending and softening of colors, and some on the building to match specific dirt and discoloration patterns. Small amounts of yellow, brown and black add contrast. Little piles of coarse white chalk duplicate the piles of spilled granules around the intake piping.

Once you're satisfied with the effect, spray on several light coats of acrylic matte varnish to secure the chalk. Then Haines-Robinson Industrial Plastics is ready to receive its first carload delivery of plastic granules. ⏻

# Welte Lumber & Millwork

## An HO kitbash that goes up and out

**BY BILL LORENCE**
**PHOTOS BY THE AUTHOR**

WELTE LUMBER & MILLWORK CO. is an old Shenandoah firm that has expanded over the years from one lumber shed to two; then as their business flourished they added to the second shed, making it long and narrow. Finally, the company expanded even further to include millwork. However, space was getting cramped, so old Clarence Welte decided to go up, building the new millwork shop atop the existing sheds directly over the tracks.

Over the years Clarence used the same basic design to expand his original lumber sheds. He did the same with the millwork shop, more or less. In fact, the motto Clarence lives by is "If it works, stick with it."

The HO scale Welte Lumber & Millwork Co. is the blending together of three Atlas Lumber Yard kits (no. 705). Figure 1 is a drawing of the partially assembled structure. Notes refer you to other figures for specific details. The original shed (the short one on the far side of the tracks) is pretty much straight from the box, except for modifications to the roof and ends to accommodate the millwork structure that straddles the track. The expanded lumber shed (on the near side of the tracks) is made from the second and third kits. And the millwork shop is made from the leftover walls of the third kit and from Grandt Line windows. The cyclone is from Magnuson Models. The remainder of the project is built up of styrene and scale lumber — lots of it — in the lumber stacks.

### LONG SHED

Since the bases are integral parts of the structures, they must be modified and spliced together. Figure 2 shows where the cuts are to be made in the two bases and walls. Note that wall B will slightly overlap base A, the peg at the bottom left end of wall B fitting in the hole in the right end of base A. Also note that the corner of the right end of wall B must be beveled at a 45-degree angle to mate properly with the beveled corner of the end wall. Since I did not intend to use the workbench on the end wall of this structure, I carefully removed the cast-on tools, etc., before gluing the wall in place.

Begin assembly by cementing the bases together, and then position and cement the walls in place.

The next step requires some cutting and splicing of the post/beam assemblies. Each kit should include a pair of these: a tall one for the inside of the building and a shorter one outside. The same cuts, moves, and splices will be made for each pair. See fig. 2. Post/beam A goes unmodified. Be careful when cutting away the post on assembly B not to break away the brace that remains with the beam. Move the post as indicated, and cement assemblies A and B together.

Before gluing the post/beam assemblies in place, the upper deck (part 29 in the kit instructions) should be glued to the rear wall in each shed section. To make the deck fit properly against the B-end wall (fig. 3), you'll need to trim or file away a little of the left end of the long stringer directly behind the catwalk. Also file away the lug at the back of the left end of the catwalk.

The loading dock walls (parts 25 and 26) that support the dock floor are next. Glue them in place in base A as per the kit instructions; next, position the same walls from the other kit in the slot in base A where the two bases meet. Notch the left edge of the dock floor to accept the relocated post of post/beam assembly B. Glue the dock floor in place, and then position the post/beam assemblies and cement them in place.

Before going any further, now is the time to fill the sheds with lumber. This task will be much more difficult as the structure gets further along. I used several Grandt Line, SS Ltd., and Campbell window and door castings left over from previous construction projects. When you have stocked the interior for Mr. Welte, assemble the catwalk and ladders according to the kit instructions.

My next step was to cut a piece of old 3/16" paneling to fit the location on the layout and draw in the spur track location. At most of the lumberyards I've visited, the railhead was the only part of the spur visible. To achieve this same effect, I routed out the right-of-way with a knife and a chisel, spiked down the rail, and ballasted the track. The rail seems to disappear into the ground, and more important than how it looks, I got just a little bit more headroom for boxcars under the upper structure.

### MILLWORK SHOP

The next step is critical. Place the two roofless sheds (the original kitbuilt shed and the new kitbashed shed) on either side of the track, making sure that freight cars will clear the handrails on the walkways. I used an outside-braced boxcar as a clearance gauge, and it's

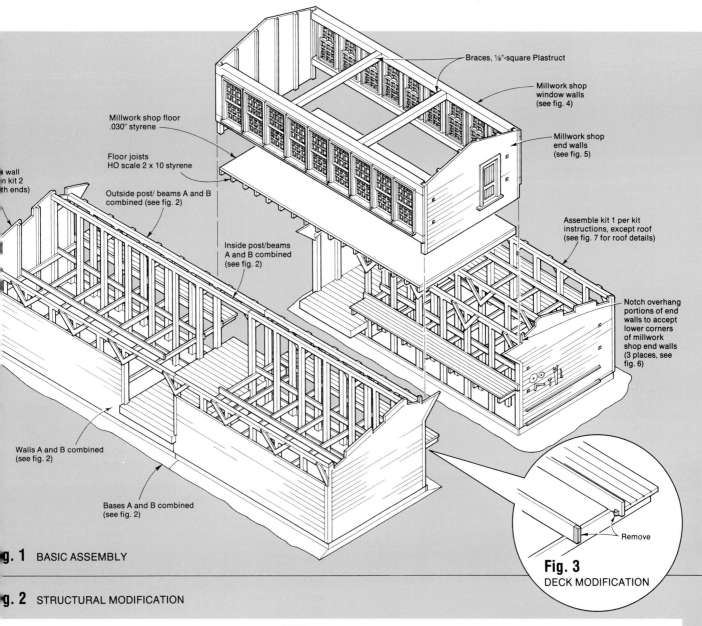

Braces, ⅛"-square Plastruct

Millwork shop
window walls
(see fig. 4)

Millwork shop
end walls
(see fig. 5)

Millwork shop floor
.030" styrene

Floor joists
HO scale 2 x 10 styrene

Outside post/ beams A and B
combined (see fig. 2)

Inside post/beams
A and B combined
(see fig. 2)

Assemble kit 1 per kit
instructions, except roof
(see fig. 7 for roof details)

Notch overhang
portions of end
walls to accept
lower corners
of millwork
shop end walls
(3 places, see
fig. 6)

wall
n kit 2
th ends)

Walls A and B combined
(see fig. 2)

Bases A and B combined
(see fig. 2)

**g. 1**  BASIC ASSEMBLY

**g. 2**  STRUCTURAL MODIFICATION

Remove

**Fig. 3**
DECK MODIFICATION

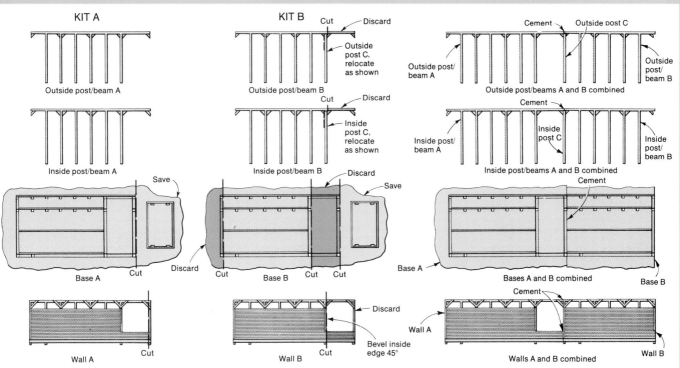

KIT A

Outside post/beam A

Inside post/beam A

Base A
Save
Cut
Discard

Wall A
Cut

KIT B

Cut — Discard

Outside
post C,
relocate
as shown

Outside post/beam B

Cut — Discard

Inside
post C,
relocate
as shown

Inside post/beam B

Discard
Save
Cut
Base B
Cut    Cut

Discard

Wall B
Cut
Bevel inside
edge 45°

Cement    Outside post C

Outside post/
beam A

Outside
post/
beam B

Outside post/beams A and B combined

Cement

Inside post/
beam A

Inside
post C

Inside
post/
beam B

Inside post/beams A and B combined

Cement

Base A

Bases A and B combined

Base B

Cement

Wall A

Walls A and B combined

Wall B

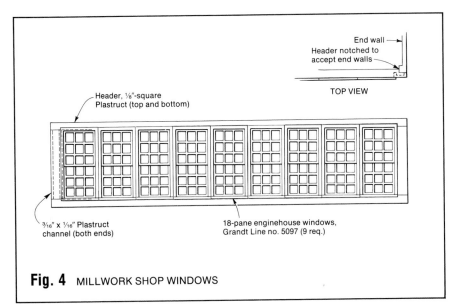

**Fig. 4** MILLWORK SHOP WINDOWS

*tight!* No clearance for a man on the car; that's for sure. Also, be careful to align the end walls of the two structures so that the end walls of the millwork shop will sit square.

Each of the two window walls (shown in fig. 4) is constructed by gluing together nine Grandt Line no. 5097 windows on a sill of ⅛"-square Plastruct stock. Use this for the header as well, notching the ends where they will meet the cast-on vertical beams of the end walls. Plastruct channel makes up the side framing and also extends the window walls. Use masking tape to maintain window alignment during gluing.

Since the window walls don't match the color of the kit walls, give them a coat of Polly S Reefer Gray mixed with White. After the paint dries, glaze the windows. And to give the building that "lived-in" look, use a hobby knife to crack a few panes and break out a piece here and there.

The end walls of the millwork shop are next. See fig. 5. These come from the two leftover ends of the lumber shed. Trim off the bottom, removing the cast-on lugs, foundation, and one wide board up from the bottom of the siding. Then, using the window walls to determine the height of the end walls, cut the sloping roof lines parallel to those of the original walls.

Temporarily place the four walls together to determine the size of the floor you'll need. Then cut the floor to fit from sheet styrene (scribed, if you plan to detail the interior) and glue scale stringers to the underside. Refer back to fig. 1. Once you have the floor completed, use this to determine the height at which the cast-on posts and studs must be removed from the bottom portion of the end-wall interiors.

Cut an opening for Grandt Line door no. 5131 in the front end wall for access from the exterior walkway. This will be built later.

One more step before assembling the walls — notch out three of the four lower walls (the wall at the far end of the long shed need not be altered) to receive the upper end walls, as shown in fig. 6.

Begin assembly by gluing one end wall in place atop the two lower walls. Next comes the preassembled floor. Position the ends of the window walls against the first end wall, and with the stringers resting on the beams from the sheds below, glue them in place. I glued the near end wall in place and then glued two ¹¹⁄₁₆" fillers in place below the window walls and butted against the end walls.

Before adding the roof to the mill, I put in a few silhouettes to look like machinery clutter and dirtied the windows so it isn't so easy to see through the building. On my structure this section has very dim interior lights.

### ROOFS

Roof sections for the sheds now need to be cut to fit around the millwork shop (fig. 7), saving the removed sections for use as portions of the roof for the millwork shop. Measure and cut the roof for the rest of the long shed, and splice it to the previous roof sections. Save the remaining piece of this roof to make the

**Fig. 5** MILLWORK SHOP END WALLS

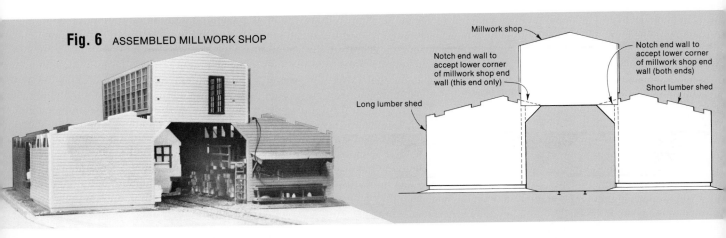

**Fig. 6** ASSEMBLED MILLWORK SHOP

fascia overhanging pieces required for the millwork shop roof.

Sand off all of the roofing details and then "reroof" them using single-ply tissue painted with Scalecoat Black. This gives the roof a tarpaper finish and blends all the sections together.

To build the roof for the millwork shop, start with the long strips left over from the lumber shed roofs. To the underside of these glue strip styrene to represent rafters, and then glue these so that they overhang the window walls. Cement pieces of strip styrene to the short leftover strips to represent fascia, and then glue these assemblies to overhang the side walls. After the overhanging pieces are in place, make up the rest of the roof from styrene sheet. Roof this over again using the tissue-paper method.

## STAIRS AND WALKWAYS

To provide access to the upper portion of the structure, a set of stairs and walkways must be constructed. Material from the original kits and some structural shapes from Plastruct form the framework for the walkways. Planking for the walkways is from scribed siding painted Polly S Reefer Gray. The steps are 3/8"-long strips of 1/8" styrene. I used Campbell stair stringers to form the stairs.

Start on the upper catwalk (fig. 8) by gluing 5-foot-long beams, made from leftover interior beams, as though they were the original lower-building roof beams extending out through the side of the building. Next, cut a length of Plastruct channel for the outside stringer under the platform, and glue it in place. Also glue in place a piece of Plastruct I-beam for a

center stringer. Finally, cement in three additional beams underneath the stringers.

While this assembly is drying, cement in place a stringer along the wall of the long shed at the same level as the kit walkway that runs across the open side of the shed. This stringer should be about 16 scale feet long and extend past the edge of the building the same as the interior walkway. To support the intermediate landing, cut and fit posts and beams from scrap material. The beams should be the same length as the width of the upper walkway.

Use channel for the stringers under this deck, but glue only the outside one in place at this point. Use a piece of the

original leftover shed siding (scribed styrene would also do) to extend the walkway from inside the building onto the intermediate platform.

Cement the stairs in place from the landing to the ground, and then glue the center stringer in place and add planking to this landing. Finally, after adding a post from the lower walkway to the upper walkway, glue the upper planking in place.

The end wall of the upper structure has some holes in it where the original structure had a workbench roof attached. On my building I used these to provide access for an electric line from the light pole in the yard, to attach supports for an access

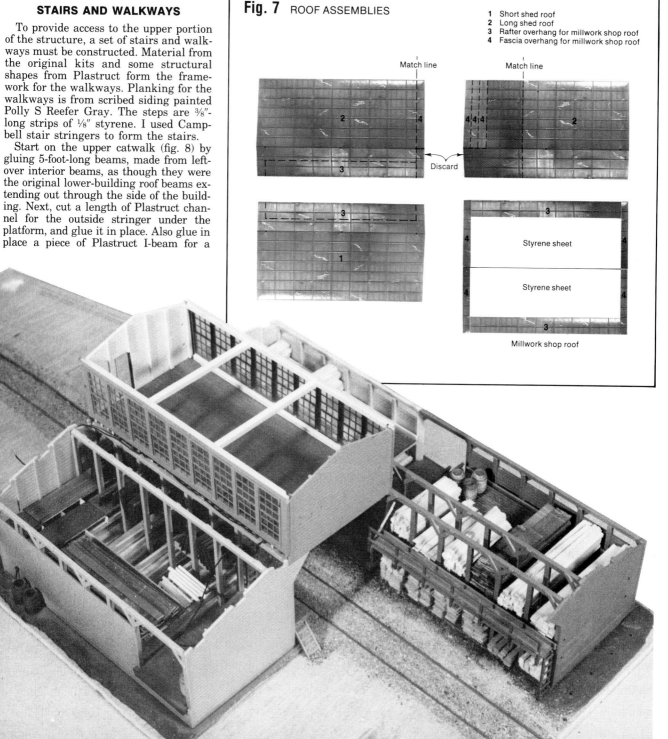

**Fig. 7** ROOF ASSEMBLIES

1 Short shed roof
2 Long shed roof
3 Rafter overhang for millwork shop roof
4 Fascia overhang for millwork shop roof

Match line

Match line

Discard

Styrene sheet

Styrene sheet

Millwork shop roof

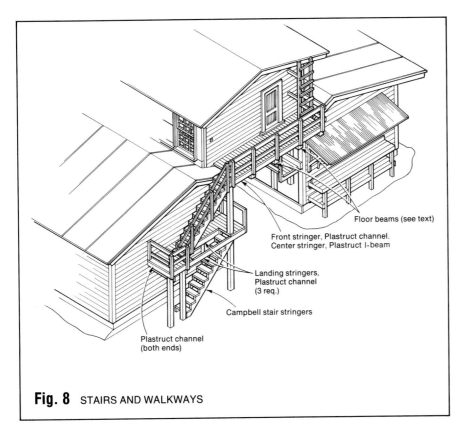

**Fig. 8** STAIRS AND WALKWAYS

Labels: Floor beams (see text); Front stringer, Plastruct channel. Center stringer, Plastruct I-beam; Landing stringers, Plastruct channel (3 req.); Campbell stair stringers; Plastruct channel (both ends)

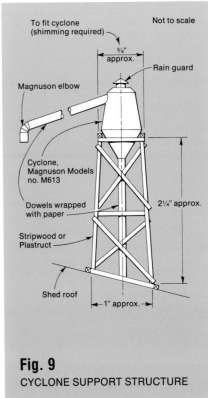

**Fig. 9**
CYCLONE SUPPORT STRUCTURE

Labels: To fit cyclone (shimming required); Not to scale; ¾" approx.; Rain guard; Magnuson elbow; Cyclone, Magnuson Models no. M613; 2¼" approx.; Dowels wrapped with paper; Stripwood or Plastruct; Shed roof; 1" approx.

ladder to the upper floor, and to glue one of the wall brackets for a portable ladder. Fill them in if you prefer.

I added handrails made from bits and pieces of the original kits and used Plastruct angle for the top rail. The legs from the unused cutting table worked out to be a great starting point for the additional handrails. The original roof supports also made good stanchions.

### WATER TANK

I formed the water tank on the roof of the long shed by wrapping scribed siding around a cardboard tube that had been cut to size and contoured to match the shed roof.

Before you glue the siding to the tube, lay it out flat and mark the location of the bands. Increasing the band spacing as you go up the tank side, score the siding along each band location. After staining the siding a suitable color, glue the siding to the tube.

After the glue has set drill one small hole through the tank at each band location, staggering the holes around the tank. To simulate the tank bands, pull a piece a thread from the inside out through each hole, run it around the tank, and back inside through the original hole. When pulled tight the thread will stay in the scored grooves; a drop of glue will hold the knot.

A piece of ABS plastic sheet painted blue/green makes good-looking water, especially when coated with white glue to give it a "wet" look.

### CYCLONE

As mentioned earlier, I used a Magnuson Models cyclone as a starting point.

However, having looked at the millwork shops in this area, I modified the cyclone to resemble some of the ones I've seen. See fig. 9. Using the elbow from the cyclone as a duct elbow at the roof line, make the duct itself from a piece of dowel wrapped with paper tape to simulate sheet metal. The rain guard came from my junk box, but I could just as easily have fashioned one out of cardstock and stripwood.

Use stripwood for the trusswork that supports the cyclone and stands on the sloped roof. Use ⅟₁₆"-square stock for the legs and the horizontal members; the X bracing is ⅟₁₆" x ⅟₃₂" stock.

### GANTRY

The gantry (fig. 10) I made is mainly ⅛"-square stripwood and Plastruct angle. The bolt-head castings are of three sizes: the largest is for attaching the upright posts with the end support braces, the intermediate size is for attaching the side sway braces, and the smallest is for attaching the ³⁄₃₂"-square cross braces at the ends of the gantry. The bridge rail is Plastruct angle.

The gantry carriage is an interesting piece to construct. The sideframes of any truck will suffice. I would have preferred archbar, but the Bettendorfs were in my junk box.

Fashion the main beam from a length of stripwood and a length of Plastruct channel for the base. A pair of Tyco trucks provided the wheelsets for my gantry carriage, one wheel from each wheelset. Cut a length of brass tubing to fit between the wheels, slipping them onto the axles to form longer axles. Blacken the brass with Hobby Black before assembly.

A length of fine brass chain, also blackened before assembly, looped over one axle acts as a "ground control." You could fashion a lifting harness from additional chain; in my case, however, I had a ready supply of blocks from ship models and so elected to form a couple of block-and-tackle lifting harnesses. Some additional ropes and chains should be left hanging around for effect.

### OFFICE BUILDING

The office building is fairly simple. First glue the rear and side walls to the base for two buildings. These bases were removed from the sheds earlier. While the cement is setting, notch the bottom of the front walls the thickness of the cast-on bottom frame. This will allow these walls to fit over a new floor and porch, as shown in fig. 11.

Glue the two fronts between the first assemblies, trimming the excess ground from the bases as necessary. Cut the scribed-styrene floor to fit between the bases and under the front walls, also forming a front and rear porch. Use the corrugated roof pieces from the unused workbench roofs as a measure of length for the floor; they'll be used for the roof.

At this point I subdued the bright yellow building with a coat of Reefer Gray and then glazed and installed the windows and doors. Then I placed some crates and boxes inside and installed a light on a brace between the peaks of the door walls.

To put a roof over the office-workers' heads, cement the two corrugated roof sections in place over the center section of the building. Next, cut the two preformed roof sections on the diagonal to

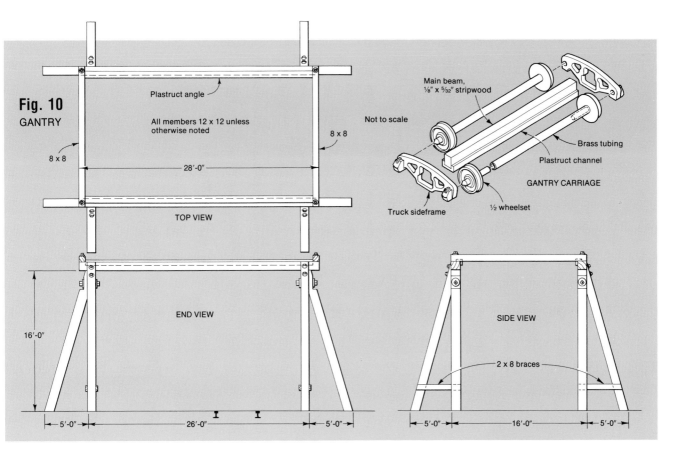

**Fig. 10** GANTRY

Plastruct angle

All members 12 x 12 unless otherwise noted

8 x 8

8 x 8

28'-0"

TOP VIEW

END VIEW

16'-0"

5'-0"

26'-0"

5'-0"

Not to scale

Main beam, ⅛" x ⁵⁄₃₂" stripwood

Brass tubing

Plastruct channel

GANTRY CARRIAGE

Truck sideframe

½ wheelset

SIDE VIEW

2 x 8 braces

5'-0"

16'-0"

5'-0"

fit on the main building walls and join with the center roof. Since these come up just a little short, use styrene to fill in the difference between the peaks. Once again, treat the entire roof to the tissue tarpaper treatment. Insert the smokejacks through the tarpaper in their original positions. To tone down the black on all the roofs, rub sifted dirt into the roofs and brush it off.

### LIGHT POLES

The light poles are also very simple. Cut the poles to about 30 feet from a length of ⅛" dowel. Notch one side for the arm (about 8 feet long) which is made from ¹⁄₁₆" x ³⁄₃₂" stock. Drill the pole just above the arm and ¼" from the top parallel to the arm.

Next, drill the arm near one end and groove it from the hole to the other end along the top of the arm. Using a grain-of-rice bulb and a Campbell lampshade, fashion a light fixture, running the wires through the arm. One wire is threaded through the upper hole and one goes through the lower hole in the pole. At this point glue the arm to the pole and glue one wire in the groove along the top of the arm.

When the glue is dry insert the post in a ⅛" hole in the base. The upper wire runs through the base as a guy wire, and the lower wire is run to the building as the electric wire.

One word of caution — make sure the brass lampshade does not short out the bulb leads!

And that's it. The rest of it is up to your imagination. Paint up anything that looks like it needs it, scatter around some lumberyard junk, erect a fence (with a gate) around the premises, and open for business your version of Welte Lumber & Millwork. ⌂

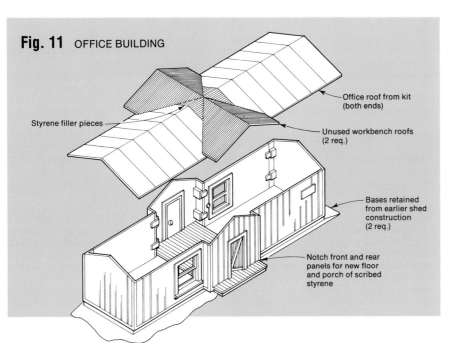

**Fig. 11** OFFICE BUILDING

Office roof from kit (both ends)

Styrene filler pieces

Unused workbench roofs (2 req.)

Bases retained from earlier shed construction (2 req.)

Notch front and rear panels for new floor and porch of scribed styrene

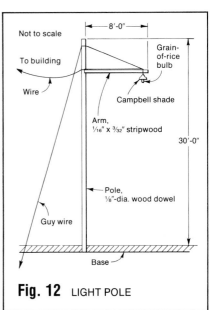

Not to scale

8'-0"

To building

Grain-of-rice bulb

Wire

Campbell shade

Arm, ¹⁄₁₆" x ³⁄₃₂" stripwood

30'-0"

Pole, ⅛"-dia. wood dowel

Guy wire

Base

**Fig. 12** LIGHT POLE

# An export elevator for the MR&T

A big HO structure made of plastic plumbing, sheet styrene, and window castings

**BY JIM KELLY**

**PHOTOS BY A. L. SCHMIDT**

WHAT I ENJOY MOST about working on a club layout is having the opportunity to build some models and try some ideas that wouldn't work out on the layout at home. In this case the club is our Kalmbach Publishing Co. employees club, and the layout is our HO Milwaukee, Racine & Troy.

The MR&T is a big layout, about 25 x 40 feet. (Andy Sperandeo's article about the club in the March 1985 issue includes a track plan.) On the layout is a large canal representative of those we have here in Milwaukee for the ocean-going vessels that come in off Lake Michigan. One structure I wanted on the canal was the big, and I mean BIG, Continental Grain Co. export grain elevator located south of downtown Milwaukee.

### THE SILOES

Look at the prototype photos in fig. 1 and it becomes apparent that the prototype structure is huge. In a straight-on side view I spotted an Alco switcher towing 50-foot covered hoppers. I could see the structure is about nine hoppers, or 450 feet, long. The siloes on the left are about 90 feet tall, and the white building on the right stands about 150 feet. A prototype-sized structure, then, would be more than 5 feet long and stand about 18″ tall. My model is only half as long, although nearly as tall. The space I had available was quite shallow, so my model could not have much depth.

I worked entirely from photos. After finishing the model I called the elevator and arranged an interview with the superintendent, Bert Nussbaum. After all, it can't hurt to find out a little about something you've modeled.

Bert told me the main building (the tall, white structure) was built in 1914-1916. The large bank of 48 storage siloes was added in 1934. The elevator can store 3 million bushels of grain (usually corn, wheat, or soybeans), making it a medium-size export elevator. (Some can handle 5 million bushels.) Ordinarily the elevator receives trains of 25, 50, or 75 cars. It can unload them at the rate of 5 cars an hour and can load a large ship in about 30 hours.

The prototype uses a leased Alco switcher to pull cars into the receiving shed. The grain is dumped through the grates between the rails into bins below. Conveyor belts carry it horizontally to the main building; then it is hoisted up the legs to the top of the structure. (A leg is a vertical shaft containing a continuous belt with buckets to lift the grain.)

At the top the grain is dumped into a huge bin, called the garner. It moves from there to a scale for weighing, then is transferred by conveyor belts to ships or storage siloes.

When grain is transferred from siloes it drops out the bottom onto horizontal conveyor belts and goes up the same legs and into the garner again.

Andy Sperandeo photos

**Fig. 1. PROTOTYPE PHOTOS**
This huge Continental Grain Co. export elevator is a local landmark on Milwaukee's Jones Island. The author's compressed version was made for the MR&T, Kalmbach Publishing's club railroad. The model has no back, but rear and end views of the prototype are included here for any readers who might want to construct a four-sided structure.

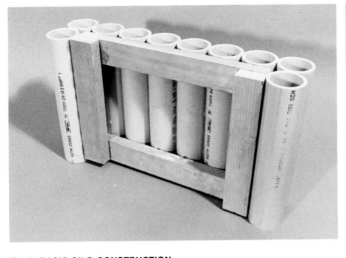

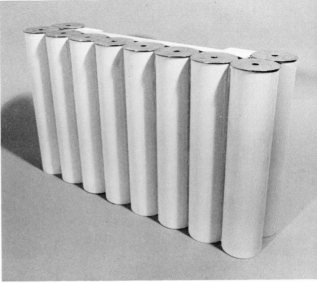

**Fig. 2. BASIC SILO CONSTRUCTION**
**Above.** The author made the siloes from plastic pipe and used scrap 1 x 2 to brace the assembly. **Right.** The round silo caps are steel fender washers.

**Fig. 3** STORAGE SILOES

Leg heads, (from 2 Kibri no. 9950 cement tower kits)

Roof vents, California Model Co. no 114

Dust collection pipe, ¼" Plastruct tubing

Windows, Alexander no. 2510 castings

Rain gutter, ⅛" Plastruct channel

Gallery, Evergreen .040" styrene (gallery is 2⅜" wide x 15⅛" long x 1⅛" high)

Legs, ¼" Plastruct tubing

Siloes, 8¼" lengths, 1½" i.d. PVC tubing

FRONT

Downspouts, ¹⁄₁₆" Plastruct rod

Base, 4" x 16⅝" x ¼" hardboard

REAR

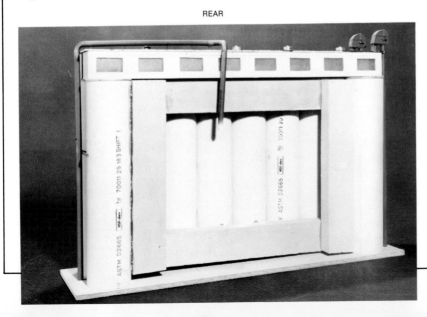

## MODELING THE SILOES

I decided to build the simplest part of the structure first, the siloes. What to make them of? Having just remodeled a bathroom I'd learned about plastic (PVC) pipe and decided it would be just the ticket. There'd never be a problem with warping, as there might be with cardboard mailing tubes. Step one was to cut 10 lengths of 1½" pipe (inside diameter) 8¼" long. I laid 8 tubes on a flat surface, lined them up, then cemented them together with 5-minute epoxy.

As shown in fig. 2, I cemented lengths of 1 x 2 across the back to brace the tubes, then added vertical 1 x 2s and an extra tube at each end. (The rear of the elevator can't be seen on the MR&T, so I didn't model it.)

I capped the siloes with 2" steel fender washers, then built the housing on the top, as shown in fig. 3, from .040" sheet styrene. Note on the rear wall that I cut in window openings, glazed them with acetate frosted by light sanding, but didn't bother with window castings.

The prototype has patched cracks here and there, so I added some to the model, carving them in with a cutting head held in a Dremel motor tool. For the most part these cracks run horizontal, following form lines in the concrete and running along where the concrete is weakest (probably at joints between pours). I hand-brushed the cracks with a fine wire brush, so they wouldn't be too stark. Mixing up a concrete color I liked (about 1 part Floquil Concrete, 1 part Reefer White, and 1 part Earth), I airbrushed the structure before installing the windows.

After airbrushing the door and window castings Boxcar Red, I let them dry a week before installing them with ACC.

To make the tar and gravel roof I tried a new technique (new to me anyway). I was quite pleased with the results and recommend it. First spray the roof heavily with Pactra's Hot Rod Primer (a flat black color), then sprinkle on Highball dirt. I had good luck shaking it on from a plastic disposable drinking cup. The trick is to apply the gravel unevenly, but without

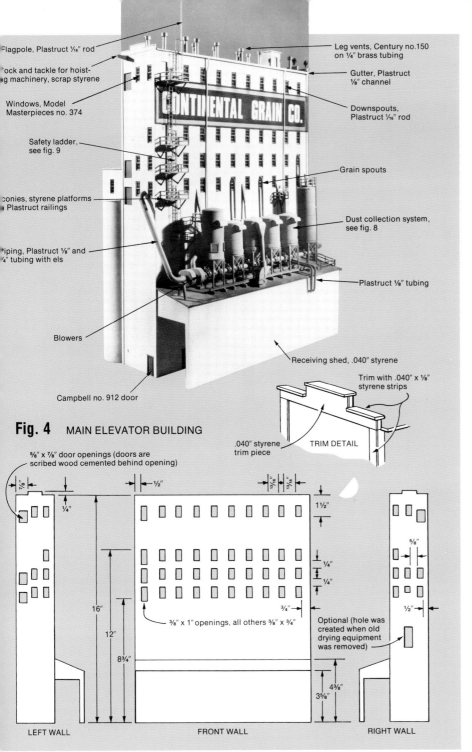

Flagpole, Plastruct 1/16" rod

Block and tackle for hoisting machinery, scrap styrene

Windows, Model Masterpieces no. 374

Safety ladder, see fig. 9

Balconies, styrene platforms & Plastruct railings

Piping, Plastruct 1/8" and 1/4" tubing with els

Blowers

Campbell no. 912 door

Leg vents, Century no.150 on 1/4" brass tubing

Gutter, Plastruct 1/8" channel

Downspouts, Plastruct 1/16" rod

Grain spouts

Dust collection system, see fig. 8

Plastruct 1/8" tubing

Receiving shed, .040" styrene

Trim with .040" x 1/8" styrene strips

.040" styrene trim piece

TRIM DETAIL

**Fig. 4** MAIN ELEVATOR BUILDING

5/8" x 7/8" door openings (doors are scribed wood cemented behind opening)

7/8"
1/4"
1/2"
13/16"   13/16"
1½"
1/4"
1/4"
3/4"
5/8"
1/2"

16"
12"
8¾"

3/8" x 1" openings, all others 3/8" x 3/4"

Optional (hole was created when old drying equipment was removed)

4¾"
3⅝"

LEFT WALL          FRONT WALL          RIGHT WALL

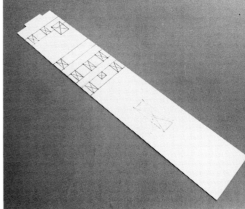

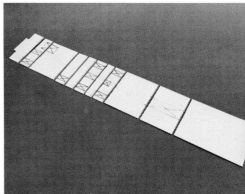

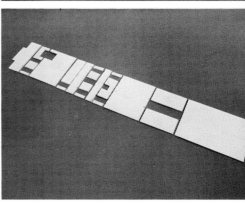

**Fig. 5. MAKING THE WALLS**
**Top.** The walls were cut from .040" styrene.
**Middle above.** They were cut into horizontal strips by scoring with a sharp hobby knife and snapping. **Above.** The window openings were snapped out and the walls were put back together with liquid plastic cement. The joints were reinforced with strips of styrene.

letting it get blotchy. You want a roof that's mostly black, but with areas of unblackened dirt here and there. Dump off the excess after the paint dries.

Figure 3 includes the details I added to complete the siloes. I weathered the structure with an airbrush, using Earth and other Floquil weathering colors. To accent the roundness of the siloes I very carefully worked Grimy Black into the joints between siloes and also used, it carefully to accent the cracks. I used Reefer White, very lightly, to highlight the round surfaces.

**THE MAIN BUILDING**

Next I turned to the tall, main stucture,

as shown in fig. 4. The walls are made of .040" styrene (illustration board would also work). As shown in fig. 5, I used John Nehrich's snap-and-reassemble method to cut all those window openings. The shed for receiving grain-loaded hoppers is also made of .040" styrene.

The open back of the building is shown in fig. 6. I braced the corners with 1/4"-square stripwood and used chunks of 1 x 2 and plywood to brace the thing and hold it square. The back is just a Masonite panel fastened on with small screws, and the suggestion of a row of siloes behind the building is built directly onto this panel.

I painted the entire building Reefer

White, then installed the window and door castings. The tarpaper roof on the receiving port was made by cementing on strips of typing paper, then painting them with Floquil's Dark Green.

**THE SIGN**

To me, the single most important detail on this structure is the big sign. Take that away and a lot of character goes with it.

It would have been a snap if I could have found some white dry transfer letters the size and type style I wanted, but I could find them only in black. The product I used is Letraset's 96-point Compacta Bold. To get white lettering I

**Fig. 6. BACK OF THE BUILDING**
**Above.** The sides, bottom, and top are braced with lengths of 1 x 2. A scrap of plywood braces the front and holds it flat. **Right.** The back is a large panel of Masonite, with two siloes and the suggestion of a housing on top.

used the old Art Curren paint-n-peel trick, as shown in fig. 7.

The first step, and a very important one, is to make a lettering guide. (You don't want to end up with a sign saying CONTINENTAL GRAIN.) To get a good idea of the spacing, I divided and subdivided the sign on my straight-on photo into quarters. (Remember what they taught you in geometry class. To bisect a rectangle draw diagonal lines connecting the corners.)

Then I traced a rough of the sign onto tracing paper and used that as a lettering guide when transferring the rub-on

letters to the building. I burnished the dry transfers only lightly, since I'd be pulling them off soon.

I masked off the sign area and airbrushed it Engine Black. After letting the paint set up for about 15 minutes, I pulled the lettering off with masking tape. Some dry transfer parts were stubborn and took an extra pull or two with the tape. Several days later I masked off the sign's red border and painted it.

## ALL THOSE TANKS AND THINGS

A neat feature on the prototype was the bank of tanks, pipes, and gee-gaws

atop the hopper car receiving port. These are part of the vast dust collection system that is woven through the entire building. (Not only is grain dust a health hazard, it can explode.)

My smaller elevator wouldn't need as much equipment as the prototype, but I followed the photo and added a lot anyway because it adds so much interest to the building.

Figure 8 shows the combination of materials I used. I winged this contraption and had a lot of fun with it. I haven't tried to show every detail. Many are just bits and pieces from the scrapbox, but the

**Fig. 7. MAKING THE SIGN**
**Left.** The author couldn't locate the lettering he wanted in white so he made his sign with black rub-on letters. **Middle.** He airbrushed the masked sign area with Floquil Engine Black. **Right.** Masking tape was burnished on the letters and used to pull them away, exposing the white underneath.

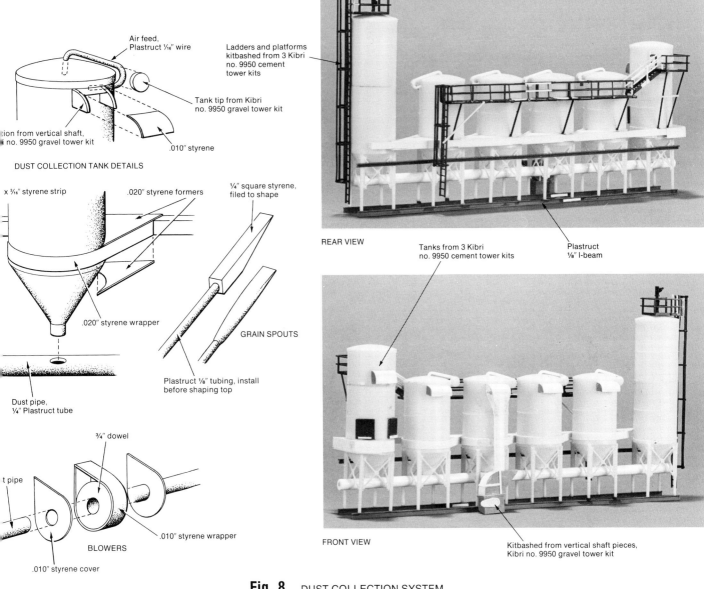

**DUST COLLECTION TANK DETAILS**

Air feed, Plastruct 1/16" wire

Tank tip from Kibri no. 9950 gravel tower kit

...ion from vertical shaft, ...i no. 9950 gravel tower kit

.010" styrene

x 3/16" styrene strip

.020" styrene formers

1/4" square styrene, filed to shape

.020" styrene wrapper

**GRAIN SPOUTS**

Plastruct 1/8" tubing, install before shaping top

Dust pipe, 1/4" Plastruct tube

3/4" dowel

...t pipe

.010" styrene wrapper

**BLOWERS**

.010" styrene cover

Ladders and platforms kitbashed from 3 Kibri no. 9950 cement tower kits

**REAR VIEW**

Tanks from 3 Kibri no. 9950 cement tower kits

Plastruct 1/8" I-beam

**FRONT VIEW**

Kitbashed from vertical shaft pieces, Kibri no. 9950 gravel tower kit

**Fig. 8**  DUST COLLECTION SYSTEM

fellows at the elevator found it a reasonable enough representation. Basically, the five tanks on the left separate dust from the air. This dust is collected in the tallest tank, right. The dust is loaded into hoppers and sold to feed mills.

I used safety cage ladders from Kibri kits and also scratchbuilt some, as shown in fig. 9. The ladders from the kit would have looked rather clunky silhouetted against the white building, particularly

where the ladder goes up over the sign.

This is not, and was not intended to be, an absolutely faithful model of the elevator. Simplifying as I did, it still took about a year's worth of stolen moments to finish the project. A more accurate and detailed contest-caliber model would have taken much longer, and that's time that can be spent building the next structure for the MR&T.

Since I used so many commercial parts

and castings, mine is a relatively expensive building (over $100). The modeler who wants to substitute other materials and scratchbuild such parts as the dust collectors could build just as good an elevator for under $20.

Very few readers will want to build an elevator exactly like mine, but I hope some of you will find the techniques and ideas here helpful in making an elevator to fit your layout. ⚙

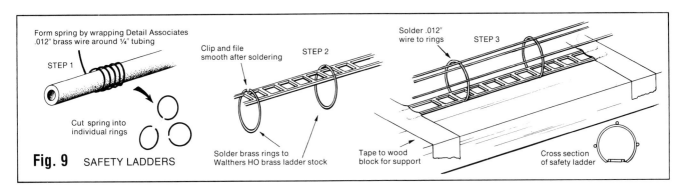

Form spring by wrapping Detail Associates .012" brass wire around 1/4" tubing

**STEP 1**

Cut spring into individual rings

Clip and file smooth after soldering

**STEP 2**

Solder brass rings to Walthers HO brass ladder stock

Solder .012" wire to rings

**STEP 3**

Tape to wood block for support

Cross section of safety ladder

**Fig. 9**  SAFETY LADDERS

This overall view shows the many different varieties of scrap that are piled along both sides of the loading track. Once a sale is made, the grapple goes to work to load the appropriate scrap material into one of the waiting 50-foot gondolas.

# D. H. Griffin Co. scrapyard

## How to build a common railroad industry

**BY MIKE SMALL**
### PHOTOS BY THE AUTHOR

WITHIN the past few years, recycling various products has received a lot of attention, especially metal, glass, paper, and plastic. This may seem like a new process to the public, but metal recycling has been going on for a long time.

Metal is generally collected for recycling in scrapyards that are often referred to as "junkyards." Many of these businesses were established years ago to handle junked automobiles and a wide range of industrial scrap. These two commodities still account for much of today's recyclable scrap, but such other household items as appliances, lawn and garden equipment, and metal furniture also enter the picture.

### SCRAPYARDS

Scrapyards have traditionally been located along rail lines for ease of shipping the various types of scrap. The ordinary open gondola has always been the most commonly used car for scrap shipments.

While scrapyards come in a wide variety of sizes, they share a number of characteristics. A main office building is needed, along with a set of truck scales, a building for processing and storing nonferrous metals, an open field storage area for steel and iron, and a rail siding. If the business is large enough, other structures may be found on the property. These include a separate scale house, a vehicle maintenance shop, garage, and other storage buildings. Metal-processing machinery like a shear, auto shredder, or baler may also be there, and some of this equipment is quite large.

All sorts of vehicles and mobile machinery inhabit scrapyards: trucks of different sizes, cranes (some equipped with magnets), grapples, front-end loaders, and forklifts. Raw scrap arrives in vehicles ranging from private pickups to tractor-trailer trucks and super dump trucks that are owned by customers or the scrapyard itself.

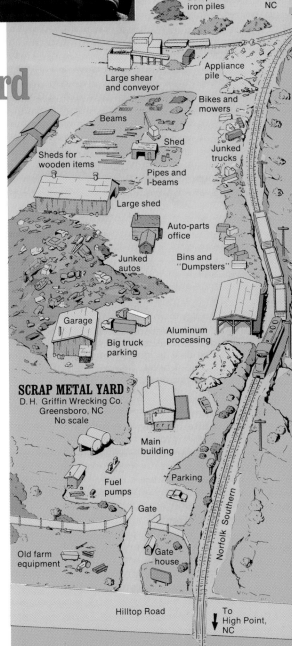

**SCRAP METAL YARD**
D. H. Griffin Wrecking Co.
Greensboro, NC
No scale

28

# An industry you can model

**Left:** The main line of the former Southern Ry. (now Norfolk Southern) runs along one side of the scrapyard. Junked automobiles are stacked up in piles that have now spread almost to the right-of-way.

**Below:** The main building houses offices in the brick section, while the sheet-metal warehouse is used to protect valuable nonferrous metals and other salvage materials that might be damaged by the weather.

## THE PROTOTYPE

To get a closeup look and photograph some typical scrapyard operations and equipment, I contacted D. H. Griffin Wrecking Co. Inc., of Greensboro, N. C. This family-owned business was founded in 1959 and is located next to the Washington-to-Atlanta main line of the former Southern Ry.

D. H. Griffin Co. specializes in demolishing and dismantling all types of structures. Many of their jobs involve early skyscrapers, and some are brought down through the implosion-blasting process that causes the structure to collapse within itself. The firm also salvages and sells building materials.

A small gatehouse is the first structure one encounters upon entering the scrapyard driveway. Its occupant provides both visitor information and security against theft. Parking is provided on both sides of the gatehouse.

The main building is just inside the gate, and it serves several purposes. Company offices are located across the front, while a combined scale and sales office is built into the side facing the driveway. A large warehouse space at the rear is used for storage and sorting nonferrous metals like copper, brass, and aluminum. These metals are sorted into forklift bins by purity and alloy. This warehouse also holds whatever saleable fixtures and furniture were taken from buildings the firm demolished.

A vehicle scale, 60 feet long, is built into the driveway. It has a concrete platform with steel edges and is level with the surrounding ground. The scale's capacity is 100,000 pounds. Inbound trucks are weighed, then head into the yard and unload. As they leave, each empty truck is reweighed so the load weight and payment may be calculated.

An aluminum baler is located directly

Grapple jaws are used on some hydraulic cranes so they can crush lightweight scrap and handle nonmagnetic items. Cranes with steel treads are utilized around the scrap piles.

Numerous hydraulic cranes, equipped with electromagnets, are used to unload and handle the various types of scrap so all of the materials can be carefully sorted into piles.

With their steel treads, the cranes can move anywhere and cross the rail siding to reach a work area. Note how each sorted scrap pile has a unique texture made up of similar items.

A single long siding marks the heart of the recycling operation. Piles of steel and iron are stacked up everywhere on both sides of the track. Most of the time, this siding is occupied by five or six gondolas.

All the metal must be separated and graded before being sold. In particular, iron has to be separated from steel and then classified according to thickness. The scrapyard separates these materials into ten different commercial grades.

A huge pile of sheet-metal household appliances (old washers, dryers, stoves, and refrigerators) marks the lighter, thinner steel area. Nearby is a big pile containing general scrap, while yet another consists of lightweight scrap from motorcycles, bicycles, lawn mowers, and yard tractors. Other piles have pipe, tubing, and galvanized sheet metal from heating and air-conditioning ductwork.

A separate area contains heavier steel such as pieces of structural beams, angle iron, steel plate, and large machine parts. Cast iron makes up another pile, along with auto engine blocks, steam radiators, sinks, and bathtubs. All of this separation is necessary due to the differing properties of the materials.

## MACHINERY

An office trailer, set in the center of the steel scrap piles, controls this entire area. Someone is always on duty to check incoming loads and direct them to the proper unloading spot. Most of the activity involving steel or iron occurs along either side of the rail siding. Inbound trucks pull in alongside the track so they can be unloaded into the gondola or onto the pile.

Two types of machinery are in continual use around the scrap heaps, and there are several varieties of each. The first are cranes equipped with electromagnets. Their magnets are used to pick up the metal and heap it higher, unload trucks, and load gondolas. Picking up the metal or dropping it is easily controlled by an electric current that passes through the magnet.

The second group of machines consists of the grapples. They're similar in appearance to the magnet cranes, except they are equipped with large grippers. Grapples may be used to lift and carry large objects and are capable of crushing small lightweight items like appliances.

Unusually large or heavy items, with thick cross sections, are reduced in size by cutting them up with acetylene torches. It's pretty common to keep one or two men busy cutting up large items with torches. A beat-up pickup truck is usually outfitted to handle this assignment.

A large shear is a recent addition to D. H. Griffin Co.'s scrapyard. This machine is used to shear or chop certain grades of scrap into small pieces suitable

across the driveway from the main building. It's protected from the elements by a simple shed-style roof. This machine compresses aluminum scrap into bales that take up less space during shipment. A midget forklift and small front-end loader work in this area.

Next comes a special parking area where different sizes of portable steel bins are stored to the east of the driveway. These "Dumpster" bins are picked up and moved on special trucks (that are equipped with hydraulic lifts) directly to customers or demolition sites to be filled with scrap material. When full, they're picked up and returned to the scrapyard.

D. H. Griffin Co. owns more than 200

vehicles (trucks, cranes, etc.), which are serviced in the combined garage and shop northwest of the main building. A parking area for this equipment is provided next to the garage.

Junked automobiles fill the area beyond the garage. A small sales office and a shed are located adjacent to the main drive to handle the auto-parts business. Hubcaps are hung up for display on the front walls of the buildings, while old car, truck, and van bodies are spread around on both sides of the drive. When necessary, a large forklift moves the bodies around. Eventually, most wind up in a trailer-mounted crusher that flattens them. The flattened vehicles are shipped on flatbed trucks.

for further recycling. It can exert as much as 1,000 tons of pressure to compress the scrap in its trough. Then the scrap passes through the shear and is moved by conveyor to storage or a waiting gondola. An elevated control room allows the shear operator to keep track of everything that's going on around the machine.

All sorts of other construction materials are salvaged and stored in the back areas of the scrapyard. These items include stacks of lumber, steel beams, pipe, doors, and windows. Items that are affected by the weather are stored in sheds.

## RAIL OPERATIONS

The scrapyard ships between 40 and 60 carloads of steel and iron scrap per month, so the Norfolk Southern switches the scrapyard regularly (usually with a GP38 or GP38-2 local freight engine). These loads are sold to steel mills throughout the country. An outbound load will ordinarily be made up of similar materials, but the various grades of steel scrap provide many load possibilities.

Shipments of copper, brass, and aluminum go to nearby customers, so D. H. Griffin Co. ships most of this material by truck. Nonferrous metals are a pretty small business for most scrapyards, but their value per pound is much greater than iron or steel. That's the reason these metals are stored indoors.

## MODELING A SCRAPYARD

Nearly all aspects of D. H. Griffin Co.'s scrapyard follow standard methods for this industry. There are many suppliers of the scrap-processing machinery, so different or additional equipment may be found in other installations. (Conveyor lines are common around shredders.)

Some scrapyards specialize in particular processes, such as shredding automobiles, while others may handle only industrial scrap. Large yards may have self-propelled cranes, and some even own locomotives to move cars around.

Anyone modeling a scrapyard needs to keep three things in mind: dirt, rust, and dents. Wherever there are scrap piles, there are rough roads leading to and around them. In dry weather, whatever moves kicks up dust that settles on everything. During wet weather, the roads turn to mud, and everything rusts. Dents and scrapes are likely whenever the equipment begins to move the scrap around. That's why most junkyard trucks are pretty battered.

Since scrapyards may be large or small, it's easy to fit one into almost any layout. One main building (with a scale alongside), a magnet crane, a few trucks, some fencing, and a rail siding are all it takes. Even if it's small, an authentic-looking scrapyard will be an asset to almost any model railroad. ◘

A huge hydraulic cylinder operates the shear blade to chop scrap metal into small uniform pieces suitable for steelmaking. The conveyor collects and carries the processed scrap metal away so it can be loaded into a gondola or dumped onto a nearby storage pile.

**Above:** The rail siding curves alongside the shear so the movable conveyor can be shifted over for direct loading of the gondolas. Then a hydraulic crane will even out the load so the scrap metal cannot slide off. **Below:** An old pickup truck serves as a rolling shop for the workers who cut large items into manageable pieces with acetylene torches. All the gas cylinders have safety chains, or they are clamped in a rack so they can't tip over.

# Build a liquid-asphalt transfer terminal

This small-yet-busy HO scale industry will fit almost any modern layout

**BY CLYDE B. MAYBEE JR.**
PHOTOS BY THE AUTHOR

During a recent vacation I discovered a compact, modern trackside facility which makes an excellent, attention-getting railroad display model. On a roadside siding I saw a row of modern 54-foot insulated tank cars engulfed in steam, a lot of piping, and several tank trucks being loaded. This turned out to be a Total Distribution Services Inc. (TDSI) asphalt bulk-loading terminal in Apex, N. C. Within a fenced-in area, liquid asphalt was being heated in the rail tank cars and pumped directly into waiting tank trucks. Since the tank cars themselves are used for storage, space-consuming storage tanks aren't necessary.

A facility like this one will fit logically on almost any modern layout, as there are a number of industries and products that use liquid asphalt, including paving and roofing.

## The asphalt business

The operation begins when a train spots 54-foot tank cars filled with liquid asphalt at one of the loading stations. For efficiency the terminal is divided into two sections, each serving eight tank cars. The siding, with a switch at each end, has unloading stations for 16 tank cars. This operation can easily be modeled as a double-ended siding or a dead-end spur with room for any number of cars. The double-ended arrangement allows flexibility in switching cars from either end.

The insulated tank cars are equipped with external heating coils (external to the tank, but enclosed in the car's insulation), and as soon as they're spotted, workers connect the cars to the terminal's steam lines. The steam, which is generated by one of two boilers in the main building, travels through insulated pipes to connections on the bottom of each car.

The steam heats the liquid asphalt enough to allow it to flow freely through insulated pipes, which are also connected to the bottom of each car. Employees may select any car and open its valve. This allows the asphalt to be pumped into a heat exchanger, which raises the temperature of the liquid to about 320 degrees. From there it flows to the loading dock and into a waiting asphalt tank truck. These 25-ton capac-

ity trucks are weighed as they're loaded. Although liquid asphalt is a potentially dangerous, hot, gooey liquid, it is handled safely, efficiently, and cleanly. I marvel at the way the staff manages to keep the terminal so neat and clean. Employees wear protective clothing, helmets with face visors, and have water showers available for emergencies. The asphalt fumes are filtered both at the tank car top hatches and at the truck loading dock. The result is a very clean, neat facility, and a model should reflect that look.

These new transfer terminals represent the culmination of a 3-year effort between TDSI and an asphalt supplier. The company has designed and built asphalt terminals in Atlanta, and in Charlotte and Winston-Salem, N. C. In fact, this new asphalt transfer concept was so innovative that it won the 1990 Golden Freight Car Award from *Modern Railroads* magazine.

The Apex terminal is a busy place. During the summer months the terminal is open from 3 a.m. to 11 p.m. 5 days a week, and in the winter it operates from 5 a.m. to 5 p.m. 5 days a week.

32

This asphalt terminal provides a perfect setting for modern 54-foot tank cars.

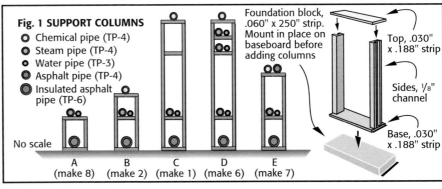

**Fig. 1 SUPPORT COLUMNS**
- ◎ Chemical pipe (TP-4)
- ◎ Steam pipe (TP-4)
- ○ Water pipe (TP-3)
- ◉ Asphalt pipe (TP-4)
- ◎ Insulated asphalt pipe (TP-6)

No scale

A (make 8)  B (make 2)  C (make 1)  D (make 6)  E (make 7)

Foundation block, .060" x 250" strip. Mount in place on baseboard before adding columns

Top, .030" x .188" strip

Sides, ⅛" channel

Base, .030" x .188" strip

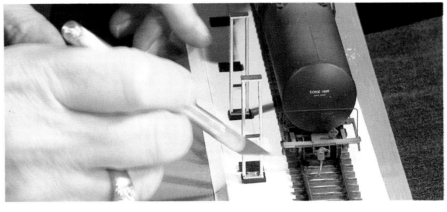

**Fig. 2. SUPPORT-COLUMN FOUNDATIONS.** Glue the foundation blocks to the foam core base before adding the support columns.

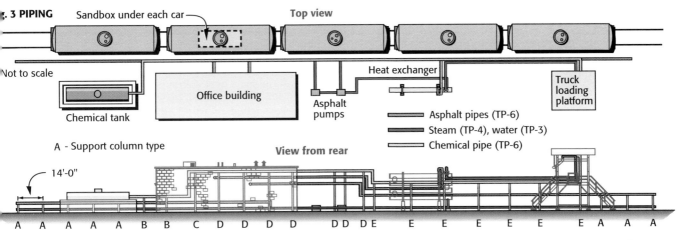

**Fig. 3 PIPING**

Sandbox under each car

Top view

Not to scale

Chemical tank

Office building

Asphalt pumps

Heat exchanger

Truck loading platform

- Asphalt pipes (TP-6)
- Steam (TP-4), water (TP-3)
- Chemical pipe (TP-6)

A - Support column type

View from rear

14'-0"

A A A A A B B B C D D D D D D D E E E E E E E A A A

### Designing the model

Although the Apex terminal has space for 16 tank cars, to conserve space I designed a 6-car facility for my display model. My model is five feet long and 10 inches wide. I decided not to include the passing track at this time so the model will be easier to install on a future layout. I cut a piece of seasoned ¾" plywood for the base dimensions, then used ³⁄₁₆" foam core as a roadbed and pipeline base. I put a piece of Atlas code 83 flextrack in place and sprayed it with Floquil Rail Brown.

### Support columns and piping

The various pipes and lines are held in place by support columns. I used

**Fig. 4. BENDING THE TUBING.** Concentrating the heat from a candle with material from an aluminum can makes it easy to bend the Plastruct tubing.

**Fig. 5 CEMENT-BLOCK BUILDING**

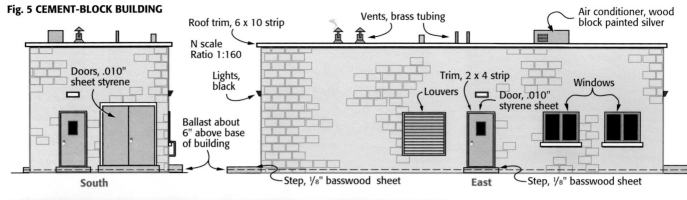

Roof trim, 6 x 10 strip

N scale
Ratio 1:160

Vents, brass tubing

Air conditioner, wood
block painted silver

Doors, .010"
sheet styrene

Lights,
black

Trim, 2 x 4 strip

Louvers

Door, .010"
styrene sheet

Windows

Ballast about
6" above base
of building

South

Step, ⅛" basswood sheet

East

Step, ⅛" basswood sheet

**Fig. 6. MAIN BUILDING.** Use stripwood to brace the interior of the structure.

five different types as shown in fig. 1. I pre-cut all the pieces to size before putting them together. After making the support columns I placed them on a strip of masking tape with the sticky side up. This held the columns upright while I sprayed them with Testor's Chrome paint. I chose Chrome rather than the prototype's duller aluminum color to give the model more sparkle.

After painting the support column foundation blocks flat black, I cemented them to the foam core base as shown in fig. 2, using the dimensions from fig. 3. Notice that the columns are located at 14-foot intervals except in the center area near the heat exchanger.

Bending and assembling the various pipes and lines is rather tricky, but these details make this model unlike other industries. I attempted to simplify the piping schematic by color-coding it in figs. 1 and 3. This should help you locate and place the pipes properly. There are three different sizes of pipes, all listed in fig. 1. The large one on the bottom represents the insulated asphalt pipe, the medium one is the insulated steam pipe, and the smallest one is the steam return pipe.

For the piping I used Plastruct material throughout, and the elbows, tubing, and tees go together nicely. However, in some less-critical places I decided to try to bend the pipe to fit. These 90-degree bends in the tubing are a challenge but I found a simple solution. By using a funnel made from an aluminum soft-drink can, I could concentrate the heat from a candle on a small section of the tubing as shown in fig. 4. This allowed me to quickly bend it around the 90-degree jig I had prepared. As a result, I can make multiple bends in one pipe. You'll be surprised how easy it becomes with a little practice.

An important note: Paint the pipes *before* assembly, again using Chrome. However, don't completely assemble the piping with elbows and tees until you thread the pipes through the support columns. Since everything is still accessible, now's a good time to add ballast to the track and surrounding area as shown in the photos. I used Woodland Scenics ballast cement to hold the ballast in place.

**Main building**

The cement-block building shown in fig. 5 houses the office at one end and contains two boilers in the other. The

**Fig. 7. PROTOTYPE HEAT EXCHANGER.** This unit uses steam to heat the liquid asphalt so that it flows easily to a waiting tank truck.

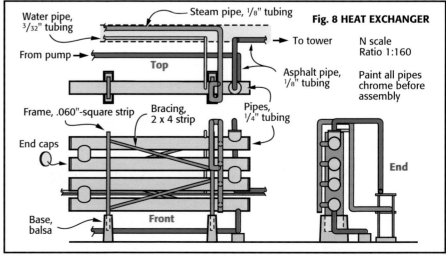

Water pipe,
³/₃₂" tubing

Steam pipe, ⅛" tubing

**Fig. 8 HEAT EXCHANGER**

From pump →

Top

To tower

N scale
Ratio 1:160

Asphalt pipe,
⅛" tubing

Paint all pipes
chrome before
assembly

Frame, .060"-square strip

Bracing,
2 x 4 strip

Pipes,
¼" tubing

End caps

Base,
balsa

Front

End

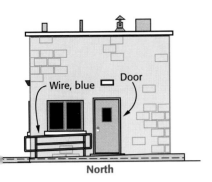

Wire, blue — Door

**North**

prototype has two office doors, but I eliminated one as I reduced the size of the building. Plastruct's embossed styrene sheet represents cement blocks fairly well. I used artist's illustration board to back the thin plastic sheet.

The office door is from Timberline but the two other doors and large rear cargo door are made from sheet styrene. I painted all of them gray, and I painted the Pikestuff sliding windows silver. I airbrushed the building before assembly with Floquil Big Sky Blue. For additional support I cemented balsa strips in the structure's corners and on leading edges as fig. 6 shows.

Because I like to operate at night, I always add lights to structures. I drilled a hole above each door and added a grain-of-wheat bulb. Using some scrap Campbell corrugated aluminum, I fashioned a light shade similar to the prototype. A screw-in socket and bulb are glued inside the office area. I made the building roof from illustration board, and covered it with strips of black masking tape. A couple of vent pipes and an air conditioning unit help to liven up the roof.

### Heat exchanger and valves

The prototype heat exchanger in fig. 7 is one of the more interesting-looking

## Bill of materials

**Builders in Scale**
250 chain

**Central Valley**
1602 stairs

**Detail Associates**
2506 .019" brass wire
2508 .028" brass wire
2509 .033" brass wire

**Evergreen Scale Models styrene**
138 .030" x .188" strip
143 .040" x .060" strip
153 .060"-square strip
159 .060" x .250" strip
169 .080" x .250" strip
188 .125" x .188" strip
4544 .040" board-and-batten siding, .125" spacing
8204 2 x 4 strip
8208 2 x 8 strip
8410 4 x 10 strip
8610 6 x 10 strip
8612 6 x 12 strip
9010 .010" sheet
9030 .030" sheet
9060 .060" sheet

**Floquil**
110007 Rail Brown
110010 Engine Black
110013 Grimy Black
110031 Reefer Yellow
110056 Big Sky Blue
110082 Concrete

**Herpa**
854000 tank truck

**Kibri**
9430 fuel tank

**Northeastern Scale Lumber Co.**
241 ⅛" x 1" basswood

**Pikestuff**
2102 windows

**Plastruct**
E-4 ⅛" elbow
GV-2 1/16" gate valve
PM-2 pump with motor
TB-2 1/16" tubing
TB-3 3/32" tubing
TB-4 ⅛" tubing
TB-6 3/16" tubing
TB-8 ¼" tubing
TP-4 ⅛" tee
TP-6 3/16" tee
102 1/16" angle
304 ⅛" channel
10103 embossed plastic sheet

**Rail Scene**
highway lights (6)

**Suethe**
9 smoke unit (2)

**Testor Corp. paint**
1147 Gloss Black
1168 Flat White
1290 Chrome spray

**Timberline**
door

**Woodland Scenics**
91 ballast cement
94 blended medium gray ballast

**Miscellaneous**
¾" plywood
3/16" foam core
balsa strips
brass screen/mesh
grain-of-wheat bulbs
hardboard
illustration board
N scale tank-car shell
wedding-veil material

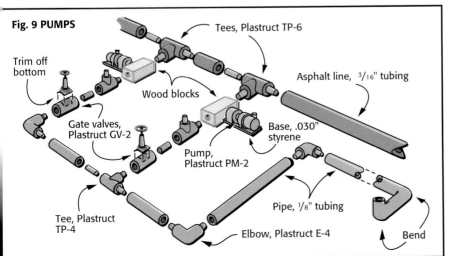

**Fig. 9 PUMPS**

Trim off bottom

Tees, Plastruct TP-6

Wood blocks

Asphalt line, 3/16" tubing

Gate valves, Plastruct GV-2

Base, .030" styrene

Pump, Plastruct PM-2

Tee, Plastruct TP-4

Pipe, ⅛" tubing

Elbow, Plastruct E-4

Bend

**Fig. 10. BASE FOR HEAT EXCHANGER.** Use foam core as a base for the pumps and heat exchanger. The pumps are already in place.

**Fig. 11. LOADING PLATFORM.** Trucks are weighed as they're loaded. The black tar paper covers the scale.

### Fig. 12 TRUCK LOADING PLATFORM

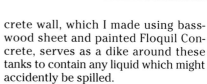

Loading pipe details

Pin through wire loop

Pin

Handrail, .019" wire    Front, 2 x 4 strip

Side, 4 x 10 strip

**Bridge step**

Tee, 1/8"    Pin

Pin

Flexible tubing

Hinge, 1/16" tubin

Pipe, 3/16" tubing

N scale Ratio 1:160

Steps and railing, Central Valley 1602

Platform base, 1/8" channel

From heat exchanger

Chain

Front

Roof outline

Crosspiece, 6 x 12 strip

Post, .060"-sq strip

Cross brace 1/8" channel

Step ba .080" x strip

Braces, 2 x 4 strip

---

units in this complex and it's also relatively easy to build. The drawing in fig. 8 shows the components. Following the prototype photo, I sprayed the pipes Chrome and painted the other parts before assembly. I made the pipe end plates by punching .010" sytrene sheet in a three-hole punch.

Since the terminal system is divided into two parts, there's a main valve and pump for each half. Fortunately Plastruct makes all of the parts required to fabricate these elements: gate valves, pump and motor assemblies, elbows, and tees, all shown in fig. 9. I added a foam core base in front of the building to hold this unit and the heat exchanger as fig. 10 shows.

### Loading dock

The loading dock shown in fig. 11 may look complicated, but it's also easy to build. On the prototype the bridge step raises and lowers, allowing workers easy access to the loading pipe and tank truck hatch as shown in fig. 12. The asphalt loading pipe should be movable as on the prototype as the drawings show. All of the incoming pipes are color-coded.

I cut the tower base from .060" styrene sheet, then sprayed it with Testor's Flat White. After masking the truck-scale area I airbrushed it with Floquil Engine Black. Yellow edging strips finish it off. I assembled the loading dock, except for the steps and handrails, and sprayed it with Chrome. I

painted steps and handrails yellow and added them to the dock.

### Tank car unloading areas

Each tank car in the unloading area has a sandbox underneath it, along with a black asphalt hose and two silver-colored steam lines as shown in fig. 13. If a bit of sizzling liquid leaks at the coupling under the car, it drops harmlessly into the sand, then cools and hardens like a lump of coal.

To represent these areas I used fine white sand, as shown in fig. 14. To secure the sand I used an eyedropper to add Woodland Scenics cement.

The black hoses and chrome steam lines are made from solder, which shapes easily. As a final detail, I added a thin strip of black masking tape on each side of every sandbox to represent sheets of tar paper.

### Fuel and chemical tanks

The facility has two storage tanks: a large one for an asphalt additive and a smaller one for boiler fuel, as shown in fig. 15. When customers purchase liquid asphalt they sometimes request this additive, which allows the asphalt to more readily accept aggregates such as stone used in asphalt paving. The boilers are fueled by natural gas but the small blue tank contains backup fuel oil if needed.

I made the larger tank from a Kibri fuel tank, and the smaller blue one from an N scale tank-car body. A con-

crete wall, which I made using basswood sheet and painted Floquil Concrete, serves as a dike around these tanks to contain any liquid which might accidently be spilled.

As fig. 15 shows, a blue gas line (3/32" tubing) comes out of the ground and goes into the back of the building. A black fuel pipe (1/16" tubing) goes into the end of the building.

### Tank cars and tank truck

This is a great opportunity to try weathering some of your tank cars just like the prototype cars. They all have some degree of spillage around the top hatch and walkway. I airbrushed some dusty tones over the entire car, then lightly sprayed Grimy Black in the midsection of the tank. After streaking a little more Grimy Black down the sides with a brush, I then stippled on a bit of Gloss Black to represent a fresh, shiny, wet-looking surface as shown in fig. 16. I painted the trucks a rusty color. The prototype tank cars vary a great deal from new, relatively clean cars to older, grime-covered ones.

To complete the unloading sequence we must have an asphalt tank truck. To be prototypical, the tank should have only one dome (with its hatch cover opened), a walkway, and a ladder. After being unable to find an exact replica, I remodeled a Herpa tank truck. The walkway on top of the tank came off fairly well, leaving just 3 holes. I covered the two outside holes with sheet

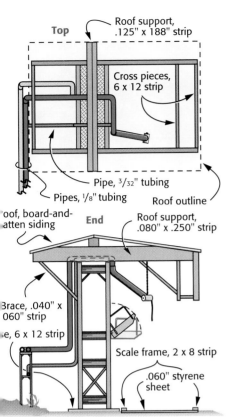

**Top**

Roof support, .125" x 188" strip

Cross pieces, 6 x 12 strip

Pipe, ³/₃₂" tubing

Pipes, ⅛" tubing

Roof outline

Roof, board-and-batten siding

**End**

Roof support, .080" x .250" strip

Brace, .040" x 060" strip

e, 6 x 12 strip

Scale frame, 2 x 8 strip

.060" styrene sheet

**Fig. 13. TANK CAR UNLOADING AREAS**. Sandboxes under each car catch spilled globs of asphalt.

**Fig. 14. UNLOADING-AREA DETAILS**. Use fine white sand for the sandboxes. Note the steam from the smoke units curling around the tank car.

**Fig. 15. STORAGE TANKS.** The large tank is a Kibri kit and the small one is from an N scale tank car. The sand storage pit at left is a necessity.

at night. The prototype Apex Terminal is open during evening hours and is very well lighted. A row of pole-mounted dual lights extends along the entire length of the facility.

For my six main light poles, I removed the base from Rail Scene's highway lights. This enabled me to add a length of 3/16" tubing to increase the height to a scale 53 feet. I left extra tubing on the bottom so the poles could be inserted into holes drilled in the baseboard, then drilled the top of the tubing open a bit to accept the light post. The lights were also carefully spread open at the wye as seen in fig. 14.

In addition to the lights already installed in the main building, I placed a grain-of-wheat bulb under the roof of the loading dock, one behind the heat exchanger, and another on the rear of the building.

### Fencing

Chain-link fencing completely encloses the prototype Apex terminal. After I drew a plan of the fence on a scrap piece of foam core, I cut .028" wire for fence posts and .033" wire for top and bottom rails. I decided not to include the barbed-wire top section, but did leave room at the post bottoms to insert the fence in the ground. With these posts taped onto my foam core template along with the top and bottom wires, it was easy to solder each joint as fig. 18 shows.

After the wires were all soldered I drilled holes in a mounting board, shown in fig. 19, which I then attached to the front edge of the baseboard.

styrene and placed a dome and walkway above the center hole. The removable hatch cover came from my spare-parts box, but could be made from styrene also.

I removed the tractor's sleeper cab and shortened the truck frame to a smaller wheelbase. This is a lot of work, but it improves the truck's looks, as fig. 16 shows.

### Steam unit

Here's where we can have some fun. Steam swirls up around the prototype tank cars, as shown in fig. 17. On my model I mounted a couple of Seuthe steam-locomotive smoke units under

the tracks opening into the sandboxes as shown in fig. 14. I mounted the switch that controls the smoke units on the rear of the building as shown in fig. 6. When it's turned on, the display comes alive. It's a real conversation piece.

To ensure that the smoke rises, the top of the stack must be almost showing in the sandbox and be off-center under the tank car. I learned the hard way that the smoke easily backs up if the unit is directly under a car.

### Lighting

Lighting always enhances a display model, and it's necessary if you operate

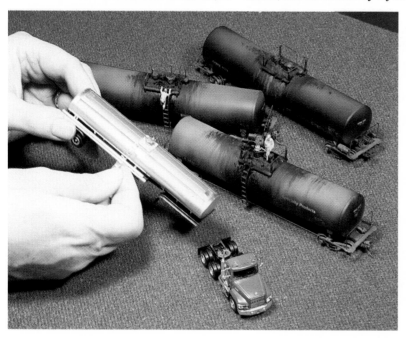

**Fig. 16. TRUCK AND TANK CARS.** A bit of weathering does wonders for the tank cars.

**Fig. 17. STEAM.** Steam rises from the cars during unloading.

Because of the model's length, I made the fence in two parts.

The chain link is made from wedding veil material, available from fabric stores. I cut the fabric to width with an X-acto knife, being sure that the strands ran diagonally. I glued this strip of fabric to the top and bottom rail, working on a small section at a time. After the fence was glued in place, I sprayed it lightly with Chrome.

I made the gates the same way. Since I wanted the gates to swing open, I worked out a simple hinge device by soldering a couple of small sections of brass tubing and connecting them with a pivot wire as shown in fig. 20.

## Final details

Details are what make a model seem real, and there are lots of opportunities with this model. Fire extinguishers, emergency water showers, signs, clothing, and workers in protective clothing and hard hats are all easy to fabricate.

There's a series of small conduit lines which run from the rear of the main building to the loading tower which can also be added as in fig. 21. A sand storage pit near the chemical tank, shown in fig. 15, is another necessary item.

To finish my model, I added a painted backdrop, trees, ground foam, and other scenery material. If you add this industry directly to your layout you can easily blend its terrain with your existing scenery.

I wish you the best in making this unique model. I guarantee it will be a conversation piece. ⚙

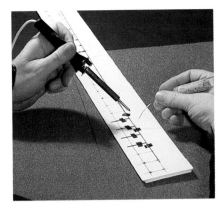

**Fig. 18. CHAIN-LINK FENCE.** Solder the fence frame on a scrap piece of foam core.

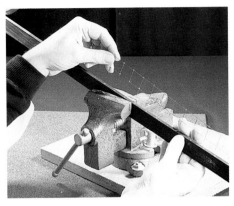

**Fig. 19. FENCE MOUNTING BOARD.** Mounting the fence on a board makes it easier to install later.

**Fig. 20. FENCE GATES.** Brass tubes soldered to the gate ends enable the gates to pivot on wire.

**Fig. 21. CONDUIT LINES.** The thin conduit lines, which run the length of the facility, are .028" brass wire bent to shape.

# Tank farm at Chateaugay

Combining several HO kits to create a large industry

### BY JOHN NEHRICH
### PHOTOS BY THE AUTHOR

CHATEAUGAY, N. Y., on the Rensselaer Polytechnic club's HO scale New England, Berkshire & Western, is a city based in part on Plattsburgh, N. Y. There is a series of tank farms just south of the Delaware & Hudson's small yard in Plattsburgh. Although these tanks are filled from barges that have plied the New York State Barge Canal up to Lake Champlain, and not from tank cars arriving on D&H rails, they seemed a sufficient reason to model a tank farm along the south end of the NEB&W's yard at Chateaugay.

Our rearrangement of the real world has put enough difference in elevation between the lake — which we call Lake Richelieu — and the Hudson River watershed to eliminate the possibility of a canal. That way all of Chateaugay's gasoline and fuel oil must come to town over Berkshire Lines rails.

Tony Steele built our tank farm, the S. Mathieu Fuel Dealer complex, using kits from four manufacturers. The large gray tanks are by Kibri, the black ones by Alexander, and the three smaller ones and the truck-loading station by Williams Brothers — see the site plan drawing. The office building/warehouse was kitbashed from a Timberline warehouse kit which is no longer available. Merely making a complex from a number of kits helps to disguise its heritage and prevents that "I've seen it before" feeling.

### TANKS

Tony stacked the Alexander tanks two-high to make them more imposing and painted them Floquil Grimy Black to suggest slightly older tanks. In order to fit the rearmost tanks into the available space, Tony made them only half round, although with full circle roofs. Trees hide the edges in the finished scene.

In fact trees are not permitted to grow so close to prototype storage tanks, but from normal viewing angles the tanks look like they're in front of a more distant row of trees, not in the midst of the woods. The effect is similar to that of a full-scale building front glued to a mountain flat, where necessarily compressed model elements can represent features miles apart.

Real tanks are typically surrounded by dams meant to hold their contents in case of a tank rupture. The volume enclosed by the dam should equal the volume of the tank, but again Tony had to use modeler's license to selectively compress the dammed-in areas.

The Kibri kits include a dam as part of the molded base. Tony painted these with glue and sprinkled on Highball N scale cinders to represent earthen dams. He used balsa strips, tapered with a rasp and similarly coated, to surround the Alexander tanks. Notice how he put these at an angle to the other tank dams, to visually break up the area. The three smaller tanks of the Williams Brothers kit were also surrounded with a balsa dam, but this was painted to represent concrete.

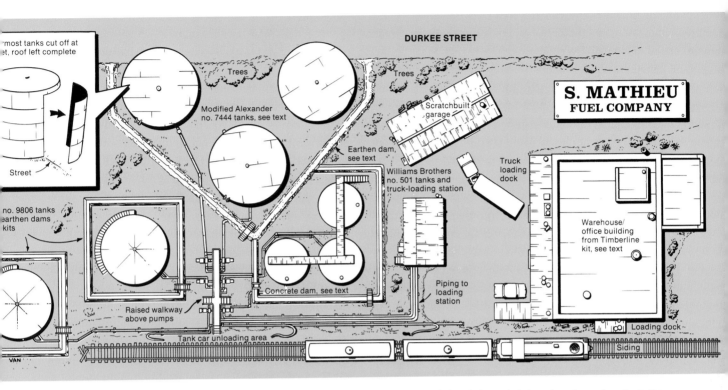

outermost tanks cut off at feet, roof left complete

Street

no. 9806 tanks earthen dams kits

**DURKEE STREET**

Trees

Modified Alexander no. 7444 tanks, see text

Trees

Earthen dam, see text

Williams Brothers no. 501 tanks and truck-loading station

Scratchbuilt garage

**S. MATHIEU FUEL COMPANY**

Truck loading dock

Raised walkway above pumps

Concrete dam, see text

Piping to loading station

Warehouse/ office building from Timberline kit, see text

Tank car unloading area

Loading dock

VAN

Siding

The S. Mathieu fuel dealership is one of several industries at Chateau-on the RPI club's HO scale Berkshire Lines. Author John Nehrich ex-ns how several kits were combined to make an imposing tank farm.

The site plan above and the photograph below show how pipes from the tanks, the truck-filling station, and the unloading hoses come together in a complex of pumps modeled with components from the various tank kits.

Each dam requires a set of access steps for the workmen, and Tony used the kit pieces for this. The piping, pumps, and so forth were cobbled up and combined from pieces in all the kits. Notice how there is a pipeline to each tank through the dams. Hose lines are coiled next to the siding to be attached to the tank cars for unloading — cars in this service usually have bottom outlets.

### BUILDINGS

The truck-loading station is the one from the Williams Brothers kit, but Tony gave it a roof so it would seem more suited to an inclement Northeast clime. The small two-stall garage is scratchbuilt, with corrugated metal siding and roofing.

After consultation with other club members about the Timberline warehouse kit, Tony made two major modifications. He left off the kit's exposed wooden roof trusses, since they are such a peculiar detail. A building such as this would be more likely to have a steel frame, and in the Northeast at least any wooden trusses would be covered. He also left the brick material off the pilasters to model the typical kind of reinforced-concrete-beam structure with brick curtain walls that was almost a standard of post-WWI industries.

If you are looking around for a kit to modify for a similar complex, keep in mind that the building should be one of

this century. This type of industry is clearly a product of the automobile age. Concrete pilasters would really change the appearance of any kit, and you might consider adding plain horizontal and vertical strips of .040″ styrene to brick structure kits like the Ramsey Journal building or the three-story building sold as

Uncle Joe's Barbershop or the Last Stop Funeral Home. Cut off the brick quoins at the corners first, and run the horizontal beams just above the windows. In the case of the Ramsey Journal Building, the oversized bricks could be painted to represent orange-red glazed concrete blocks, also typical of the period. ✿

# Build a modern furniture

## Kitbashing Pikestuff kits into a large HO structure

**BY BILL MORRISSEY**
PLANS AND PHOTOS BY THE AUTHOR

**P**ikestuff's modular kits make steel factory construction easy in HO, while modelers in other scales will have to do a little more "engineering" to use Evergreen corrugated siding and strip materials. My factory is free-lanced from Pikestuff kits, with detail parts from other manufacturers. Off-the-shelf materials are used wherever possible to minimize scratchbuilding. The techniques and materials I use represent typical construction applicable to any structure, large or small.

### Free-lancing with a purpose

Designing a free-lanced model is deceptive. At first glance, it seems fairly simple to put four walls and a roof together, stick in a few doors and windows, and the model's done. Unfortunately, the result is often a structure that just doesn't look convincing.

A better approach is to start with the basic need for the structure and then ask yourself the same questions that architects ask their clients:

• What kind of freight cars will be used? I wanted a source of boxcar traffic on a modern-era layout.

• What kind of business will provide that? A warehouse or a small factory, preferably some sort of light industry. A

An interesting combination of rooflines adds to the apparent size of this modern steel building

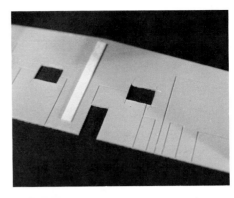

**Fig. 1. WALLS.** Cut out the window and door openings after the wall joint has set hard.

**Fig. 2. BAY WALLS.** Cut out all wall openings and doorways before the bays are assembled.

**Fig. 3. AIR CONDITIONER.** A styrene box, with diesel louvers, simulates a large industrial air conditioner that cools the plant's manufacturing bay.

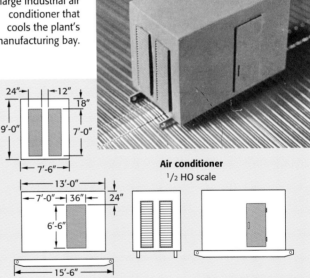

Air conditioner
1/2 HO scale

24"  12"  18"
9'-0"  7'-0"
7'-6"
13'-0"
7'-0"  36"  24"
6'-6"
15'-6"

# factory

**Fig. 4. TRIMMING GUTTER.** Trim off the molded gutter so the office fits flush against the warehouse wall.

furniture factory is a good choice, as it requires specialized structures and has lots of traffic. Wood, upholstery materials, stains and varnishes, hardware, and packaging supplies come in, while bulky packaged items are shipped out.

• What will the structure look like? Modern factories look like a series of steel boxes built on an elevated concrete slab: a big box to house manufacturing, a few smaller ones for storing materials and finished products, and a small box for plant administration.

• What space is available? There's room for a fair-sized structure, 90 feet wide, along a straight siding that will handle at least three 50-foot boxcars. That's pretty lavish by model railroad standards, but this is a major industry.

A large overhead door makes it easy to bring raw materials into the manufacturing bay. The small door in the rear wall is an emergency exit only, so it doesn't have a stairway.

Pikestuff makes a number of generic steel structure kits, so I combined five of them into my furniture plant. Each kit comes with a standard sprue of doors and windows, which meant I had plenty of parts to choose from. I test-fitted some of them and realized there wasn't room for a truck dock. By elevating the office, I cleared the dock and added some interesting detail and another shape to the roofline.

### Manufacturing bay

The manufacturing bay is a good place to start. It's built from a Pikestuff distribution center kit, with one extension module inserted in the middle. Assemble the end walls first, using the reinforcing strips furnished in the kit. After the cement has set, cut the openings in the west wall as shown on the plans and in fig. 1. The east wall has no openings.

Pikestuff walls come with molded grooves marking typical door and window locations, or you can cut your own. I put a pair of high windows in the west wall, with their sills 10 feet above the floor so machinery won't block the light. A single door is included as an emergency exit.

Cut these openings carefully. Pikestuff's doors and windows have overlapping frames to cover some sizing problems, but they aren't very wide. The Pikestuff plastic is thick, so cutting window openings can be frustrating. I get the best results from scribing the outline on the back of the wall, drilling a hole in the center, and using an X-acto no. 11 blade to enlarge the hole until it matches the outline. Don't install any doors or windows yet, as they must be painted separately.

**Fig. 5. CYCLONE VENTILATORS.** File the ventilators so they fit over the peaks on the warehouse roof.

**Fig. 6. OFFICE WALL.** The rear wall of the office has partial corrugations that help position it over the loading dock.

Both sides of the manufacturing bay are made from the distribution center wall panels, with an extra center section added from the extension kit. Assemble both sides according to the Pikestuff directions.

A roll-up freight door is necessary on the north or track side of the bay. The kit has two roll-up doors. Trim the larger one until it's a scale 13 feet high. Otherwise, it will tower above any boxcar spotted next to it. After the wall joints have hardened, cut a centered opening for the freight door as shown in the drawing and fig. 2.

Assemble the walls, taking care to match the beveled corners for a nearly invisible joint. Pikestuff doesn't provide any corner reinforcements, so I add pieces of Evergreen 6 x 6 to keep everything square.

Building the roof is next. Make each side using two roof panels from the distribution center kit, a panel provided in the extension kit, and the appropriate ridge caps. Join the roof halves with three ridge cap/reinforcement pieces. Test-fit, but don't cement the roof to the walls at this time.

Add an industrial air conditioner to the roof, as shown in fig. 3. It's a .020" styrene box detailed with an access door, louvered air intakes, skids, hinges, and latches.

### Stretched sprue

Plastic sprues can be heated and stretched into fine filaments for detailing purposes. Use a small candle as a heat source, holding a piece of sprue well above the flame so it doesn't catch fire. Hold the sprue by both ends, rotating it as you apply the heat until the plastic warms up evenly. The plastic will gradually soften until it becomes pliable. Draw it out with a smooth, even motion, release one end, and let the thread dangle straight down. This keeps the soft filament straight for the few seconds it takes to harden.

Stretching doesn't change the styrene's physical properties, but the stretched styrene gains a toughness that allows it to bend and spring back better than bits of wire.

### The warehouse

Building the two-bay warehouse is a little more complex since it combines parts from a pair of enginehouse kits. When the two kits are assembled side by side, they're about 5 feet wider than the manufacturing bay. I didn't try to change this because it enhances the "prefabricated" appearance of the finished building.

Varying the roof levels makes a more interesting model, so I reduced the overall height of the warehouse. Trim 5 scale feet off the bottom of two enginehouse side walls and two end walls. Make the cuts on the corrugated side of the panel to get a cleaner edge. Use an X-acto no. 11 blade

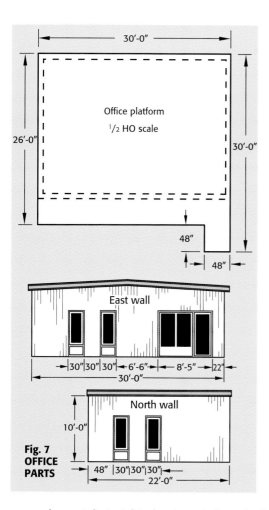

Fig. 7 OFFICE PARTS

East wall

North wall

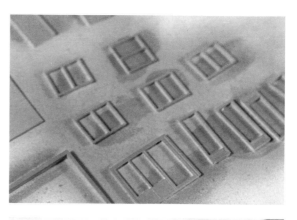

**Fig. 8. PAINTING SMALL PARTS.** Secure small detail parts with dabs of rubber cement so the airbrush spray does not blow them away.

**Fig. 9. OFFICE STAIRWAY.** Commercial parts greatly simplify construction of the office stairway and its safety railings.

and a metal straightedge to cut about halfway through, bend the panel at the scored line to separate the parts, and smooth any ragged edges with a file. Use these shortened pieces as patterns to cut two plain end walls and a side wall from .040" styrene sheet.

Cement two end walls together, side by side, to make the east end of the warehouse. You'll need to remove the small gutters that interfere near the top corners and add a reinforcing strip across the joint. After the joint has hardened, cut door and window openings as shown in the drawing.

You'll also need to trim part of the gutter off the east end so the office wall can fit flush against the warehouse wall. Since the office is 30 feet wide, trim 15 feet of gutter on each side of the right-hand peak. See fig. 4. Neatness isn't necessary, as this area will be covered later.

Cut the door and window openings in the north side of the warehouse as shown in the drawing. Once again, there are no openings in the south side. Cement together the north, east, and south walls, keeping the corners square and reinforcing them with more 6 x 6.

Cement together the plain .040" styrene ends to make the hidden west end wall, saving the extra Pikestuff ends for future use. Reinforce the joint and let it harden. The completed west wall must match the Pikestuff east wall, or it won't support the roof properly. Install the west wall and reinforce the corners with 6 x 6 styrene.

Test-fit the intermediate wall, make any size adjustment that may be needed, and cement it in position with 6 x 6 corner reinforcements. Make this wall just wide enough to fit inside the end walls and the same height as the roof support lip along the tops of the walls. See fig. 2.

The warehouse roof is really two Pikestuff roof assemblies jointly supported on top of the center wall. You may

want to add extra material along the top edge of this wall to make it thicker and ensure good roof support.

Install the cyclone ventilators at this point so they can be painted the same color as the roof (aluminum). Shape the castings to match the roof slope, and install the ventilators so they're evenly spaced along the peak, as shown in fig. 5. Fill the gap between the roof halves at the peak with strips of l x 2 styrene. Set the roof assemblies aside for now.

**The office**

The office/showroom kit includes three end walls and two sides. Discard the wall that has openings for large display windows. Another wall has corrugations that stop at a molding about a third of the way down. See fig. 6. This wall becomes the back wall of the office, with the molding acting as a positioning guide against the warehouse roof.

Shorten the side walls to match the dimensions shown in the drawing. Cut the door and window openings and carefully fit, but do not install, the windows. Assemble the office walls, but don't install the roof at this time.

The office sits on an elevated platform made of .020" styrene, cut to the dimensions shown in fig. 7. Frame the edges with strips of 2 x 12 styrene. Sand the edges after the cement has dried, and set it aside for now.

**The concrete floor**

Prototype steel buildings are generally constructed on a reinforced concrete slab. In this case, it's built high enough to serve as a loading platform.

My platform is made of .020" styrene sheets, cemented edge to edge and reinforced underneath with splice strips. Some plastic suppliers in large cities sell 4 x 8-foot styrene sheets that will allow you to cut the slab in a single piece.

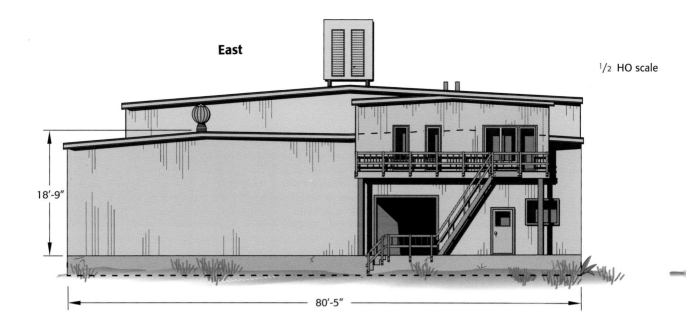

East

$^1/_2$ HO scale

18'-9"

80'-5"

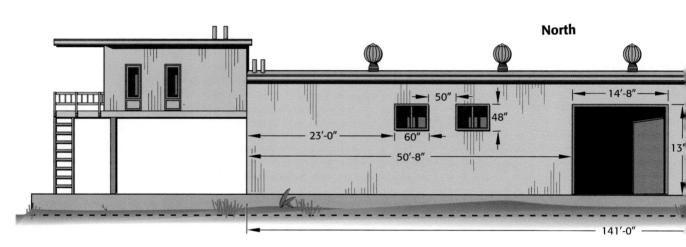

North

50"

14'-8"

48"

23'-0"

60"

50'-8"

13"

141'-0"

It should be carefully sized for an exact fit beneath the manufacturing bay and warehouse with an open area for the loading dock. My dimensions are shown in the drawing, but you should match it to your factory.

Cut .020" styrene into strips a scale 42" wide, and cement them in position to form sides around the bottom of the platform, not the edges. Cut and add internal stiffeners, just like the outside strips, in a grid pattern with about 6" between the elements. When all the stiffeners are in place, cement 6 x 6 reinforcements at all the joints.

Add concrete steps to the platform. I made mine by stacking and laminating pieces of .020" styrene, but you can substitute Pikestuff's plastic casting. After the cement has set hard, sand the seams so the base looks solid.

### Painting

I used Testor's Model Master paints throughout, spraying the walls with a light beige mixed from Military Brown and white. The trim is straight Military Brown that I brushed onto the eave moldings and sprayed on the doors and window frames. You may prefer some other color combination, so look at real buildings for ideas.

Put a dab of rubber cement on a piece of cardboard to hold small parts that would get blown away. Rubber cement holds the parts nicely, as shown in fig. 8, yet they lift off without difficulty. Scrape off any paint that gets onto the cementing surfaces, as it will interfere with the bond.

All of my roofs are sprayed silver, but white is another commonly used color. Either way, the ventilators should still be silver. Paint the base edges and dock area with a light gray to represent relatively new and unweathered concrete. (The yellowish concrete color we usually see appears as concrete weathers over the years.) The air conditioner is an industrial green.

### Roof details

Prototype factories have pipes sticking up all over them. Plumbing vents appear above every drain for toilets and sinks, water-cooler drains, shop sinks, and so forth. These vents are usually 2" or 4" pipes projecting 18" to 36" above the roof. Exhaust vents are found over every combustion site, ranging in size from 6" to 36" in diameter, with similar heights above the roof.

Decide where the plumbing and heating equipment would be located in your building and add suitable vents made of $^1/_{16}$" and $^3/_{32}$" tubing. Add the air conditioner so it straddles the roof ridge on the manufacturing bay.

### Final assembly

Cement the manufacturing bay to the warehouse, then position and cement it onto the concrete platform. Use a small brush to carefully apply cement from the inside. Don't apply too much cement at any spot, as the excess can run down the outside and mar the paint job. It's much

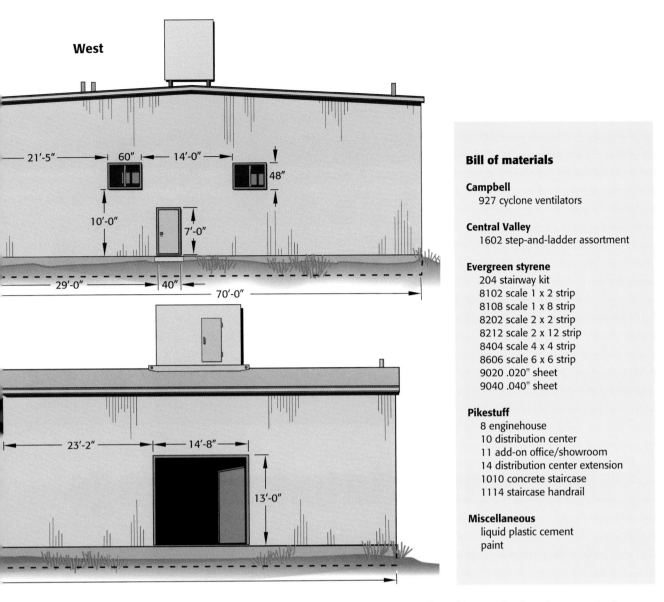

West

**Bill of materials**

**Campbell**
    927 cyclone ventilators

**Central Valley**
    1602 step-and-ladder assortment

**Evergreen styrene**
    204 stairway kit
    8102 scale 1 x 2 strip
    8108 scale 1 x 8 strip
    8202 scale 2 x 2 strip
    8212 scale 2 x 12 strip
    8404 scale 4 x 4 strip
    8606 scale 6 x 6 strip
    9020 .020" sheet
    9040 .040" sheet

**Pikestuff**
    8 enginehouse
    10 distribution center
    11 add-on office/showroom
    14 distribution center extension
    1010 concrete staircase
    1114 staircase handrail

**Miscellaneous**
    liquid plastic cement
    paint

better to come back later to add more cement. Be sure to add reinforcing strips wherever the walls meet the base.

Cement the office and its platform together so its back wall is flush with the floor. Join the office to the warehouse, supporting it with H columns made from 1 x 12 styrene.

### Window glazing

Add glazing to all the windows. I used Microscale's Micro Kristal Klear. These windows are a little larger than Microscale recommends, but I've found that they work fine with the right technique.

Load up a tapered round toothpick with Kristal Klear, and run a bead of compound around the inside of the entire window opening. With a fresh load of liquid on the toothpick, insert it in the window opening and lay the toothpick over, next to one end of the frame and with the toothpick touching opposite sides (touching three sides of the frame). Then, drag a film of compound the length of the window and pull the toothpick out gently. If the film breaks, reload the toothpick and try again.

Keep the window horizontal until the glazing compound has dried. If you set the model upright too early, the glazing compound sags to the bottom of the window frame.

### Final details

Build the staircase leading to the office from an Evergreen stairway kit. Be careful to keep the treads square from side to side and front to back, as inaccuracies here are conspicuous. Paint the steel staircase flat black and cement it in place.

The platform steps and the office stairs are guarded with railings from the Central Valley step-and-ladder assortment, as shown in fig. 9. Carefully free a railing from the sprue, and cut it a little oversize so you can trim it to exact length after installation.

The horizontal railings are sections of the Central Valley industrial ladders with 2 x 2 styrene posts. Keep the posts at right angles, as this railing catches visitors' attention. Paint the railing assemblies flat black, and cement them in place. Install the railings so they're 36" high and level.

The last step is to install the roofs. Fit them carefully and use cement sparingly. You need to cement them only at the corners and the middle of each side. The more cement you use, the more likely you are to damage the paint.

There's an emergency exit at the west end of the factory that intentionally doesn't have a stairway or ladder. This door isn't an entrance; it's strictly an emergency exit, and anyone using it is expected to jump.

Any profitable factory is a busy place, so you'll want to include a forklift, a couple of palletized cartons, and workers on the shipping dock. Preiser has some nice figures, including men in hard hats and some climbing stairs, that would fit right in. Don't forget to add a parking lot and vehicles as part of the surrounding scenery. ✿

A. L. Schmidt

# Modeling Hansen Storage

## A modern warehouse with loads of potential for operation

### BY GORDON ODEGARD
#### PHOTOS BY THE AUTHOR

I'VE WANTED to build a model of Hansen Storage ever since I first noticed it back in 1978. It seemed so typical of modern warehouses, and I thought it would be easy to model and would provide an opportunity for lots of model railroad operation.

In fact, about the only problem with modeling such a structure is its size — it's huge. See fig. 1. A full-scale HO model of Hansen Storage would come out an actual 4'-3" x 11'-0". It would completely cover a typical 4 x 8-foot layout and hang out over the edges!

I built my scaled-down version of Hansen Storage for the Milwaukee, Racine & Troy, our MODEL RAILROADER Magazine HO club layout. The model is a scale 268 feet long, still large by model railroad standards, but reducing it any further would mean sacrificing character and proportions. This is a simple building, basically a pair of boxes, and you can easily alter it to fit whatever site you have.

#### ABOUT THE PROTOTYPE

Warehouses handle almost every material and product you can think of. Typical present-day items are foodstuffs,

paper goods, tools, manufactured products, and parts. Besides cooled and heated areas, some facilities have refrigerated storage facilities for meats and frozen foods.

Located in Wauwatosa, a suburb of Milwaukee, Hansen Storage is just one part of an enterprise that the Hansen family has operated for almost 90 years. A large portion of the business at this facility is manufactured food products, but they also handle a fair amount of rolled paper for printing plants.

Originally two tracks entered the enclosed loading dock, for a total capacity of 30 cars. Rail shipments have declined in recent years, though, and one indoor track has been removed.

A rolling steel door shuts out the elements. Products are unloaded with forklifts and stacked as high as possible, with some reaching close to the 28-foot height. As much as possible items are stored on pallets.

When the maximum number of 50-foot cars was handled, they were spotted on

the two tracks with the car doors lined up. Then metal bridge plates were laid to interconnect the cars and the dock.

In those days the Chicago & North Western switched the warehouse daily, but now it's every other day. Even though the rail traffic has dwindled, it's the most appealing feature of this industry to us as model railroaders and I'm sure most of you building such a structure will want to emphasize that aspect.

The north side of the Hansen building has a truck dock with 33 doors, alternately painted red, yellow, blue, and orange. As goods are needed by various distributors, retailers, and manufacturers, they're loaded into trucks and shipped.

#### BUILDING THE MODEL

My "cutoff" model is placed against the backdrop with the tracks extending through to the other side, where they're hidden under the scenery. Each track will hold seven 50-foot cars. A lucky result of this arrangement from a model railroader's point of view is that I didn't have to model the more complicated truck dock.

Figure 2 shows the ¾" plywood base I built for my structure. Yours may

**Left:** Gordy's HO model has been selectively compressed, yet it retains the character of the real structure. The Alloy Forms chain link fence is a vital detail for a modern warehouse where good security is a major concern.

**Fig. 1. THE PROTOTYPE.** Hansen Storage, beside the green field in the upper right photo, is in Wauwatosa, Wis., and is typical of modern warehouses found on the outskirts of major metropolitan areas. The building is nearly 1,000 feet long. Goods are delivered by rail or highway, then stored until called for by their owners. Gordy didn't model the north side of the building with its 33-door truck dock, shown in the lower photo. Note all the ducts on the roof.

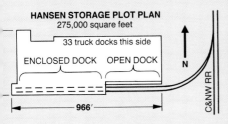

HANSEN STORAGE PLOT PLAN
275,000 square feet

33 truck docks this side

ENCLOSED DOCK   OPEN DOCK

N

C&NW RR

966'

vary, depending on your model's size and location. I covered the base with Midwest cork sheet to match the other roadbed on the MR&T.

Next, I laid out the building site and the track center lines, using 1¾" spacing. After locating the necessary opening in the backdrop, I cut it out with a saber saw. Then I added a plywood extension to the other side and covered it with the sheet cork.

Once both base pieces were in place, I installed Kadee no. 308 uncoupling magnets flush with the top of the cork. Then I laid Walthers code 83 track, making sure joiners came near the splice of the two plywood base pieces so that later I'd be able to easily remove the structure portion for scenicking and detailing.

A sturdy 1 x 1 wood bumper at the track ends helps keep cars off the floor. Also there's a 2"-high cardboard fence tacked to the sides of the plywood. You may want to add a detection circuit near the ends of the tracks so you can tell when the cars are getting close.

### THE ENCLOSED DOCK

I built the closed and open dock sections as separate pieces so it would be easier to remove the closed portion if a car got derailed inside.

Let's start with the enclosed section. The construction details are shown in fig. 3. I made my walls by laminating Evergreen corrugated styrene to styrene sheet. Where I needed a little time to position the parts I used Testor's liquid plastic cement. When I wanted the parts to bond immediately, I used the much faster-setting Tenax 7R.

For large structures like this I prefer to use sheet styrene purchased from Cadillac Plastics, a local supplier. It comes in 4 x 8-foot sheets and saves you

**Fig. 2. THE BASE, Left.** Here we see the wedge-shaped plywood base that Gordy installed to support the building, with the two tracks extending about 30" through the backdrop and below the scenery on the other side. **Above.** Gordy installed Kadee's large uncoupling magnets under the ties by cutting recesses through the cork roadbed and into the first layer of the plywood.

49

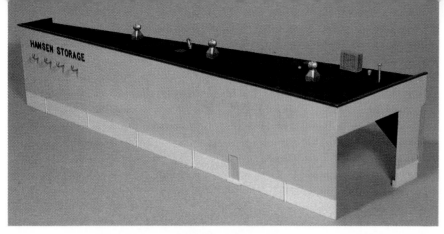

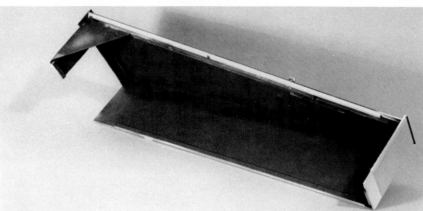

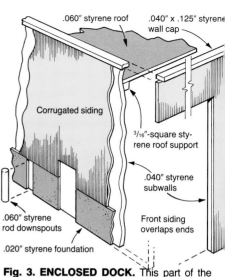

.060" styrene roof

.040" x .125" styrene wall cap

Corrugated siding

3/16"-square styrene roof support

.040" styrene subwalls

.060" styrene rod downspouts

.020" styrene foundation

Front siding overlaps ends

**Fig. 3. ENCLOSED DOCK.** This part of the structure is a simple box with a corrugated overlay and a few details. Gordy braced the interior with styrene strips and painted it flat black.

the work of having to splice together smaller sheets. You also save money, but unless you plan to build a lot of big structures, it probably isn't worth the effort it takes to find and transport.

First I cut the subwall panels from .040"-thick sheet. Then I took a strip of .020" styrene that's 5'-3" wide and applied it along the bottom edges to represent the foundation wall. Note that on the long wall you'll be leaving five spaces a scale 12" wide to accommodate the downspouts.

I added the corrugated siding, making sure it extended past the corners on the long wall and overlapped the ends. Next, I cut the opening for the Pikestuff door and installed it. Five 5'-3" lengths of .060"-diameter styrene rod were used for the downspouts.

Then I cut a .060"-thick roof section to fit and assembled the walls and roof. The insides of the walls and roof were braced with large styrene strips for

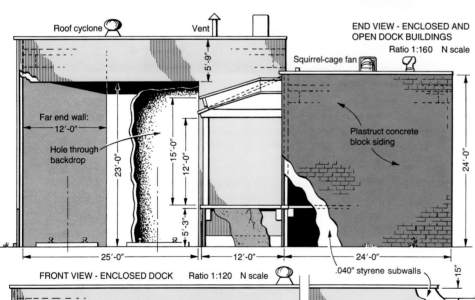

Roof cyclone

Vent

5'-9"

END VIEW - ENCLOSED AND OPEN DOCK BUILDINGS

Ratio 1:160    N scale

Squirrel-cage fan

Far end wall: 12'-0"

Hole through backdrop

23'-0"

15'-0"

12'-0"

5'-3"

Plastruct concrete block siding

24'-0"

25'-0"

12'-0"

24'-0"

.040" styrene subwalls

15"

.040" x .125" styrene wall cap

.060" styrene roof

Air conditioner

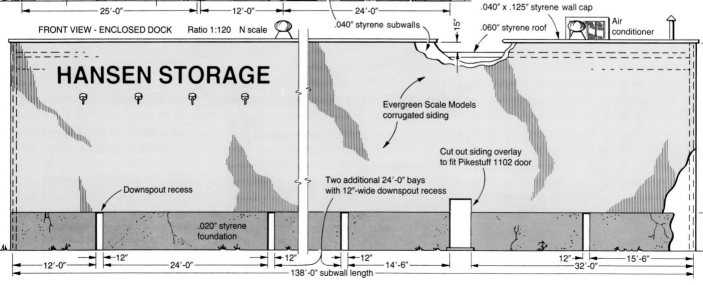

FRONT VIEW - ENCLOSED DOCK    Ratio 1:120    N scale

# HANSEN STORAGE

Evergreen Scale Models corrugated siding

Cut out siding overlay to fit Pikestuff 1102 door

Downspout recess

.020" styrene foundation

Two additional 24'-0" bays with 12"-wide downspout recess

23'-0"

5'-3"

12'-0"    12"    24'-0"    12"    12"    14'-6"    12"    32'-0"    15'-6"

138'-0" subwall length

50

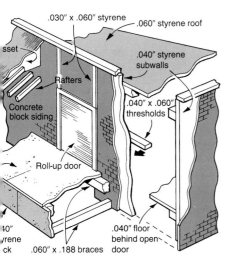

.030" x .060" styrene

.060" styrene roof

sset

.040" styrene
subwalls

Rafters

.040" x .060"
thresholds

Concrete
block siding

Roll-up door

.040" floor
behind open
door

40"
rene
ck

.060" x .188 braces

**Fig. 4. OPEN DOCK.** The canopies add interest to this section. The upside-down view shows the bracing that keeps the dock from warping. The open door required a fake floor.

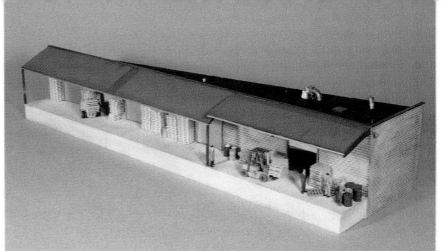

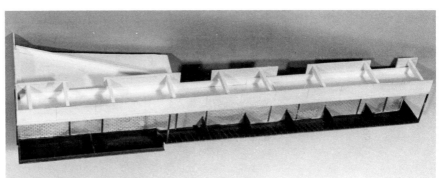

strength and to prevent warping. You can use whatever is in your scrap box. Finally, I added a large triangular support between the roof and large end wall to keep it vertical.

### THE OPEN DOCK SECTION

This section is a little more complicated. See fig. 4 for the construction details, and cut the subwalls to size. This time we're using Plastruct concrete block for the overlay.

I started by cutting the Pikestuff roll-up doors 9'-3" high with a razor saw, except for one I modeled open by leaving the side rails and cutting away all but 12" of door at the top. After making sure the doors fit, I waited to install them after the entire structure had been painted.

Assembling the two main walls and adding the interior bracing came next. Again, the size of the bracing wasn't critical. I added a .060" styrene roof panel and installed a .040" styrene floor behind the open door, cutting it to extend into the opening to form the threshold. I cut .040" x .060" strips for the thresholds of the closed doors.

After cutting out a dock platform and wall, I scored them into 13 panels, each about 10 feet long. The edge of the dock should extend over the wall about 3". Be sure the dock edge clears *all* your freight cars. (Some models are oversize, you

know.) I braced the dock underneath with cross pieces of styrene strip.

To finish both structure sections, I added .040" x .125" styrene cap material to the tops of the walls, set flush with the inside wall surfaces.

FRONT VIEW - OPEN DOCK    Ratio 1:160    N scale

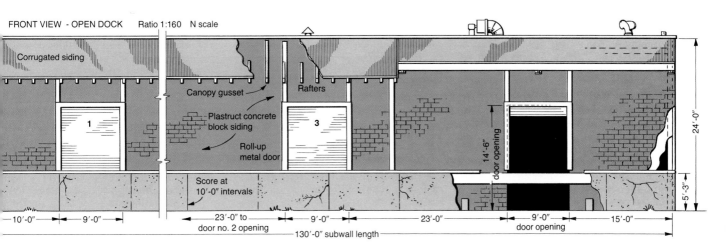

Corrugated siding

Canopy gusset

Plastruct concrete
block siding

Rafters

Roll-up
metal door

Score at
10'-0" intervals

1

3

14'-6"
door opening

9'-0"
door opening

24'-0"

5'-3"

— 10'-0" — — 9'-0" —     — 23'-0" to — — 9'-0" —     — 23'-0" —     — 9'-0" —     — 15'-0" —
door no. 2 opening

— 130'-0" subwall length —

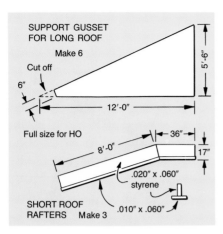

SUPPORT GUSSET
FOR LONG ROOF
Make 6

Cut off

6″

5′-6″

12′-0″

Full size for HO

36″

8′-0″

17″

.020″ x .060″
styrene

.010″ x .060″

SHORT ROOF
RAFTERS    Make 3

**Fig. 5. CANOPIES.** Corrugated material fills the vertical gap between the two levels of the canopies, above right. Gordy modeled only the visible ends of the rafters, below right, and he shortened the Pikestuff doors, below.

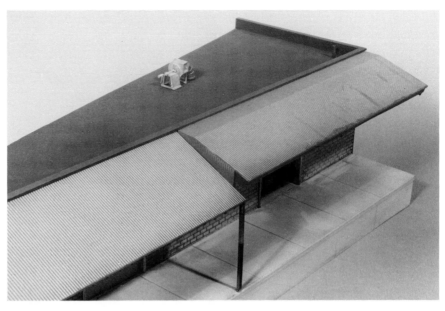

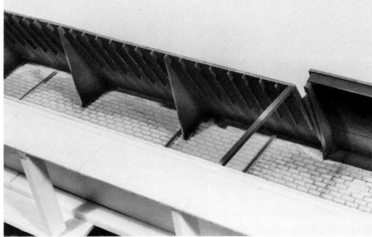

## THE CANOPY

These roof sections were the hardest part of the project, but then let's face it, without them the model wouldn't have much character at all.

First I cut the long roof from corrugated styrene. Then I cemented six triangular gussets made from .020″ styrene to the underside, as shown in fig. 5. I placed one gusset on the far left, set against the wall of the enclosed dock, and put a .020″ x .060″ styrene rafter at the other end. Then I spaced the remaining gussets equally along under the canopy.

I cemented seven equally spaced .020″ x .060″ rafters between each pair of gussets and between the end rafter and its adjacent gusset. Then I attached the canopy to the wall and added a .060″-square corner post at each end.

For the short, peaked canopy, I cut and then scored and bent another piece of the corrugated material. I made the rafters for this shorter roof from .020″ styrene, capping the underside with .010″ x .060″ strip. A .020″ x .125″ fascia strip cemented across the front of all three supports dressed up the edge.

Next, I cut a piece of corrugated roof material to fill the gap between the two canopy sections. For gutters, I cemented lengths of Plastruct 1/16″ channel to the edges of both sections of the canopy.

One last detail completed the open dock wall. I cut pieces of .030″ x .060″ styrene to fit vertically between the top of the rolling door frames and the underside of the canopy and painted them and the loading doors Floquil Old Silver. I didn't install the doors or the verticals until I'd painted the rest of the model.

I applied a numeral to the middle of each loading door (1 through 4), using 3/16″-high dry-transfer numbers from Woodland Scenics.

## MAIN ROOF DETAILS

From most layout viewing angles the roof is a dominant surface, so there should be a variety of details here. These can be plain as long as they're recognizable and look functional.

Soil pipe vents for lavatories can be scale 6″-diameter pieces of metal or plastic tube. You can use blocks of wood or plastic to represent heating and air-conditioning units, as shown in fig. 6. Air vents and stacks are available from several manufacturers. Don't forget a few access hatches.

## PAINTING

I painted my model with an airbrush and Floquil paints. For the enclosed dock corrugated walls I blended Depot Buff and Reefer White 50:50; the wall caps were done in Tuscan Red.

For the concrete foundation and dock I used a mix of 4 parts Reefer White to 1 part Depot Buff. I applied a thin wash of Polly S Grimy Black to the concrete finish and the Plastruct block material.

I painted the flat roofs Grimy Black and covered them with Woodland Scenics cinders. For the canopy roofs I used Floquil Gun Metal. I added a little Floquil Engine Black to some of this color and highlighted one section. Then I painted my loading doors, gutters, and

## Bill of materials

**Alloy Forms**
2009 chain link fence
2015 squirrel-cage exhaust fan

**California Scale Models**
241 roof vent
244 roof vent

**Campbell Scale Models**
927 cyclone vent (2)

**Evergreen Scale Models styrene**
103 .010" x .060" strip
126 .020" x .125" strip
133 .030" x .060" strip
153 .060" x .060" strip
156 .060" x .125" strip
158 .060" x .188" strip
189 .125" x .250" strip
196 ³/₁₆"-square strip
222 .062" tubing
4526 .040" x .040" corrugated sheet
4527 .040" x .060" corrugated sheet

**Floquil paints**
110010 Engine Black
110011 Reefer White
110025 Tuscan Red
110087 Depot Buff
110100 Old Silver
110108 Gun Metal

**Gloor Craft**
883 building lights (2)

**Kibri**
1002 forklift (2)

**Pikestuff**
1102 solid door
1109 roll-up door (2)

**Plastruct**
302 channel
10103 concrete block sheet
PABT 10 plastic alphabet

**Polly S paints**
410013 Grimy Black
410073 Rust

**Scale Scenics**
3505 LP gas tank
5002 pallets (4)

**Selley**
151 oil drums

**Tenax**
7 plastic welder

**Testor**
3502 liquid plastic cement

**Woodland Scenics**
DT-508 Gothic black dry transfers

**Miscellaneous**
.020" styrene sheet
.040" styrene sheet
.060" styrene sheet

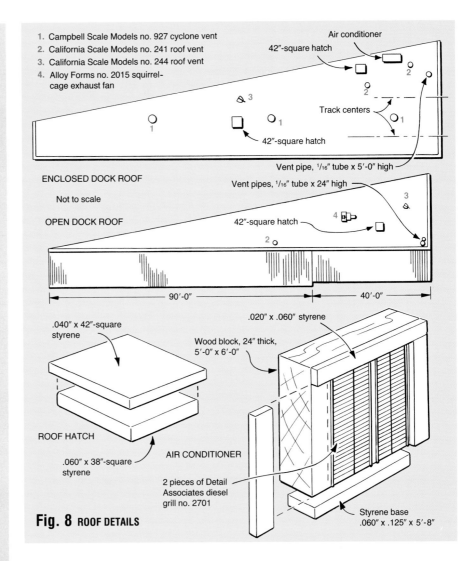

1. Campbell Scale Models no. 927 cyclone vent
2. California Scale Models no. 241 roof vent
3. California Scale Models no. 244 roof vent
4. Alloy Forms no. 2015 squirrel-cage exhaust fan

**Fig. 8** ROOF DETAILS

roof details Old Silver. I applied a few touches and streaks of Polly S Rust to weather the gutters and corrugated roofing. All the interior surfaces were sprayed Grimy Black.

With the open door I thought I'd have to partially detail the interior. While this would have made an interesting scene, I found it unnecessary with the black interior. Have at it if you like; it's too much work for me.

For the HANSEN STORAGE lettering I cut individual letters from a Plastruct plastic alphabet set, then fixed them to a strip of upside-down masking tape and sprayed them Floquil Tuscan Red. Using cyanoacrylate adhesive (CA) I cemented the letters to the wall.

Next, I bent four Gloor Craft light castings so they would illuminate the sign from below and drilled holes to mount them. Also, I mounted one to the end wall of the open dock. I painted these Old Silver.

### FINAL DETAILS

One problem with a low-profile structure is getting it to blend into the backdrop. Part of the solution is to make the structure and the scenery in front of it interesting and colorful so they'll draw the viewer's eyes to the modeled area and away from the background. Correspondingly, the background should be subdued so as not to detract from the the three-dimensional models.

I recommend adding lots of detail to the dock. You can include figures, hand trucks, forklifts, boxes, crates, barrels, a scale or two, and piles of empty wood pallets. Be sure you match the equipment and packaging to the era being modeled. Wooden barrels haven't been seen much since the 1940s, for instance, and forklift trucks were rare before that time. Until the '40s, most materials were moved with two- or four-wheel hand trucks or carts pulled by a small motor tractor.

As a finishing touch I enclosed my structure with chain link fence. It was a big job yet worth it, as it really sets off the structure. I added splotches of rust to the fencing to give it character.

I hope you enjoy building a version of Hansen Storage for your layout. One special perk I enjoy is the satisfaction of having visitors to the MR&T recognize my model: "Oh, yeah, that's the place alongside Highway 45." ☼

# Modeling Maxon Mills

## A pike-sized HO scale industry compressed from a prototype

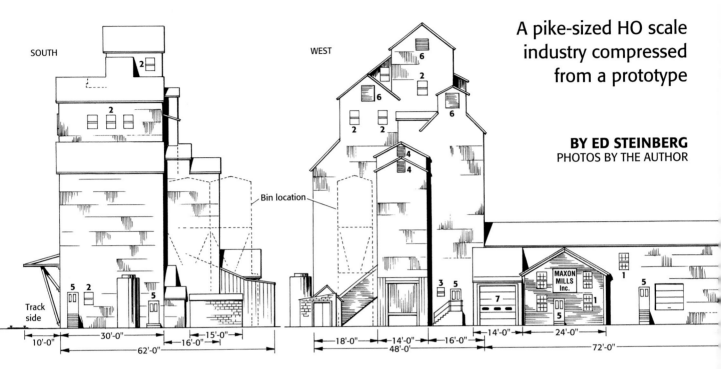

SOUTH

WEST

Bin location

Track side

**BY ED STEINBERG**
PHOTOS BY THE AUTHOR

The real Maxon Mills in New York State has seen better days. All of the deliveries and shipments move by truck today but the mill was once an important railroad customer.

The east side of Maxon Mills shows the doors and chutes once used for railroad cars. If you're strapped for space, model only this side of the building.

When you compare it to the prototype it's hard to believe the author's HO model is selectively compressed. It still has all the flavor of the real thing.

**M**y HO model of the Maxon Mills feed mill is mostly a result of Jim Kelly's Bull Session comments in the September 1992 MODEL RAILROADER about the relative size of industries served by rail. Often we model structures too small to warrant rail service. Unless an industry is larger than the freight cars spotted on its siding, it probably would ship by truck and look strange with a railroad car next to it.

To avoid this problem we can, and sometimes do, model only the track-side part of a large establishment, suggesting the rest is unseen. We also take relatively small examples from the real world and make them even smaller. This is called selective compression, and that's exactly what I've done with Maxon Mills.

### Locating a prototype

One day as I drove north through Wassaic, N. Y., looking around for country scenes to photograph, I spotted the roof of what turned out to be Maxon Mills, a Midwestern-looking grain elevator in eastern New York state.

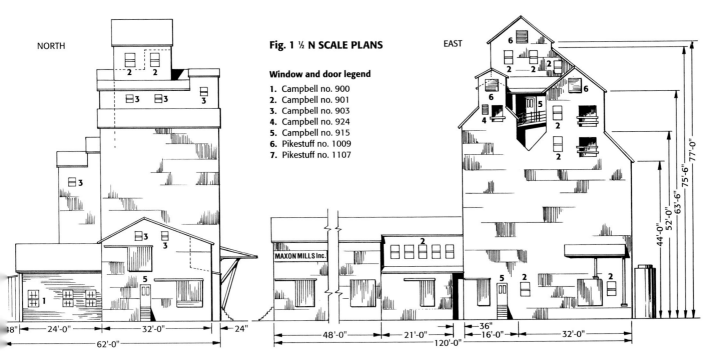

NORTH

**Fig. 1 ½ N SCALE PLANS**

EAST

**Window and door legend**

1. Campbell no. 900
2. Campbell no. 901
3. Campbell no. 903
4. Campbell no. 924
5. Campbell no. 915
6. Pikestuff no. 1009
7. Pikestuff no. 1107

MAXON MILLS Inc.

It took three trips to get all the information I needed, including photos, notes, and measurements. I made one trip just because the tree south of the office wing dropped its leaves to reveal what it was hiding.

My first impression of Maxon Mills was that it was quite old with a succession of additions. I later learned the mill was actually built in the 1950s, but the office was a remnant of a 19th-century hotel.

At one time grain was delivered by rail, lifted, ground and blended into livestock feed, stored in the tower, and discharged into trucks in the narrow extension on the west side of the building. The large steel storage bins were added later.

A trackside bin east of the tower building once received grain from boxcars and a pit and auger beneath the track was added in the 1960s to unload covered hoppers.

## Compressing the mill

I first drew the full-length building in HO scale, all 180 feet of it. That's over two feet of layout space, and with the fuel tank on the north end and some room to get around the south I'd have needed nearly 30 inches of layout real estate! Clearly selective compression was in order.

My model is reduced by approximately one-third in length and width, and 20 percent in height. Figure 1 shows 1/2 N scale drawings of the compressed mill. Enlarge them on a photocopier 368 percent for HO scale, 500 percent for S, and 666 percent for O.

## Getting started

My model of Maxon Mills is a series of plastic boxes with window and door openings punched in. I cemented the boxes together, wrapped them in corrugated aluminum, and then installed the windows and doors.

Start with the main elevator tower. I used mostly .060" sheet styrene for the core building, but if I were doing it again I might use .080" styrene instead for more strength.

Cut out the windows before assembling the walls. First score the back of the styrene with an X-acto no. 24 blade, then chisel out the opening with an X-acto no. 18 blade or a sharp 1/4" wood chisel. Finish with a small, flat file.

Assembly comes next. To make a really strong joint, apply liquid cement to both of the surfaces and press them together firmly. Reinforce the joints with .100"-square styrene strip, and make sure they are straight, true, and square. They don't have to be beautiful, though, since they'll be covered with siding later.

Now add carefully squared floors, one near the bottom and one near the top. These keep the box square and rigid, and the upper square also serves as a platform for the upper structure's walls and partitions. See fig. 2.

## Other styrene notes

Build the rest of the boxes that will be covered with metal in the same way. Use Evergreen no. 4062 novelty siding for the interior visible through the loading door. I detailed this interior wall with columns, studs, and a loading door, painting them all tan to represent bare, worn wood.

Make sure all the corners are square. I used a 12" steel framing square and a combination square. If the walls are out of plumb at this stage it will be hard to square subsequent modules.

As you complete each module, add styrene "plugs" to receive the next one. See fig. 3. In most cases you can use a frame of .100"-square styrene strips, but for the board-and-batten garage use a piece of .015" styrene slightly smaller than the end wall. Line the inside edge of each roof gable with .100"-square styrene. These plugs and liners provided surfaces for good plastic-to-plastic joints instead of plastic to aluminum siding.

## Adding the aluminum

Use scale 48" strips of Campbell corrugated aluminum for the sheathing.

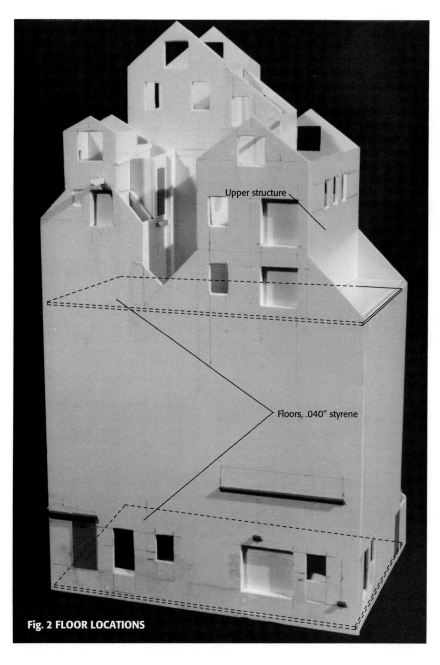

**Fig. 2 FLOOR LOCATIONS**

Upper structure

Floors, .040" styrene

See fig. 4. It adheres nicely with rubber cement, but can be a messy operation.

Use a carpenter's square to draw pencil lines around each module, the first line 48" from the bottom and all the others at 42" intervals to allow the aluminum to overlap the course below. Without guide lines it's impossible to keep the aluminum strips parallel.

Simply lay the aluminum across the door and window openings. After the rubber cement has dried for several hours, you can cut out the openings in the aluminum. Use a sharp blade, and work very, very carefully.

The sheathing goes slowly, partly because of the need to allow cement to dry, partly because of the obstructions previously cemented to the plastic core, and partly because there's so much aluminum to install!

Spray-paint and glaze the Campbell windows and doors before cementing them in place with rubber cement. See fig. 1 for notes about the scratchbuilt doors and other details.

### Garage and office

Make three sides of the garage from Evergreen no. 14544 board-and-batten siding, and use .040" plain styrene on the back. Airbrush it with Polly S no. 400414 Roof Red.

The prototype office is sheathed in white asbestos siding and has a somewhat elaborate cornice owing to its hotel heritage. Since I wasn't trying to build an exact replica I simplified the office, building it out of Evergreen no. 4062 novelty siding.

Before painting the office white, mask where the sign will go so you'll be able to cement the sign to bare styrene. Make both signs of .030" styrene with dry-transfer lettering.

### Building details and roofing

Build the bridge between the gables on the east side of the elevator tower using .060" styrene. Make the railing out of .040"-square strip styrene as shown in fig. 5.

You can use Pikestuff no. 1015 shingle roof sheet for almost all the mill's roofing. It's nicely detailed material and easy to shape but I wish it came in longer sheets. You'll have to splice two pieces for the long warehouse roof, and on my model the joint leaves a lot to be desired.

At the top of the tower, the prototype mill has what looks like a chimney treated with excess growth hormone. It must be some sort of ventilator stack. I made mine out of scraps from commercial building kits.

The next task was the shed roof over the unloading pit. Make it from

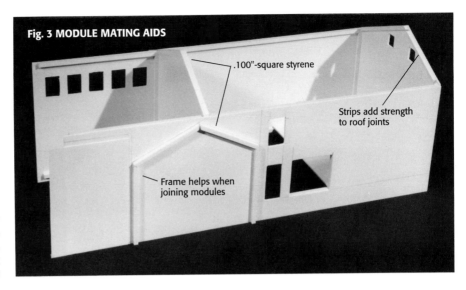

**Fig. 3 MODULE MATING AIDS**

.100"-square styrene

Strips add strength to roof joints

Frame helps when joining modules

**Fig. 4 ADDING CORRUGATED SIDING**

Lines drawn 42" apart as guides to line up sheathing

Cut angles and openings after rubber cement cures

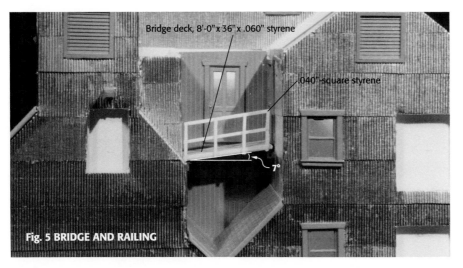

Bridge deck, 8'-0"x 36" x .060" styrene

.040"-square styrene

7°

**Fig. 5 BRIDGE AND RAILING**

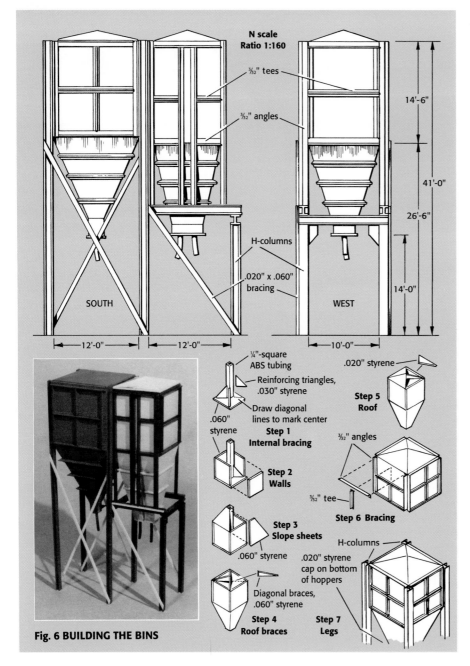

N scale
Ratio 1:160

³⁄₃₂" tees

³⁄₃₂" angles

14'-6"

41'-0"

26'-6"

H-columns

.020" x .060"
bracing

14'-0"

SOUTH

WEST

12'-0"  12'-0"  10'-0"

¼"-square
ABS tubing

Reinforcing triangles,
.030" styrene

Draw diagonal
lines to mark center

.060"
styrene

**Step 1
Internal bracing**

**Step 2
Walls**

**Step 3
Slope sheets**

.060" styrene

**Step 4
Roof braces**

Diagonal braces,
.060" styrene

.020" styrene

**Step 5
Roof**

³⁄₃₂" angles

³⁄₃₂" tee

**Step 6 Bracing**

H-columns

.020" styrene
cap on bottom
of hoppers

**Step 7
Legs**

**Fig. 6 BUILDING THE BINS**

Evergreen no. 12060 V-groove siding facing down, with .020" x .060" rafters and joists cut from the same material.

After painting the underside, I used rubber cement to apply a strip of 8-foot corrugated aluminum roofing to the top. The whole assembly warped badly overnight, so I removed the aluminum and laminated another layer of .060" styrene to reduce the warp. After roofing it with 48" aluminum strips, the bow now looks like a natural sag.

## The loading bins

Figure 6 includes HO scale drawings of the loading bins, construction steps, and a photo of the finished bins. On the prototype, the smaller bin is actually two bins, back-to-back, so I built my model the same way, each half 9'-0" wide and 4'-0" deep, separated by .060" sheet styrene.

Make the cinder-block building next to the steel loading bin from Pikestuff no. 1004 cement block wall sheet. Paint it with Testors no. 1258 Flat White spray. On mine the coverage is poor, so it looks like weathered whitewash – just what I wanted. Make the roof from .060" sheet styrene painted flat black on both sides.

Use .060" ABS sheet for a base for the bins and the cinder block building. If you sand the shine off the material it looks a lot like concrete without having to be painted.

## Planting the mill

Since the spot for Maxon Mills on my layout isn't ready yet, I "planted" it on a piece of ¼" plywood painted brown on both sides with ordinary latex house paint.

I made the pit and trough from .030" and .060" Plastruct ABS and ¼" angle. See fig. 8. After airbrushing this assembly with Polly S Roof Red, I cemented it into the plywood base with a small amount of Walthers Goo.

Next I added a piece of Shinohara code 70 flextrack with the ties trimmed and removed to fit around the pit and over the trough. Concrete aprons made from lightly-sanded .060" ABS should be cemented in place on each side of the trough assembly.

## Site details

Make the fuel tank from a 14'-0" length of 1" PVC pipe with a top shaped from .060" ABS. Use a double thickness of sanded .060" ABS for its concrete pad. Spray the tank silver and cement it to the base with Goo.

I used a gas pump from a Model Power gas station kit. The filling hose is no. 22 insulated wire with a nozzle from stripped wire bent in a loop.

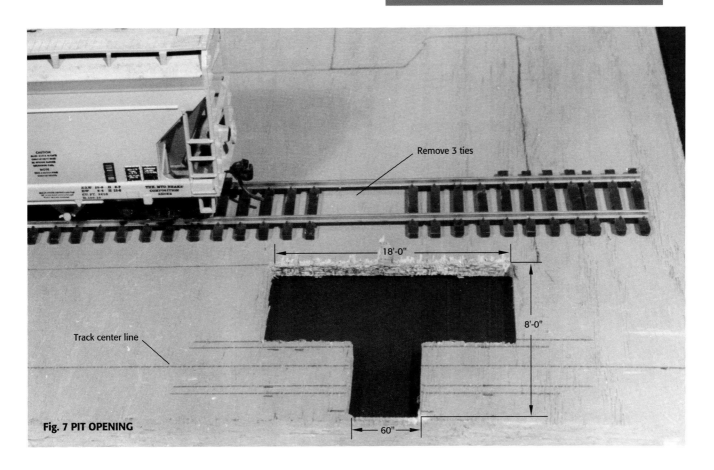

Remove 3 ties

18'-0"

8'-0"

Track center line

60"

**Fig. 7 PIT OPENING**

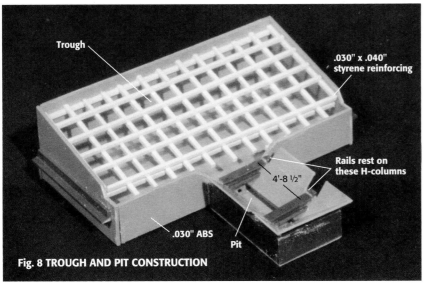

Trough

.030" x .040"
styrene reinforcing

Rails rest on
these H-columns

4'-8 1/2"

.030" ABS

Pit

**Fig. 8 TROUGH AND PIT CONSTRUCTION**

## Bill of materials

**Campbell Scale Models**

| | |
|---|---|
| 804 | corrugated siding |
| 900 | windows |
| 901 | windows |
| 903 | windows |
| 915 | doors |
| 924 | vents |

**Evergreen styrene**

| | |
|---|---|
| 132 | .030" x .040" strip |
| 142 | .040"-square strip |
| 175 | .100"-square strip |
| 223 | 1/16" tubing |
| 4062 | novelty siding |
| 4544 | board and batten siding |
| 9015 | .015" sheet |
| 9020 | .020" sheet |
| 9030 | .030" sheet |
| 9040 | .040" sheet |
| 12060 | V-groove siding |
| 19060 | .060" styrene sheet |

**Pikestuff**

| | |
|---|---|
| 1004 | cement block sheet |
| 1009 | louver vents |
| 1015 | shingle roof sheet |
| 1107 | garage door |

**Plastruct**

| | |
|---|---|
| 103 | 3/32" angle |
| 404 | 1/8" H-columns |
| 503 | 3/32" tees |
| 708 | 1/4"-square tubing |
| 7003 | .030" ABS sheet |
| 7006 | .060" ABS sheet |

The bollards (bumping posts) are 48" lengths of 1/16" Evergreen round styrene painted bright yellow and cemented into 1/16" holes.

Weather the mill using *very* dilute Polly S no. 410083 Mud paint in an airbrush. Apply it heavily around the unloading bin, loading tower, and exterior bins, where dust is likely to be concentrated. Look at the prototype photos for some ideas.

### Reflections on the project

If I were starting over I'd change a few things, which explains why some details in the drawings don't exactly match the photos of my model. All in all, though, I'm satisfied my model captures the character of the prototype. And even though I found it in New York, you could add Maxon Mills to a layout set just about anywhere in the United States. ✿

# Great Western Chemical Co.

## A simple structure that doesn't need compression

### BY HARRY BONHAM
### PHOTOS BY THE AUTHOR

THERE'S an unwritten rule in model railroading that structures must be compressed to fit on our layouts. Often they're compressed to the point that if they were real, they couldn't justify rail service for their products.

Great Western Chemical Co. (GWC), located along the Southern Pacific's Coos Bay branch in Eugene, Oreg., is an interesting exception to this unwritten rule. The 40 x 95-foot main building, along with its 50 x 50-foot fenced storage yard, will drop onto a layout of any size with little or no compression.

Best of all, despite the small size of the building, GWC did a lot of business by rail. As part of a large chemical company with outlets in seven western states and British Columbia, the Eugene facility moves chemicals by rail from suppliers to the warehouse, and then by truck to the customer.

### HISTORY

Great Western Chemical Co. purchased the building and property in 1952 from the Atlas Gas Co., also a railroad customer. It began to receive shipments of lime, wheat flour (used to manufacture particle board and special wood product glues), and nearly 4,800 other products ranging from acetic acid to zinc sulfate. These shipments arrived in boxcars and 10,000-gallon tank cars. Since the site doesn't have storage tanks, liquid chemicals were and still are left in tank cars and off-loaded as needed into company-owned trucks for customer delivery.

During the 1950s and '60s, GWC owned its own 10,000-gallon tank car. The top two-thirds of the car's single-dome tank were painted kelly green, with the lower third, underframe, and

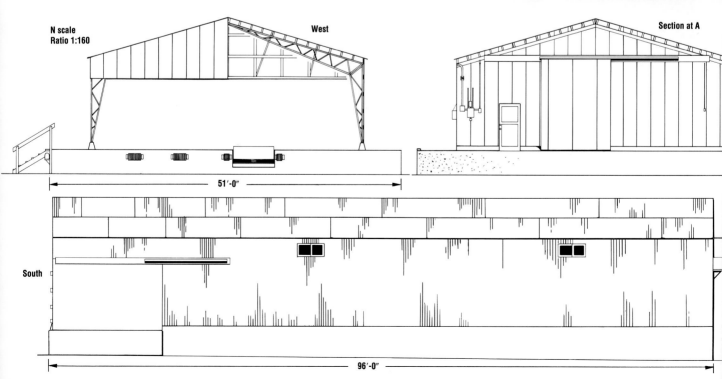

N scale
Ratio 1:160

West

Section at A

51'-0"

South

96'-0"

60

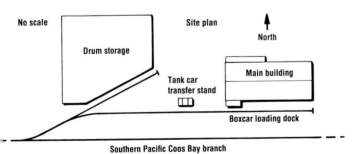

No scale

Site plan

↑
North

Drum storage

Tank car transfer stand

Main building

Boxcar loading dock

Southern Pacific Coos Bay branch

Although the sun is setting on Great Western Chemical's rail traffic, you can model this company when rails were a big part of its business.

Drawn for MODEL RAILROADER MAGAZINE by
**RON DUGAS**
Magazine purchaser may have photocopies of these drawings made locally as an aid to his personal or commercial modelmaking or tool designing, but purchaser does not have the right to distribute copies of the drawings to others.

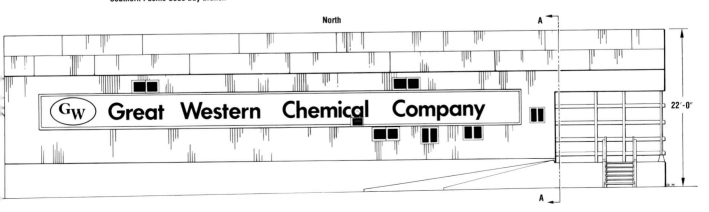

North

A

22'-0"

A

With windows, stairs, loading dock, and door, the northwest side of the building has the most character. The metal wall at the end of the shipping dock is where boxcars once were unloaded.

The fenced-in area to the west of the main building is used to store drums of chemicals. Don't forget to model safety equipment like the employee rinse station at the left of the photo.

This portable stand is used to transfer chemicals from tank cars to trucks. Since most modern chemical tank cars don't have bottom openings, all loading and unloading is done from the top. Note the shower for flushing chemicals off personnel. It will make a neat detail to model.

trucks painted black. The company name was stenciled in yellow across the entire width of the green area in 12"-high letters. The GWC logo, also in yellow, was located in the black area on the right end of the tank. Reporting marks (GWX 314) were located in the black area on the left end.

### THE STRUCTURE

Although the building is a little spartan, various additions have enhanced its character. In October 1949 a loading dock was added to the west side of the building. A ramp was built and later extended to accommodate a forklift, probably when the fenced-in storage area was erected.

The roof over the dock came later, and for a time boxcars were unloaded at the dock. Eventually, a wall was built next to the dock when rail shipments dropped off. Today, only large volumes of liquid caustic soda and bentonite come by tank car to the Eugene site.

### MODELING

Great Western Chemical's structure should be easy to model in any scale since it's covered with corrugated metal siding. The metal siding is nailed to 2 x 4 framing that's exposed inside.

As the photos show, there are only a few windows. These are located in the small office, storeroom, and bathroom. A good match for the windows in HO scale would be Pikestuff no. 2101 vertical slide windows. That firm's no. 1103 door would be a good match for the dock door.

The interior of the warehouse has three large, three-tier metal storage racks with enough room between them for the small forklift to maneuver. The parking lot is paved today, an improvement over the gravel and packed earth of the past.

For tank car traffic, you'll need to model the tank car unloading tower. The prototype is constructed of iron L beams and other shapes and painted oxide red. It can be modeled with Plastruct structural shapes.

Though it isn't fancy, Great Western Chemical Co. can be a great destination for box and tank cars without taking up much space on your layout. ✿

Great Western Chemical Co. has its own truck for making local deliveries. The trailer has a side door for less-than-truckload shipments.

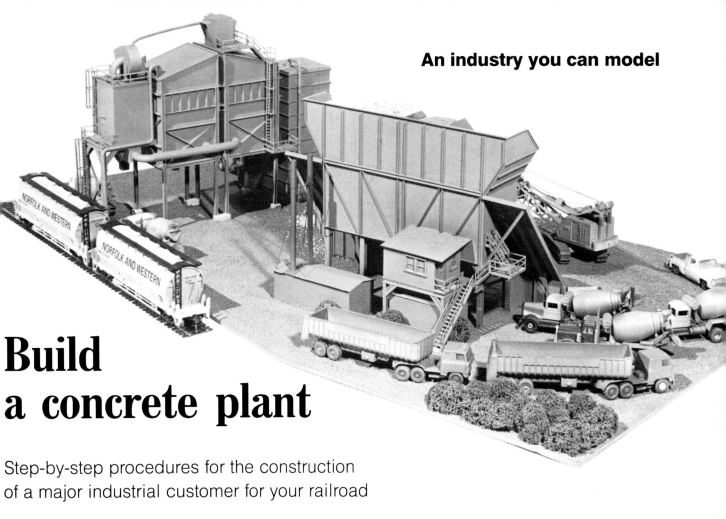

# Build a concrete plant

Step-by-step procedures for the construction
of a major industrial customer for your railroad

**BY ED STEINBERG**
**PHOTOS BY THE AUTHOR**

I AM always on the lookout for new and different industries to build for my layout, ones that are unlike structures other modelers have built. That way I have the pleasure of finding and solving its particular modeling challenges without depending on solutions others have offered. I'm sure structures *similar* to this concrete batch plant have been modeled before, but the prototype variations are so numerous that I'm certain the structure I built can safely be considered unique.

For several years I have photographed every concrete plant I have come across. I like them for several reasons. For one, they are part of the construction industry, which is important to me for reasons both professional and personal. Second, they are unusual, stark steel structures consisting of bold shapes, angular hoppers, bins, pipes, and fans. Third, they offer an opportunity to display my collection of scale and near-scale construction equipment and vehicles.

At this point it is worthwhile to distinguish between concrete plants and cement plants; they are related, but they are not the same. A *cement* plant, obviously, is where cement is made by roasting the water out of certain types of stone — primarily limestone — and then crushing and pulverizing the result. A *concrete* plant is where cement, sand, aggregate, and water are mixed together to produce concrete. These days the mixing is usually done in the big trucks with their revolving drums, not at the plant. In reality, the concrete plant is mostly a loading facility where precisely measured quantities of each component are charged into the mixing drum of each truck. The mix is made according to the contractor's order, which matches the structural engineer's specification.

The plants I have seen generally fall into two major categories with lots of subcategories. One category is made up of big, sprawling affairs such as the prototype Colonial Plant upon which my model is based. These are characterized by several large structures, some small buildings, heaps of sand and aggregate covering acres of land, and cranes loading the charging hoppers. The other major category is characterized by tall, compact facilities usually on small, crowded sites with little on-ground storage of material. The cement towers are narrow (often round), and their charging hoppers

are loaded using conveyors fed by cranes, dump trucks, or front-end loaders.

For a model railroad, some relationship between the industry and railroading is needed. Most of the concrete plants I've seen are along a rail line; however, some do without the railroad, receiving their quarry stock (sand and aggregate) and cement by truck, usually huge dump trailers. The cement comes in bulk-carrier trailers and is blown into the cement towers by compressed air. I have never seen a concrete plant receive sand or aggregate by rail, although they may in some areas. They frequently do receive cement in Center Flow covered hoppers. My model of the Colonial Plant gets its cement this way.

Without trespassing I could not obtain direct measurements of the facilities. So, being a fundamentally impatient man, I decided to build directly from the photographs of the prototype that accompany this article. Since I knew that the transit-mix trucks are 8 feet wide and about 12 or 13 feet high, I could reasonably scale out the structure from the photos. As it turned out, I think my selectively compressed model does a good job of conveying the effect of a large, busy facility.

## CONSTRUCTION

I began the project with the largest cement storage silo. Actually, the one shown

**4**

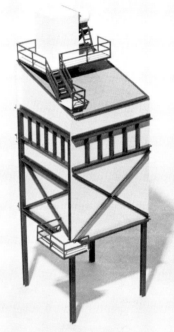

**5**

**6**

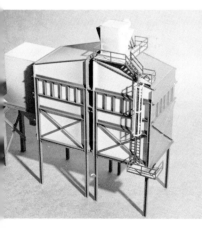

**7**

in fig. 1 was to be part of another batch plant I had started at another time. To use it in this plant, I sawed off the original sloping roof and rebuilt it to a flat surface, as shown in the plans and the finished model. The silo is a simple box of .030″ styrene with pieces of 5/16″ and 3/8″ Plastruct ABS angle reinforcing the corners. The outside horizontal bracing is made of 1/16″ ABS angles. I marked the locations with a scribing tool and cemented the angles in place so they overlap at the corners. I salvaged the safety ladder from a Kibri concrete plant kit. It is the only thing on the structure that is not scratch or parts built.

The sand/aggregate hopper came next. I really don't know what the inside looks like or exactly how it works, but it covers the necessary scales, delivery augers, and controls that measure and deliver the materials. I built a flare-topped box as shown in fig. 2. The legs and joists are made of 3/16″ ABS H section, and the walls, bottom floor, upper floor, and bin dividers are made from .030″ styrene. All corners are braced with 3/32″ ABS angle. For the external bracing, along with the reinforcing on the sloping spill sheets, I used 1/16″ and 3/32″ ABS angle and T material. The delivery pipes shown in fig. 3 are 1/4″ ABS square tube. I cemented them to the center of the bottom of each panel and set the unit aside to be detailed and completed later.

The steps in construction of the large cement loading towers are shown in fig. 4. The legs are made from 1/8″ ABS H material, and the walls are from .030″ styrene. I used scraps of ABS angle to stiffen the inside corners and the inside of the roof.

Figure 5 shows where detailing goes on one of the cement loading towers. The stairs, railings, and ladders are from Plastruct; the platforms are .030″ styrene. I made the motor from several bits of telescoping Plastruct tubing, mounting the assembly on a styrene platform with ABS angle braces and supports.

Figure 6 shows loading tower no. 2 with the extra little tower that will eventually be trackside. I added a couple extra bits of 3/32″ ABS angle to the short side of tower no. 2 to support the small bin. The small bin, including the inverted pyramid bottom, is made of .040″ styrene.

### ASSEMBLY

My next step was to paint the facing surfaces of the towers light green. I had to do this at this point since it would be impossible to paint these facing walls after assembly. To securely join the units, I cemented two scraps of 1/4″ Plastruct H material between them, being sure to cut the pieces short enough that they would be all but invisible among the external bracing. See fig. 7. The paint interferes with the bonding of liquid solvent cements so I used Ambroid tube glue for this and similar joints.

Figure 7 also shows the first of three safety ladders needed for this project. Since the publication of my article detailing the construction of these ladders [MODEL RAIL-ROADER, January 1980 issue], I have found a slightly different technique which results in a more durable ladder. The ladder itself is a length of Plastruct ABS ladder stock and the cage is built from Evergreen HO scale 2″ x 4″ styrene strips. I clamp a piece of 5/16″ brass tubing in a bench vise and heat it up with a propane torch. As it cools I

drape bits of the styrene strip over it. The temperature is critical, as too much heat melts the styrene and makes it stretch and deform. At just the right temperature the styrene assumes the curve of the tube. It took me several cycles and several strips of styrene to make enough curved loops to produce all of the cages.

After the brass tube has cooled, I clean it off and tape it to the proper length of ladder stock for the specific location. Then I cement the loops to the ladder, around the tube, one side at a time. I have found that ACC works much better than solvent cement for this. Next, I clamp each joint with a self-locking tweezers for 10 to 15 minutes while the cement sets up. Then, with all the loops on, I cement five straight strips to the loops with solvent-type cement. And that's it.

The centrifugal fan on the roof of the small cement tower was next up. I used drafting dividers to scribe circles into .020″ ABS sheet. Then I cut two pieces for the outer sides, with the full discharge chute, two inner formers (with only a stub of the discharge chute), and a scrap of big ABS square tube for a spacer. See fig. 8. Then I cemented these formers and outer sides together with the spacer between them.

Using a large, self-closing tweezers to hold it, I cemented in place a scale 48″-wide wrapper of .015″ styrene. (I had to notch the wrapper to make it fit between the sides of the discharge chute.) After letting this joint set up and harden, I brushed solvent cement on the mating surfaces and bent the wrapper around the fan. I clamped it to the discharge chute, making sure that it was wrapped tightly and reasonably square. See fig. 9.

After letting the unit dry for a couple of days, I filed and sanded the edges flush and smooth. A bit of scrap wrapper was all

**8**

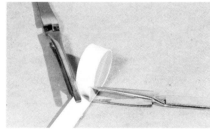

**9**

**10**

**11**

**12**

it took to cover the bottom of the discharge chute. The next step was to cement smaller circles of .015″ styrene at the center of the fan on each side as shown in fig. 10.

To complete the detailing, the centrifugal fan needed a motor to drive it, a protected belt to connect the motor to the fan, a shaft between the belt and the fan housing, and some system to support and maintain the alignment of all this. As a base for this assembly I used a piece of .060″ ABS. Another piece of .060″ ABS supports the drive shaft and one side of the fan. The other side of the fan is supported on ³⁄₃₂″ ABS angle. The motor simply consists of three bits of telescoping ABS tube cemented to a mount of ³⁄₁₆″ ABS channel. The belt housing is .060″ ABS, carved and sanded to appropriate shape as shown in fig. 10.

### ADDING THE DETAILS

With this task accomplished it was time to go back and detail the sand/aggregate hopper. The stairways, platforms, and door

are all shown in fig. 11, and the underside is shown in fig. 12. I used Plastruct stairs and railings; .030″ styrene landings; and assorted I beams, angles, and T shapes for support and bracing. The door is just a bit of .015″ styrene.

Figure 13 shows the control office that sits on the rear platform at the first landing. The walls and roof are from .030″ sty-

rene. I used modified Campbell windows and a door from Model Hobbies to save time, but I could have fabricated my own parts. The corrugated metal building that fits under the control office is also made of .030″ styrene. I covered it with Campbell corrugated siding and added a Campbell plastic door at one end.

The other corrugated building, the model

**13**

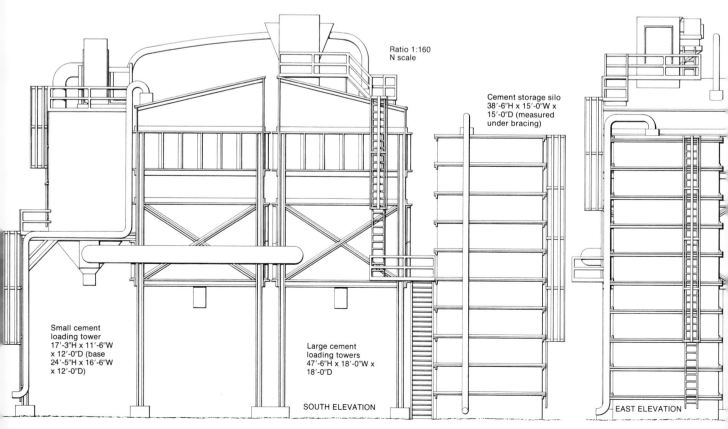

Ratio 1:160
N scale

Cement storage silo
38′-6″H x 15′-0″W x
15′-0″D (measured
under bracing)

Small cement
loading tower
17′-3″H x 11′-6″W
x 12′-0″D (base
24′-5″H x 16′-6″W
x 12′-0″D)

Large cement
loading towers
47′-6″H x 18′-0″W x
18′-0″D

SOUTH ELEVATION

EAST ELEVATION

**14**

To install the big pipe visible along the lower portion of the cement towers, I had to box out one side of the pyramidal hopper bottom. Installation of the box (built up of .030″ styrene and 3/32″ ABS angle reinforcing) was pretty much a trial-and-error operation. See fig. 15.

The large pipe that runs along the lower rear of the cement towers and the one that runs into the centrifugal fan on top of the small bin are both 5/16″ ABS tubing. These are shown in fig. 16.

Figure 16 also shows the smaller piping (made from 1/8″ ABS) needed to blow bulk cement into the towers. The long, curving pipe which arches over the towers is just a length of insulated electrical wire. I was going to use the copper conductor to stiffen a piece of ABS, but I found that the insulation was exactly the same outside diameter as the tubing and the conductor slipped inside the ABS tube perfectly.

I cemented the ends of the pipes into bits of 1/4″-outside-diameter tubing to provide a larger surface for more strength in the joints. I had to custom-fit each of these pipes to its location. I used both solvent and tube glue to install them as shown in figs. 16 and 17.

At this point, everything that was not done previously had to be painted. I used an airbrush for this job. I applied Floquil Barrier first and then applied two coats of Floquil Light Green. When the paint had dried, I mounted the assembled unit of three cement towers on foundations made of 1/4″ x 3/8″ ABS rectangular tubing with the ends sealed with .020″ ABS.

Once I had securely cemented the unit to the foundations, I installed the stairway to the landing on tower no. 1 and clamped it in place. See fig. 18. And that takes care of the structures.

The prototype plant has huge heaps of sand and aggregate around it. These materials are delivered by dump trailers and heaped up by bulldozers and front-end loaders. Eventually, the material is hoisted by clamshell crane and delivered to the hoppers for loading into the mixing drums. To maintain room for maneuvering trucks under and around the charging hopper, these piles of material are retained by steel-and-timber walls. I used ABS H material and 1/16″ x 1/8″ stripwood (see fig. 19) to model these walls, adding 3/8″ ABS angle brackets to hold the retaining walls in place on the base. I added another timber retaining wall, made from the same size stripwood, along the back legs of the charging hopper.

Next, I cut a base from 1/8″ tempered Masonite and painted it with latex-base gray house paint. I positioned each unit on the base in a test-fitting operation to make sure there was enough room for the mixing trucks to maneuver (things are a bit tight, but that's the price of selective compression). When I was satisfied that all was well, I used Ambroid tube glue to cement each piece to the base. See fig. 20.

With all the structures installed, I added the piles of sand and aggregate. I wasn't anxious to waste bags and bags of ballast or to accumulate all that weight, so I decided to try to preshape the material using

**15**

of which is shown in fig. 14, is some sort of boiler house (perhaps to heat water for winter concrete production). I also used .030″ styrene to build this structure. First, I scribed the doors into the styrene and then framed them in with scale 2″ x 4″ Evergreen styrene strips. The two stacks are 3/16″ ABS tube cemented into the building. I used a carpenter's combination square to check that they were plumb. The guy wires are lengths of thread running through tiny holes drilled in the roof of the building and tied to the stacks.

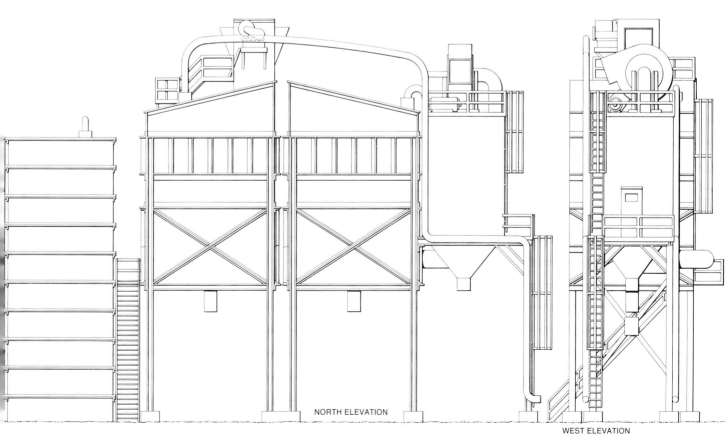

NORTH ELEVATION

WEST ELEVATION

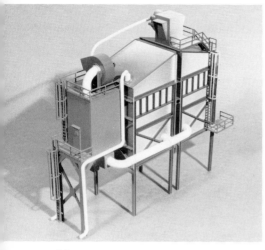

**16**

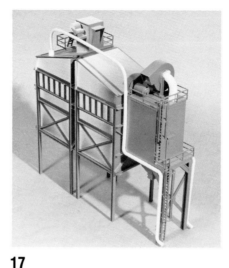

**17**

**18**

**19**

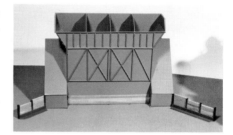

Styrofoam (from a 1"-thick sheet) underneath, cutting and carving it with a razor saw. If I had needed more height, it would simply have been a matter of using white glue to affix another layer of Styrofoam. Everything else attacks the foam! I painted the foam with the same latex house paint I used for the base.

After I had glued the piles in place with white glue, I applied the first coat of sand and aggregate onto the surface of the Styrofoam and on the base by painting Life-Like ballast cement over the area and spreading ballast over it. I vacuumed up the excess after the cement had dried. Then I spread more ballast cement and applied the fine, dark gray of the predominant sand. I heaped the sand and aggregate into their final shapes and fixed them

with detergent-water spray and diluted white glue applied with a large dropper. I used the same procedure in the charging bins so the piles all have natural slopes. See fig. 21.

Next, I sprayed several shades of heavily diluted gray Floquil paint over the tops and upper portions of the cement towers and, to a lesser extent, on the charging hoppers to give the complex a weathered effect. I also oversprayed the whole area to

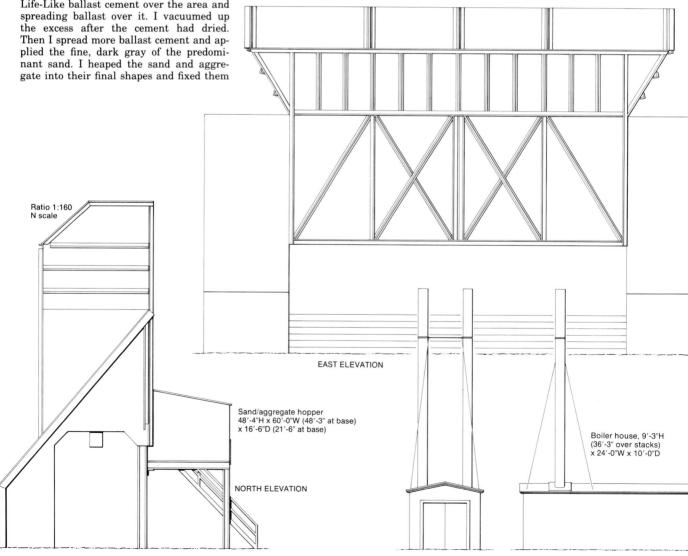

Ratio 1:160
N scale

EAST ELEVATION

Sand/aggregate hopper
48'-4"H x 60'-0"W (48'-3" at base)
x 16'-6"D (21'-6" at base)

NORTH ELEVATION

Boiler house, 9'-3"H
(36'-3" over stacks)
x 24'-0"W x 10'-0"D

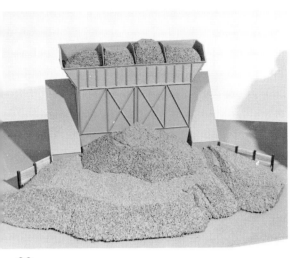

**20**

**21**

produce a proper dulling effect. You don't really want any streaking; instead, there should be a pervasive, dull-gray overlay on everything, including the "brush" growing in one back corner and around and under the stairs and rear platform.

At last the scene was ready for the vehicles. Four of the six concrete-mixing trucks in my photos are kitbashed; the other two are Wiking models. The crane is a Shinsei model of a P&H clamshell. It is really too

short to charge the hoppers, so I placed it in the down position for maintenance. The pickup truck is a Matchbox toy with tires cannibalized from a properly sized Wiking model. The wheeled loader is a Wiking; the crawler loader is a Tomica. The tractor-dump-trailers are Road Champs with tires from Athearn and Wiking. All of the equipment is heavily weathered with the airbrush to give it a prototypically dirty and well-used appearance.

It should be noted that the prototype and, therefore, the model exhibit no signs or lettering of any sort on any of the major structures. This is not uncommon. Some concrete plants do have signs, but many do not. Either way is "right."

Though time-consuming, this project is not especially difficult. In fact, I consider the time well-spent, since my railroad now has a realistic and unique destination for its covered hoppers. ✿

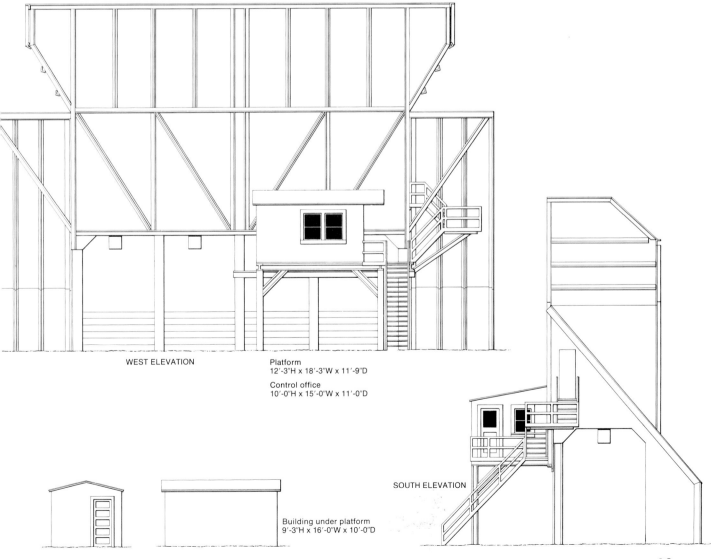

WEST ELEVATION

Platform
12'-3"H x 18'-3"W x 11'-9"D

Control office
10'-0"H x 15'-0"W x 11'-0"D

SOUTH ELEVATION

Building under platform
9'-3"H x 16'-0"W x 10'-0"D

# A solution to your short siding problems?

## This little one-evening project needn't be limited to loading effluvium

### BY JIM FINDLEY
### PHOTOS BY MALCOLM FURLOW

FITTING large buildings onto a model railroad is never easy. Take a look, for example, at the March 1971 issue of MR [out of print] to see what we had to do to Leming's Compressed Gas to fit it into John Allen's Gorre & Daphetid. Another version of the same building, Allen's Effluvium Co., presented the same problem — and others — on my Tioga Pass.

While Leming's Compressed Gas was not placed alongside the tracks, Allen's Effluvium was. Whenever you place a large building such as this along a short siding it takes up a disproportionate share of the space, crowding out other industries you'd like to have along the siding and limiting the value of the siding for operation. In addition to that, Allen's Effluvium Co. was large enough to completely hide cars behind it. It was next to impossible to spot cars over the uncoupling ramp behind the building.

My solution to these problems was a simple one: I built a small loading/unloading facility physically apart (along the tracks between the factory and a junkyard) from the industry itself. After all, a loading point need not be directly adjacent to the structure it serves, and separating the two can add visual interest to the scene.

Because I used "disguised" readily available parts, it took me only one evening to build the facility, and most of that time was spent waiting for the paint to dry.

I started out with the dock base, a 7 x 17-foot piece of balsa painted with Pactra Camouflage Grey. For the complex of piping I turned to my parts box. I was happy to find an unused casting for a Cal-Scale steam turret, complete down to the valve handles (no. 323). To put your mind at ease, no one has yet identified it for what it actually is . . . at least they've been courteous enough to not say so.

The two outer pipes on the steam turret casting (ordinarily leading to the locomotive injectors) I bent at right angles to serve as pipes going to the pumps on the dock. The next two larger pipes I also bent at right angles, but in the opposite direction, to simulate pipes going to the car being loaded or emptied. I simply stuck the last two pipes into the dock. Painting the pipes different colors improves their ap-

pearance; I also painted the valve handles bright red.

Do you recognize the centrifugal pumps? They started out as SS Ltd. bench grinders (no. 2210). I altered them only by removing one of the emery wheels. In addition to looking like pumps, they conceal the joint between the cast pipes and the wire pipes coming from the pumps.

The sections of hose on the platform are simply lengths of resin core solder bent and flattened to shape in a vise.

This open-air-type loading dock could serve any industry whose sign proclaims it to be involved in the manufacture or distribution of liquid or gaseous products and whose main storage facility isn't immediately trackside. And *that's* the real beauty of it! ✿

Charles Smiley assembled the HO scale Del Norte Canning Co. from Design Preservation Models' new modular wall system. It's a low-relief building for a location against a wall or backdrop.

# Del Norte Canning Co.

Building an HO cannery with Design Preservation Models' modular wall system

**BY CHARLES R. SMILEY**
**PHOTOS BY THE AUTHOR**

GROWING UP in Oakland, Calif., in the 1940s and '50s left me with lasting visions of buildings like the one portrayed by this HO scale model. It's a cannery, and the Alameda and Contra Costa Counties around Oakland grew and packed a variety of nationally recognized food products. The name of my canning plant is as close as I wanted to come to a recognizable brand. Del Norte happens to be the name of a small county in the most northwestern part of California. I hope the contrived brand name triggers associations with the food business.

As I'm between layouts, this low-relief building was designed for a dual purpose. For now, I want a long industrial building that can serve as a photographic background for locomotives or passenger cars. When I build my next railroad I'll install this structure along a back wall.

### CHARACTER, AND A SYSTEM

This model was built as a character with a role to play. It had to be brick and have arched windows, and also had to have at least four loading doors for as many different switching spots. I wanted it to receive produce in refrigerator cars and ship canned goods in boxcars, with the possibility of trucks sharing the same loading dock and roadway.

After sketching out what I wanted and looking at several epoxy kits that I didn't really care to saw apart, I still wasn't sure of how to create the model I wanted. As if the company had guessed my needs, Design Preservation Models' HO scale modular wall system showed up at the local hobby shop. One glance was all it took. I went home with an armful of DPM packages and a bunch of other stuff — see the bill of materials.

The DPM system consists of 15 different sections. All the wall sections have a common width of 20 scale feet, but there are four basic heights: 26'-9", 19'-9", 13'-6", and 4'-6". There's also an eight-piece cornice kit to cap the walls.

Each section comes with several pilasters of 18" and 24" widths and appropriate

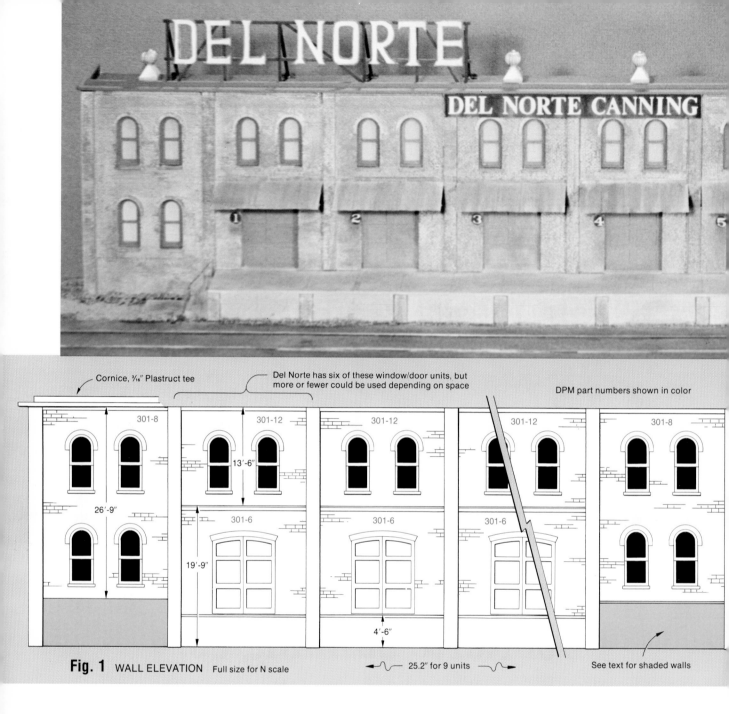

Cornice, ³⁄₁₆″ Plastruct tee

Del Norte has six of these window/door units, but more or fewer could be used depending on space

DPM part numbers shown in color

301-8

301-12

301-12

301-12

301-8

13'-6"

26'-9"

301-6

301-6

301-6

19'-9"

4'-6"

**Fig. 1** WALL ELEVATION   Full size for N scale

25.2″ for 9 units

See text for shaded walls

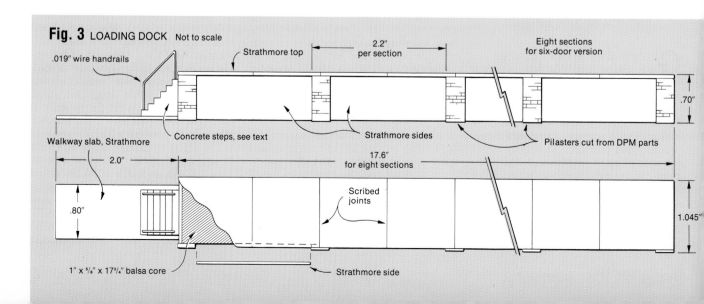

**Fig. 3** LOADING DOCK   Not to scale

.019″ wire handrails

Strathmore top

2.2″ per section

Eight sections for six-door version

.70″

Walkway slab, Strathmore

Concrete steps, see text

Strathmore sides

Pilasters cut from DPM parts

2.0″

17.6″ for eight sections

.80″

Scribed joints

1.045″

1″ x ⁵⁄₈″ x 17³⁄₄″ balsa core

Strathmore side

heights. The pilasters are a realistic, clever way to hide the vertical seams between sections, and the narrow pilasters are for corners. This is all covered in the direction sheet included with each package. While Del Norte Canning uses only a few of the DPM sections, I invite you to review them all and try variations on my theme.

## CUTTING AND SPLICING

I used two basic wall units in this model. Six have both doors and windows and are made from DPM no. 301-12s stacked on top of no. 301-6s as in fig. 1. In fact, the store was already out of 301-12s, and I had to cut down taller no. 301-09s to make the parts I needed.

The wall sections can be cut by scoring along a horizontal mortar line with a new X-acto no. 11 blade, a metal straightedge, and the care and caution these moldings deserve. Make several passes with the knife, then break the pieces apart as shown in fig. 2. Work the material until it gently yields rather than forcing it to crack suddenly.

The three window-only units — see fig. 1 again — are made from 301-08 sections on top of .90"-tall sections from the remains of the 301-09s.

To bond the sections, I used Alteco Super ST cyanoacrylate adhesive (CA). It's important to make a tight seam between the top and bottom pieces so as not to reveal how they were assembled. Drag the edges over 280- or 360-grit sandpaper laid on a flat, hard surface until the matching edges are straight. When done correctly, the seam won't be noticeable.

When all the units are assembled, check them for uniformity in height. Lay them out side by side with slight gaps (about .030") between them for the pilasters. Follow the DPM instructions, and use a long straightedge as an alignment guide — I used a metal yardstick on the top edge. After the entire assembly was glued together, I stiffened it along the bottom edge with a strip of ⅛" x ⅜" basswood cemented with Walthers Goo.

After allowing all the glues to dry overnight, I used a sanding block to even out the bottom of the wall. The same 280- to 360-grit sandpaper will do if the units are basically even to start.

I made one extra window-only unit, then split it down the middle to make the ends. They give the building enough depth to make the roof vents and space-frame sign possible. Use the same score-and-break method described earlier.

Of course, you could make a full-depth building if you have enough room, but you're on your own as to the arrangement of the other side. I'd probably make some sort of recessed lobby entry with concrete stairs leading up to the same height as the freight doors.

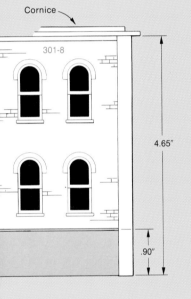

**FIG. 2. CUTTING WALL MODULES**
First score along a horizontal mortar line with a sharp knife and a steel rule. Then place the scored line over a raised edge as in the photo, and apply pressure until the plastic starts to fatigue (whiten). Work the piece to be separated up and down, to break it off gently rather than with a sudden snap.

## LOADING DOCK

I made the loading dock from a 36″-long piece of 1″ x ⅝″ balsa as shown in fig. 3. Balsa is cheaper than basswood, and we don't have to worry about its porous surface because the top and three visible sides can be covered with Strathmore illustration board to represent concrete.

Strathmore is found in art- and drafting-supply stores. It's cardboard of a high quality that can be cut, sanded, and generally treated like milled wood. It's available in various surface finishes and colors, but all we need is the smooth stock that comes light gray on one side and white on the other. All the Strathmore I've ever seen is a uniform .045″ thick (³⁄₆₄″ if you prefer).

I used a new X-acto no. 11 blade to cut the Strathmore, and I lightly beveled the edges with sandpaper to prevent fraying. The pilasters shown in fig. 3 are laid between sections of Strathmore to appear embedded in the concrete. I assembled all parts of the dock with Walthers Goo — water-based glues might cause warping.

For a concrete color, I brushed on Floquil Concrete paint. I also use Floquil D&H Gray on occasion to vary concrete colors from building to building. I was careful not to get paint on the brickwork, and let it dry overnight.

The photo in fig. 3 shows typical cracks in the concrete added with a sharp X-acto no. 11 blade. Remember that cracks, once started, generally run unchecked until they come to a seam or another crack. After scribing the cracks, burnish the surface with an old sock or dry washcloth. This will smooth and

slightly polish the surface. Later on I'll explain the final touches that make the concrete and mortar convincing.

The concrete stairway is a milled wood piece from California Model Co. on a Strathmore slab. You could use Pikestuff's molded plastic stairway, which is also listed in the bill of materials.

### PAINT AND MORTAR

Since the Floquil paints I use can attack some plastics, I first sprayed the walls, and the doors and windows on their sprues, with Barrier. This was followed the next day with Oxide Red

for a brick color on the walls. The brickwork on the loading dock had to be brush-painted. The windows and doors were sprayed BN Green. The weathering will tone this green down a bit. If you prefer to keep weathering to a minimum, use Coach Green instead.

I used Kiwi Scuff Magic water-based white liquid shoe polish for the mortar. I use a stiffened old brush, dipping it in water to thin the polish and then making jabbing motions with the surface laying flat. I use paper towels to blot up excess polish. You can paint the unused walls for practice.

**Fig. 4** AWNING FRAMES

Rafters, .025″-square brass (see text) inserted in holes, drilled at a 25-degree angle, and cemented from inside with CA

Stringers and braces, .019″ wire soldered to rafters and cemented inside wall with CA

5′-6″

**Fig. 5** SPACE-FRAME SIGN

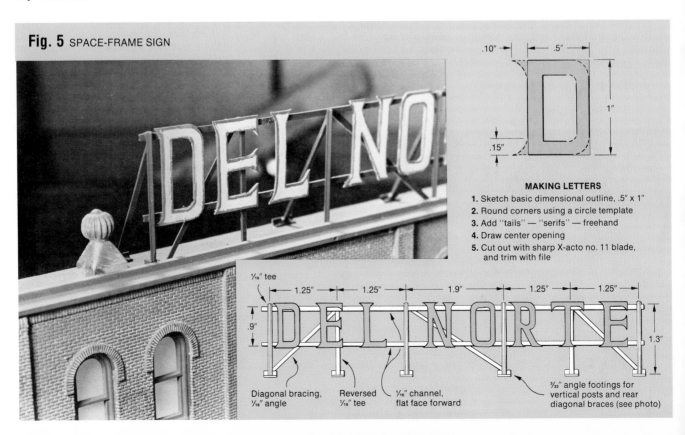

.10″  .5″  1″  .15″

**MAKING LETTERS**
1. Sketch basic dimensional outline, .5″ x 1″
2. Round corners using a circle template
3. Add "tails" — "serifs" — freehand
4. Draw center opening
5. Cut out with sharp X-acto no. 11 blade, and trim with file

¹⁄₁₆″ tee
1.25″  1.25″  1.9″  1.25″  1.25″
.9″
1.3″

Diagonal bracing, ¹⁄₁₆″ angle
Reversed ¹⁄₁₆″ tee
¹⁄₁₆″ channel, flat face forward
³⁄₃₂″ angle footings for vertical posts and rear diagonal braces (see photo)

## Bill of materials

**California Model Co.**
106 5-tread concrete steps (wood),
   1 pkg.

**Campbell Scale Models**
805 corrugated roofing, 1 pkg.
927 cyclone vents, 3 pkgs.

**Design Preservation Models**
301-6 door modules, 2 pkgs.
301-8 tall 4-window modules, 1 pkg.
301-11 tall blank modules, 1 pkg.
301-12 short 2-window modules, 2
   pkgs.

**Detail Associates**
2506 .019" brass wire, 1 pkg.
2508 .028" brass wire, 1 pkg.

**Evergreen Scale Models styrene**
9220 .020" sheet, 1

**Floquil paint**
110010 Engine Black
110013 Grimy Black
110017 Weathered Black
110019 Barrier
110035 BN Green
110082 Concrete
110100 Old Silver
110132 SP *Lark* Dark Gray
110186 Oxide Red

**Pikestuff**
1010 concrete staircase (plastic,
   optional substitute for California
   Model Co. wooden steps), 1

**Plastruct ABS shapes**
103 ³⁄₃₂" angle, 1
502 ¹⁄₁₆" tee, 2
506 ³⁄₁₆" tee, 2
302 ¹⁄₁₆" channel, 2

**Testor's paint**
1949 Model Master Flat Black spray

**Woodland Scenics' Model Graphics**
MG714 ³⁄₈" and ½" white Railroad
   Roman dry transfers, 1 sheet

**Miscellaneous**
³⁄₈" x 1" x 36" balsa, 1
⁵⁄₈" x 1" x 36" balsa, 1
code 70 or 83 rail
frosted Mylar drafting sheet
Kiwi Scuff Magic white liquid
   shoe polish
Strathmore illustration board,
   .045" x 32" x 40" sheet, 1

## ASSEMBLY

After all the paint and mortar had dried, I attached the loading dock to the front wall. I had to touch up some of the door sills with a flat file to match the height of the dock. Next, I brush-painted the door sills with the concrete color.

I installed the doors and windows using CA. The doors are slightly short, and it's best to leave gaps at the top of the archways, where they won't show, than at the bottom. To keep light from showing through, I glued a scrap of black paper behind each door.

## AWNINGS

I built the door awnings using brass stock soldered into a framework to support Campbell 6-foot-wide corrugated aluminum. See fig. 4. The four rafters in each of my awnings are .025"-square brass removed from wire-wrap connector headers used in breadboard electronic circuits. This material is hard and resists accidental bending, but you could substitute Detail Associates .028" brass wire.

I used small clips as heatsinks to protect the plastic, and worked quickly using a 30-watt pencil iron. When finished, I brush-painted this framework with Floquil Weathered Black.

To prepare the Campbell roofing, I painted the aluminum strips Floquil Concrete — I already had some in the airbrush — and dried this base color in the oven for an hour at 150 degrees. Then I cut 30 panels ½" wide and glued them to the awning frames with Walthers Goo. Each panel overlaps the next by two or three corrugations.

For a rusty look, I drybrushed the corrugated metal with various orange and brown Floquil colors, using downward strokes.

## ROOF

Rather than use DPM's fancy cornices, I substituted Plastruct ³⁄₁₆" tee beams as indicated back in fig. 1. Since the building is longer than the Plastruct stock, I had to make a neat butt-splice. I mitered the ends 45 degrees and hid the cracks using a plastic filler. Then I brushed the homemade cornice Floquil SP *Lark* Dark Gray — Barrier is unnecessary on this ABS plastic.

The roof itself is 1" x ³⁄₈" balsa covered with Strathmore cut to fill the area inside the walls. I brushed the Strathmore with Weathered Black to represent the common tar roof.

The roof vents are Campbell cyclone vents painted with Barrier followed by Old Silver. The air-conditioning unit is merely a block of ⁵⁄₈"-square basswood cut 1½" long. I brush-painted the unit Old Silver after adding a few "panel doors" of thin cardstock.

## SIGNS

The small sign is a piece of .025"-thick Evergreen styrene sheet that I painted Testor's Flat Black with a spray can. The styrene was cut as a ½"-wide strip somewhat longer than its final 5¾" length. That way I could apply the dry-transfer letters without worrying about where the center of the sign would be. The white Roman-style letters are from Woodland Scenics.

The letters for the large space-frame sign were cut from Evergreen .020" styrene sheet — see fig. 5. I cut a 1" strip off the short side of the sheet and sanded one side with fine sandpaper. You can draw the letters on this sanded finish with a sharp pencil or a .5-mm mechanical pencil. Cutting out the letters as in fig. 5 was easier and produced better results than I anticipated. I remade a few letters before I was satisfied, but still had all I needed in about an hour.

I erased and sanded off the pencil markings and painted the borders of the letters with Floquil BN Green to match the windows and doors. Then I mounted the letters on parallel lengths of Plastruct channel as shown in fig. 5. I used CA to tack them in place, and added five-minute epoxy in a small fillet at each joint. The rest of the bracing was bonded the same way.

After cutting the footing angles and cementing them to the roof, I cemented the sign to the footings with five-minute epoxy. I brushed the sign frame with Floquil Weathered Black and streaked it with Reefer Orange to represent rust.

The round door-number signs help switching crews spot cars just where the customer wants them. I used a paper punch to cut them from scraps of .015" styrene sheet. I sprayed the disks Testor's Flat Black and applied white dry-transfer numbers, then glued the disks in place with Walthers Goo.

## BASEBOARD

Del Norte Canning is mounted on a 5½" x 28" piece of ¾" plywood, for use as a photo backdrop until I install it on my layout. I glued it in line with the back edge of the baseboard.

For the track I spiked preblackened code 70 nickel-silver rail directly to the plywood. Ties aren't needed since the track will be buried in an "asphalt" road. The rail nearest to the building is .55" from the loading dock.

The asphalt roadway consists of three pieces of Strathmore board as in fig. 6, painted Floquil Grimy Black. Be sure to paint the edges that go alongside the rails before gluing the Strathmore down. I've made similar roadways with plaster, and had constant trouble with chipping and abrasive debris fouling the track area. The Strathmore looks as good, and doesn't chip into grit or dust.

## WEATHERING AND GLAZING

I weathered everything with pastel chalk dust brushed on using a ¼"-wide, stiff-bristle brush. You'll find pastel sets of 20 to 30 pieces for around $5 at art stores. Generally only the brick-reds, browns, blacks, whites, and grays are useful for weathering, but I still find it handiest to start with a set and replace chalks that I use up with individual pieces.

To apply, simply use a blade to scrape dust from a piece of chalk onto a sheet of paper, then brush the powder onto the model. For brick buildings I start with a red-brown similar to the brick color to tone down the paint and mortar. This also makes the overall finish very flat, which gives the look of older, crumbling brick. On the windows and doors, I used gray chalk to tone down the green paint. White is good in slight downward streaks from the cornice and window ledges to suggest years of dripping water.

I smudged black and gray onto the roadway to break up the uniform look of the paint. The Strathmore asphalt can also be painted in rough squares with thick Floquil Engine Black to resemble fresh patches. You can add to the distressed look by denting the surface with a screwdriver blade. Practice on scraps first until you can do this without tearing the surface of the

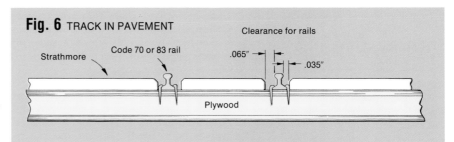

**Fig. 6** TRACK IN PAVEMENT

Strathmore, but be prepared to touch up the paint on your finished roadway.

I sifted real dirt and glued it to the bare plywood areas with white glue. Then I added ground foam and bits of rope fiber at random to represent weeds.

To represent windows with that neglected, soaped-up look, I used frosted Mylar for the glazing. This is available at most drafting-supply stores, and a few dollars will buy a lifetime supply. DPM's acetate window material can

also be sanded with fine sandpaper for a similar effect.

The DPM system certainly helped me create a purposeful-looking industrial building with that old-side-of-town look. If I make another building from DPM modules, I'll have to try to make it look different from this one. Those arched freight doors are almost too distinctive, but that only adds to the challenge. ✿

The fuel company complex added much depth to its narrow shelf location and provided both visual interest and a car-spotting location.

# Modeling Consumers Fuel

## A selectively compressed model of this prototype
## in Martinsburg, W. Va., serves as an important customer for the South Penn

### BY JEFF MADDEN
### PHOTOS BY THE AUTHOR

W HEN I LIVED in Martinsburg, W. Va., I passed Consumers Fuel Co. almost daily on my jaunts through town. My modeling instincts drew my attention to this century-old building complex, which stands angled away from the old Baltimore & Ohio tracks. I saw the modeling possibilities of this structure as a long, narrow industrial flat that would be suitable for any era since the 1880s and attract attention.

Today the building houses a coal and home heating-oil dealership, but it has served other uses over its long history. Consumers Fuel is an independent dealer ordering Pocahontas coal, both pea-size stoker and nut size, from southern West Virginia. The coal's shipped here via trains of the Norfolk Southern and the Chessie System.

Some anthracite coal arrives by 25-ton trucks. Trucks also bring in the fuel oil.

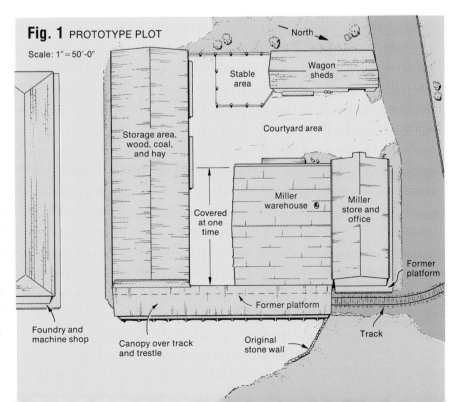

**Fig. 1** PROTOTYPE PLOT

Scale: 1" = 50'-0"

North

Storage area, wood, coal, and hay

Stable area

Wagon sheds

Courtyard area

Covered at one time

Miller warehouse

Miller store and office

Former platform

Former platform

Foundry and machine shop

Canopy over track and trestle

Original stone wall

Track

A photo from the late 1880s shows how the complex looked as first built. **Above right:** Contemporary view of the covered unloading trestle.

This recent photo shows how little the structure has changed over the years. **Above right:** Here's a ground-level view of the coal trestle.

Most of the coal and oil is sold locally, though there occasionally have been some interesting exceptions. About 20 years ago Consumers Fuel sold about 400 pounds of coal to a physician living in California, who intended to use it in his live steamer!

### BACKGROUND

The complex was built in 1886 by J. H. Miller for use as a wholesale grocery store and warehouse. In 1940 Fine Distributors purchased the property and used it primarily as a fuel dealership, even though a travel agency and a beer distributor also had offices in the complex. For the past 30 years the buildings have been used strictly as a fuel dealership.

Today, as fig. 1 shows, the Consumers Fuel complex consists of an office, warehouse, covered trestle, storage areas, and sheds. Hopper cars loaded with coal are spotted on the trestle, and their contents are dumped into storage bins below. The loading dock of the warehouse has doors facing the trestle so that boxcars and refrigerator cars can also be unloaded.

### MODELING APPROACH

The idea struck me several years ago that if I condensed the overall structure it would make an ideal industry to angle across one of those worrisome corners or place along a backdrop as a flat. I thought it would be a waste of layout space to model the prototype full size. So I selected the narrow profile.

I decided to model the complex the way it looks today and call it the Berne Bros. Fuel Co. It could be backdated to the turn of the century by installing the proper windows and doors in the storefront, using correct signs for the period, and including the wooden platform shown in the old photo. From the 1920s to the present, the building would have looked much the same except for the signs.

Since no blueprints were available, I measured the portions of the structure I could reach and estimated others by counting boards and using known dimensions on photos. I had to selectively compress the prototype, so I eliminated 20 feet from the warehouse front and the trestle next to the store section (fig. 2).

Even after this compression there was room for two hopper cars to fit in nicely. Reducing the length eliminated a window and a door.

I also eliminated 3 feet from the last trestle section and reduced the length of the warehouse to 37 feet. The main side of the store was reduced until it was only a scale 10'-6" deep. The warehouse sides would be 4 scale feet deeper because of the setback at the end of the trestle adjoining the store. The setback shows a rough planked door and two windows, but I omitted these to simplify construction.

### BUILDING SHELL

After completing the drawings, I obtained the supplies I'd need to build my HO version of Consumers Fuel. You'll find these listed in the accompanying bill of materials. Rather than adding the structures directly to the layout, I decided to mount them on a base, add scenery and detailing as though it were a diorama, and then install it on my South Penn layout.

Construction began with my laying out the storefront, the four visible side

78

**ove:** The coal yard is sandwiched between the trestle and the road. **Below:** An interior view
the covered coal trestle. Note that two of the doors for unloading boxcars are boarded up.

### Bill of materials

**Alexander Scale Models**
2705 chimney

**Campbell Scale Models**
904 double windows (2)
914 double doors (2)

**Faller**
614, 615, or 616 stone foundation

**Grandt Line**
5032 36" x 52" single windows (3)

**Kappler Mill & Lumber Co.**
KP006P12 6" siding (4 pkgs. for siding)
KP010P12 10" siding (trestle platform
and porch floor)
KP101P12 $1/32$" stripwood (corner molding and wood railings)
KP102P12 $1/32$" x $1/64$" stripwood (window
framing and snow boards)
KP140P12 $1/8$"-square stripwood (1 pkg.
for interior bracing and vertical
trestle bents)
KP151P12 $5/32$"-square stripwood (1 pkg.
for horizontal trestle bents)
KP152P12 $5/32$" x $3/16$" stripwood (2 pkgs.
for stringers)
KP1115P12 $1/16$"-square stripwood
(1 pkg. for trestle roof supports)

**Northeastern Scale Models**
18BABP board-and-batten siding
(roofing)

**Miscellaneous**
Cardboard or artist's board (rear
walls and sloping ground under
trestle)
Drain pipes and gutters, available
from several manufacturers

pieces for the store and warehouse (I also used siding for the left side of the store), and the warehouse front that sits behind the trestle. I found it necessary to glue the warehouse front and storefront siding sections on top of one another for one-piece construction.

Next, I located the window and door openings using the commercial castings as templates. I cut the openings with an X-acto knife. For the window and door framing I used $1/32$" x $1/16$" stripwood, which I cut to size and glued edgewise. To simulate the boarded up windows and planked doors, I turned scrap pieces of siding vertically and glued them to the backside of the walls.

After trimming the front and side walls to size, I braced them with $1/8$"-square stripwood and joined them with white glue. I used artist's board for the peaked rear wall of the store and the warehouse end. I added framing behind the false front of the warehouse to form the front roof supports.

When the shell for the warehouse and store had been completed, I glued in the window and door castings. At this point I sprayed the walls of both buildings with

a couple of coats of Floquil Zinc Chromate Primer (a sort of barn red color). I made sure to spray the insides of the walls to prevent warping.

### THE TRESTLE

Now I turned my attention to building the trestle. My model is 23 feet shorter than the prototype, but still long enough to hold two cars.

For more strength I departed from prototype construction and attached four $5/32$"-square pieces of stripwood paralleling the two stringers. These pieces support the bents below and the flooring above. I used $1/32$"-thick scribed siding with $1/8$" spacing for the trestle flooring because the trestle shed would hide any detailing anyway. If you want to use stripwood, be my guest!

I partially stripped the ties from a section of Shinohara code 70 flextrack and spiked the rails to the trestle stringers. The remaining section of track just hung out at the end of the trestle until scenery was added to the diorama. See fig. 3.

I built 12 trestle bents of increasing heights from right to left for the slope I

wanted. I didn't bother to simulate the partial stone foundations under some of the prototype's bents. The bents were glued to the stringers and the paralleling supports. I squared the bent sides facing the warehouse so they fit flush.

Before gluing the completed trestle to the warehouse, I stained it with Minwax walnut stain. I let this dry thoroughly before attaching the trestle to the warehouse.

### DIORAMA BASE

First I cut a 6" x 21" base for the diorama out of the back of a scrap of $1/4$" paneling. Then I mounted the trestle and warehouse on a piece of cardboard to form the required slope down to the base (fig. 4). I extended the cardboard in front of the trestle to form the open yard area. The fencing was left out, along with the road that descends in front of the yard since I didn't know how this diorama would fit into my layout.

I glued this unit to the base, shimming as necessary under the cardboard so the unit was level. Then I built up the raised terrain where the store was going to be located. I used a 2 x 2 under

The author's completed Berne Bros. Fuel Co. complex, circa 1950, is ready to be dropped into place on his HO scale South Penn layout.

the track and scrap balsa to form the framework, then fitted artist's board around the extended track. The track section, previously hanging in space, was spiked down.

For the final steps I added pre-painted ³/₃₂″ stripwood posts and roof bracing to form the trestle canopy. Then I attached the railing and the triangular decorative siding.

## COMPLETING THE BUILDINGS

I cut out the roof pieces and spray-painted both sides aluminum. Before gluing the roofs in place, I added window glass that I'd simulated with dull Scotch tape. Masking tape was added to represent shades. I added signs before fastening the store to the complex.

Like the prototype, my red buildings have white lettering. For that I first brush-painted white over the areas to be lettered. When the white had thoroughly dried, I spelled out the words for the various signs using stick-on letters. Then I oversprayed the letters with Floquil zinc primer, the building color. When the paint dried, I peeled off the letters and found some nice looking white signs underneath.

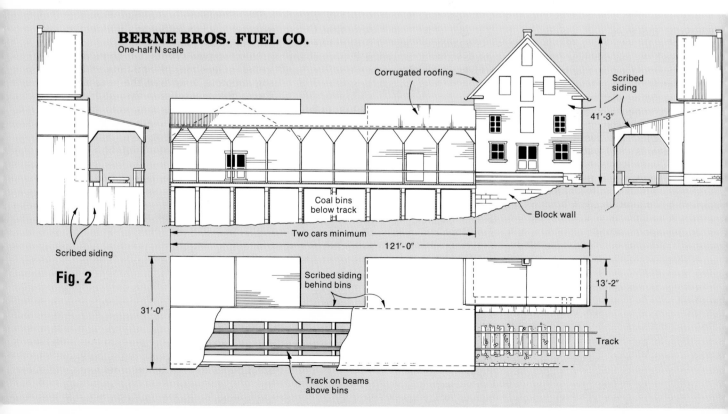

**BERNE BROS. FUEL CO.**
One-half N scale

Corrugated roofing

Scribed siding

41'-3"

Coal bins below track

Block wall

Two cars minimum

121'-0"

Scribed siding

**Fig. 2**

Scribed siding behind bins

31'-0"

13'-2"

Track

Track on beams above bins

Now I was ready to add decorative siding to the trestle ends using leftover scrap siding that was already painted. The store's roof edge trim and fascia boards, snow boards, and chimney came next, after which I glued Faller embossed stone around the base of the store and braced it inside.

The next step was gluing the store building to the diorama base and adding corner trim. I made the store platform and stairs out of scraps of stripwood and glued them in place. Then I added drain pipes and gutters that I fabricated from scrap plastic and painted them silver.

### SCENERY AND DETAILS

It was time to add the retaining walls. I used wallboard compound to form the terrain (including the road), which I painted with earth-brown latex paint. I sprinkled ground foam over the wet paint. Then I formed coal piles using clay rolled in scale coal. I then poured white glue over the bare spaces and added more coal. Coal and earth-colored foam were sprinkled over the paint I'd brushed on all flat surfaces of the yard and beneath the trestle.

I lightly weathered the buildings using chalks applied with an eye-shadow brush. The last step involved adding such details as vehicles, figures, telephone poles, barrels, and crates.

The finished Consumers Fuel Co. makes a quaint industry that fit nicely along the backdrop of my South Penn. You could deepen the warehouse and store buildings, and the resulting complex could be worked into an inside corner location on your layout (fig. 5). Also, by changing the signs, vehicles, windows, and other details, you could make the complex match about any era in the past century.

I hope that many of you will come away as enthused about this structure as I am. On some future layout tour I look forward to seeing a model of Consumers Fuel built by someone else. ⚙

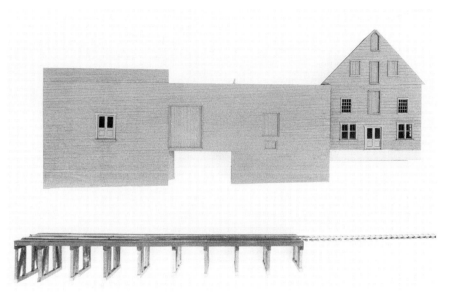

**Fig. 3.** The major components of the model are the trestle, warehouse, and storefronts.

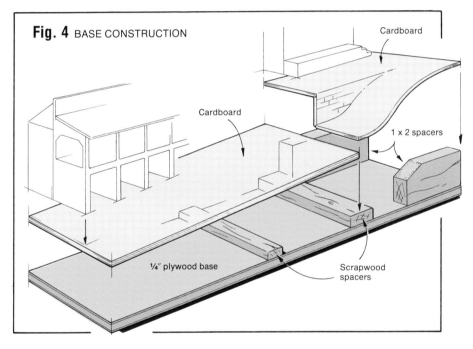

**Fig. 4** BASE CONSTRUCTION

Cardboard

Cardboard

1 x 2 spacers

¼" plywood base

Scrapwood spacers

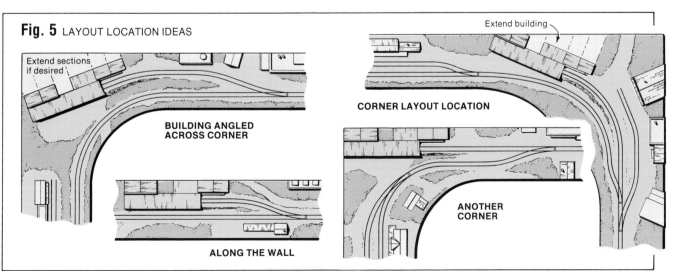

**Fig. 5** LAYOUT LOCATION IDEAS

Extend sections if desired

**BUILDING ANGLED ACROSS CORNER**

**ALONG THE WALL**

Extend building

**CORNER LAYOUT LOCATION**

**ANOTHER CORNER**

This HO scale wood-treatment plant on Cyril Durrenberger's Houston, East & West Texas RR is a major industry that ships and receives by rail, and has its own narrow gauge railroad too.

# Build a wood-treating plant

## This industry prepares poles and ties and has its own tram railroad

### BY CYRIL DURRENBERGER
### PHOTOS BY THE AUTHOR

M Y HO SCALE Houston, East & West Texas RR serves a number of East Texas wood products industries. On the real HE&WT these included several wood-treating plants, so I wanted to model one.

A wood-treating plant's main function is to add preservatives to various wood products. The most common operation is to creosote railroad ties and utility poles. Ancillary operations can include sawing, notching, and drilling ties; debarking and sizing poles; and other kinds of timber preparation. These plants also include areas for storing both treated and untreated poles, ties, and timbers.

As an added attraction, many wood-treating plants used narrow gauge tram railroads to shift timbers within the plant. About the time I was getting ready to build my treatment plant, a friend came up with a couple of AHM Mini-Train sets he wanted to sell. These are models of industrial railroad equipment that run on N gauge track, equivalent to 30″ gauge in HO, so I planned on having an HOn2½ tram road to serve my treating plant.

[The Roco Mini-Trains once imported by AHM are no longer available, but Wm. K. Walthers sells Roco's current HOn2½ or "HOe" equipment. This includes many of the same cars and European-prototype steam and diesel locomotives. — Ed.]

#### PLANT DESIGN

The next step was to fit the plant into my layout. There wasn't room at the town of Lufkin, Tex., where such a plant had been located on the prototype. I had planned to have a small sawmill at the town of Humble with a handle plant at the end of a spur. After a little figuring I decided to move the handle plant to Diboll, make the sawmill a tie mill to be located where the handle plant would have been, and put the wood-treating plant on the former sawmill site!

Before designing the model I did some research. In the University of Texas engineering library here in Austin I found articles showing equipment and new plants in a magazine called *Wood Preserving News*. I concentrated on ads and articles that were published in the 1920s, so I'd get an idea of how these plants looked during the era of my model railroad. Most of my model is based on a Taylor-Cloquitt Co. plant in South Carolina, various parts of which were shown in advertisements in *Wood Preserving News*.

Actually there has been little outward change in these plants over the past 50 years, except for the addition of devices to control air pollution. You could probably even find plants today that still operate steam-powered trams!

Hobby magazines have published articles on wood-treating plants too. For examples see the Winter 1972 *Slim Gauge News*, page 29, wood-treating plant in Seattle; October 1975 MODEL RAILROAD-ER, page 78, Burlington Northern tie plants at Brainerd, Minn., and Somers, Mont.; and February 1980 MR, page 93, Union Pacific tie plant at Laramie, Wyo.

The most important step in designing the plant is to decide what buildings will be included and where they will go. Then you can lay out the tram tracks to serve the buildings. The centerpiece of my model is the retort building where the wood is treated, but it also has a boiler house, creosote storage tank, office, pole debarking and trimming area, and storage yard for poles, ties, and timbers. It's adjacent to a tie sawmill and connected to it by both standard and narrow gauge tracks. The layout of the plant is shown in fig. 1.

Since all the wood-treating plants I have seen are constructed with corrugated-metal exteriors, most of my structures have metal walls and roofs. I made the plant office a little nicer by giving it

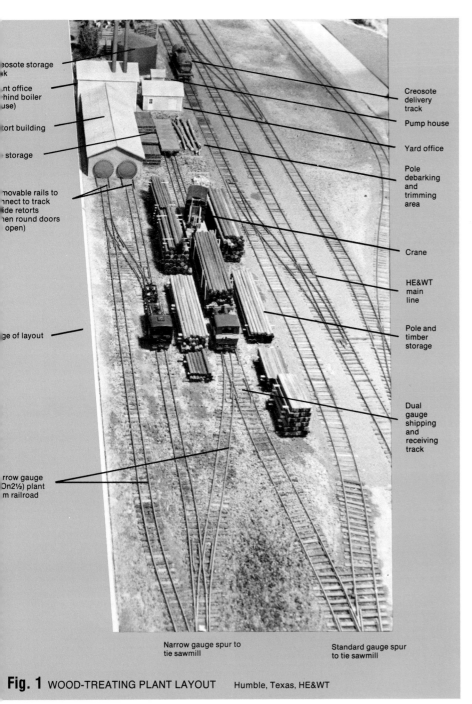

Creosote storage
[ta]nk

[Pla]nt office
[(be]hind boiler
[ho]use)

[Re]tort building

[Pole] storage

[Re]movable rails to
[con]nect to track
[(sli]de retorts
[wh]en round doors
[are] open)

[Ed]ge of layout

[Na]rrow gauge
[(]On2½) plant
[tra]m railroad

Creosote
delivery
track

Pump house

Yard office

Pole
debarking
and
trimming
area

Crane

HE&WT
main
line

Pole and
timber
storage

Dual
gauge
shipping
and
receiving
track

Narrow gauge spur to
tie sawmill

Standard gauge spur
to tie sawmill

**Fig. 1** WOOD-TREATING PLANT LAYOUT    Humble, Texas, HE&WT

## Bill of materials

**Wood (all basswood except as noted)**
1/32" scribed siding, 1/32" thick
1/16" clapboard siding, 1/16" thick
1/16"-thick balsa sheet
1/32" x 1/16" strip
1/16"-square strip
3/16"-square pine or spruce strip
  (1/8"-square would be okay)
1" x 4" HO scale lumber
1" x 6" HO scale lumber
8"-square HO scale lumber
12"-square HO scale lumber
1/8"-diameter dowels
3/16"-diameter dowels
Campbell Scale Models no. 798 bridge
  ties

**Grandt Line**
5032 windows
5072 doors
5093 nuts-on-washers

**Miscellaneous**
.010" styrene sheet
Alexander Scale Models no. 7443 oil
  tank
Clear plastic window "glass"
Heavy-duty aluminum foil or Campbell
  Scale Models no. 803 corrugated alu-
  minum (see text)
Life-Like 36-foot HO tank car, any road
  name
Plastruct 5/16"-diameter ABS tubing

---

clapboard siding and a metal roof. Also, the boiler house could be brick.

I wanted the buildings in my plant to look like they were built at the same time and to have the same general style, so I scratchbuilt all of them except the oil tank. They aren't hard to build, so this would still be a good project even if you've never scratchbuilt a structure.

### RETORT BUILDING

The retort building is the simplest to build, but is the most important since this is where the wood is treated. The retort building is joined to the boiler house, but to make assembly easier, I built them as two structures. See fig. 2.

Figure 3 shows the basic construction methods I used for all the buildings. I cut my own bracing material with a Dremel table saw, but many hobby shops carry 3/16"-square spruce strips which work just as well. I cut out the walls and braced them, then added the corrugated-metal sheathing. Note that the end of the retort building that will adjoin the boiler house doesn't need to be sheathed.

I like the effect of using individual sheets of metal for the sheathing, and they don't take much extra time. The actual dimensions of these pieces aren't important as long as the sheets are a reasonable size. I usually make mine a scale 3 feet wide and 5 feet long.

To attach the metal to the walls, I first covered an area with Elmer's contact cement and added one row of sheets while the cement was still wet. This way you don't have to apply cement to the metal before placing it on the walls. I gave the glue a number of hours to dry before adding the second row.

The whole wall could be sheathed in one sitting, but then it's very easy to accidentally move the sheets you applied earlier. That's why I like to do just one row at a time. I built the walls for all the plant's structures at one time, then added the metal sheathing. By the time I had one row of metal on each wall, I was ready for something else!

You could use Campbell's corrugated-aluminum siding, but I prefer to make my own from heavy-duty aluminum foil. I tear off a strip of aluminum foil and lay it over a corrugated surface as a pattern. A section of corrugated roofing from a molded plastic structure kit can make a good pattern. I lightly rub the foil with a pencil eraser to form the corrugations, then cut it to sheathing size with scissors.

When all the walls were sheathed I glued the sides and ends together, making sure everything was square and leaving space in each corner joint for the stripwood corner trim. Next, I painted the assembled walls with an airbrush, using Floquil SP Lettering Gray to represent galvanized iron that's only lightly weathered. Then I painted the corner trim strips Floquil Reefer White and cemented them in place.

To add the roof I first cemented the ridge pole in place. Then I cut out the roof sections and covered them with corrugated metal. After cementing the roof sections in place I added the ridge cap, then sprayed the roof with SP Lettering Gray, like the metal walls.

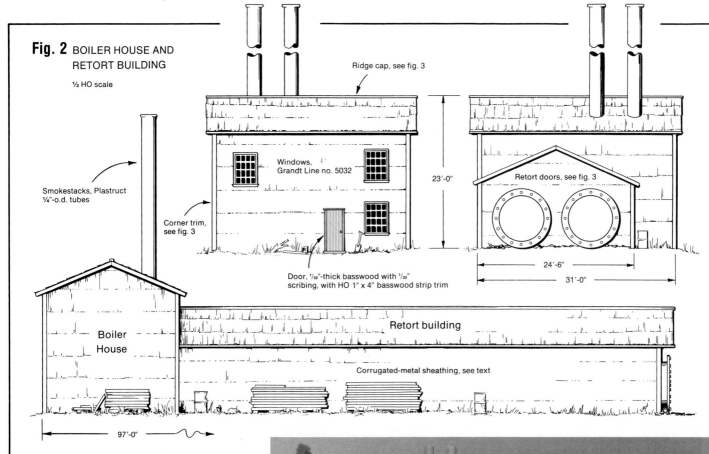

**Fig. 2** BOILER HOUSE AND RETORT BUILDING

½ HO scale

Ridge cap, see fig. 3

Windows, Grandt Line no. 5032

Retort doors, see fig. 3

Smokestacks, Plastruct ¼"-o.d. tubes

Corner trim, see fig. 3

23'-0"

Door, ¹/₃₂"-thick basswood with ¹/₃₂" scribing, with HO 1" x 4" basswood strip trim

24'-6"

31'-0"

Boiler House

Retort building

Corrugated-metal sheathing, see text

97'-0"

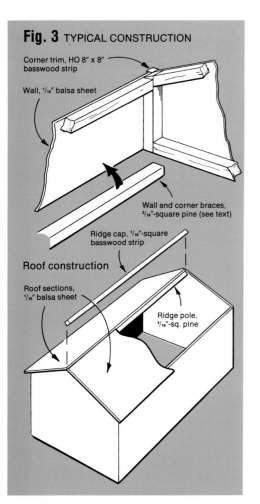

**Fig. 3** TYPICAL CONSTRUCTION

Corner trim, HO 8" x 8" basswood strip

Wall, ¹/₁₆" balsa sheet

Wall and corner braces, ³/₁₆"-square pine (see text)

Ridge cap, ¹/₁₆"-square basswood strip

Roof construction

Roof sections, ¹/₁₆" balsa sheet

Ridge pole, ³/₁₆"-sq. pine

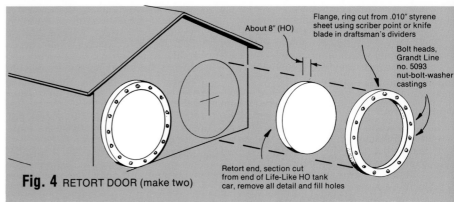

About 8" (HO)

Flange, ring cut from .010" styrene sheet using scriber point or knife blade in draftsman's dividers

Bolt heads, Grandt Line no. 5093 nut-bolt-washer castings

Retort end, section cut from end of Life-Like HO tank car, remove all detail and fill holes

**Fig. 4** RETORT DOOR (make two)

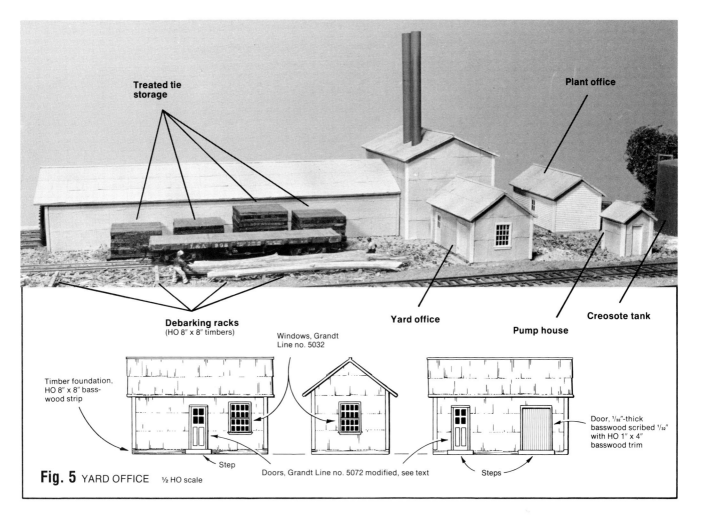

**Treated tie storage**

**Plant office**

**Debarking racks**
(HO 8″ x 8″ timbers)

Windows, Grandt
Line no. 5032

**Yard office**

**Creosote tank**

**Pump house**

Timber foundation,
HO 8″ x 8″ bass-
wood strip

Door, 1/32″-thick
basswood scribed 1/32″
with HO 1″ x 4″
basswood trim

Step

Doors, Grandt Line no. 5072 modified, see text

Steps

**Fig. 5** YARD OFFICE   ½ HO scale

---

### RETORT DOORS

The retorts in which the poles and ties are treated are long pressure cylinders. They are opened by unbolting the doors which form their exposed ends, then loaded by shoving in tram cars carrying the wood to be treated. The doors are bolted shut, and creosote and other compounds are forced into the wood by steam pressure. When the treating process is complete, the cylinders are depressurized and opened, and the tram cars are removed so the process can be repeated.

While the cylinders themselves are inside the retort building, their doors have to be modeled, so I did a lot of thinking about how to make decent-looking replicas.

Retort doors are usually convex, so I decided to model them using the ends of an HO tank car. See fig. 4. After airbrushing the completed doors with Floquil Grimy Black, I glued them in place.

### BOILER HOUSE

The boiler house is the tallest structure in this plant. Its construction is similar to the retort building's, except for the doors, windows, and smokestacks. Referring to fig. 2 again, notice where the retort building butts to the boiler house — that area of the boiler house wall needs no metal sheathing.

After assembling and painting the walls, I cut the door trim pieces to size and painted them Floquil Reefer White,

then cemented them in place. Similarly, I airbrushed the Grandt Line windows white, installed them after the walls were assembled, then added clear plastic "glass." The Plastruct tubing smokestacks were cut to size, sprayed Grimy Black, and glued in place.

### YARD OFFICE

This is the building used by the storage yard crew for an office, shop, and equipment storehouse. See fig. 5. It's also sheathed with metal, and its construction is similar to that of the previous buildings. It has Grandt windows and doors, the latter with the transom windows removed above the lintels.

The yard office has a timber foundation.

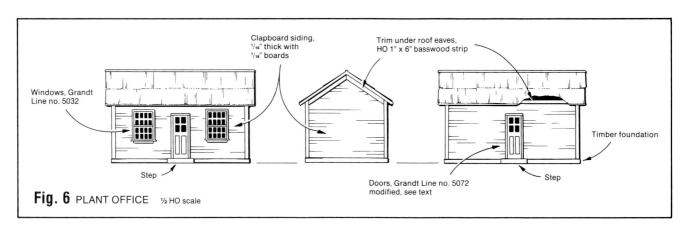

Windows, Grandt
Line no. 5032

Clapboard siding,
1/16″ thick with
1/16″ boards

Trim under roof eaves,
HO 1″ x 6″ basswood strip

Timber foundation

Step

Doors, Grandt Line no. 5072
modified, see text

Step

**Fig. 6** PLANT OFFICE   ½ HO scale

**Fig. 7. TIMBER AND POLE STORAGE.** The HO 12″ x 12″ timbers and the poles made from ⅛″- and ³/₁₆″-diameter dowels were stained with black shoe polish diluted with denatured alcohol (shellac thinner) and glued together. The layers of timbers and poles in each stack are separated by lengths of ¹/₃₂″ x ¹/₁₆″ basswood stained with Flo-Stain Driftwood. The 25-ton crane peeking up behind the poles is from Walthers kit no. 932-5500.

I modeled this with scale stripwood stained with Flo-Stain Driftwood, a wood stain made by Floquil.

### PLANT OFFICE

As I mentioned earlier, the plant office shown in fig. 6 (and the fig. 5 photo) is the only building that has wood siding. After locating the window and door openings, I cut them out to fit the Grandt doors and windows. Again I removed the transom windows from the door castings. This time I airbrushed the castings with Floquil Barrier before cementing them in place, then airbrushed the assembled walls with their windows, doors, and trim with Reefer White. This building also has a timber foundation.

### CREOSOTE STORAGE TANK AND PUMP HOUSE

The creosote storage tank is from an Alexander kit. I simply assembled it according to the kit instructions and airbrushed it with Grimy Black. I built the small pump house just like the other metal-sheathed buildings. It measures about 6 x 8 scale feet and has only one door, and it's so simple that I haven't bothered to include a drawing of it. See the fig. 5 photo.

### POLE DEBARKING AND TRIMMING

Before they can be treated poles must have their bark removed, be trimmed to length, and then checked for defects. Logs to be used for poles were placed on a simple rack formed by parallel timbers, as shown in the fig. 5 photo, and the debarking and trimming were done by hand. (Modern treatment plants have automated the debarking and trimming processes.) The poles were inspected before being stored or treated.

The ground under and around the rack should be covered with bark and trim pieces. Periodically this debris was removed and burned, although today it frequently is bagged and sold for mulch.

### STORAGE AREA

Every wood-treating plant has an area for storing finished products. This area should have tram and standard gauge tracks nearby so that treated products from the retorts can be unloaded from tram cars, and products sold to customers can be loaded on standard gauge cars. At least one crane is needed for loading and unloading poles and ties. See fig. 7.

I made stacks of ties using Campbell bridge ties — not the shallow profile ties — stained like the poles. Ties are usually stacked in layers, with ties in each row being perpendicular to the previous row. For economy I made my tie stacks hollow as shown in fig. 8. I stained the ties before assembling the stacks, then re-stained the exposed cut tie ends as necessary.

### WEATHERING AND DETAILS

I wanted my model to look like a plant that had been in operation for a few years, so I lightly weathered all its buildings with Floquil Grimy Black and Dust. An airbrush is the best way to apply this weathering in light coats.

Removable rails carry the tram cars into the retorts when the doors are open, so I cut some suitable lengths of rail and laid them on either side of the doors.

Various kinds of debris and a few weeds should be placed in the storage area, but don't overdo it. Piles of combustible materials would be a fire hazard, so they'd be quickly removed, and vegetation doesn't grow well where creosote soaks into the ground. A small earth containment dike should be built around the creosote storage tank, and a hose for unloading the tank cars could be added.

Workmen add life to the treating-plant scene, and Preiser figure set no. 44 is suitable for this plant. These figures are also included in one of Preiser's unpainted figures sets.

This wood-treating plant receives and ships products in several types of freight cars. Tank cars bring in creosote, while flatcars and gondolas bring in loads of logs, poles, and ties to be treated and take out the finished wood products. At least one crane is needed to load and unload logs, poles, and ties. Put in an operating narrow gauge tram line and you'll have an eye-catching addition to your layout. ⌀

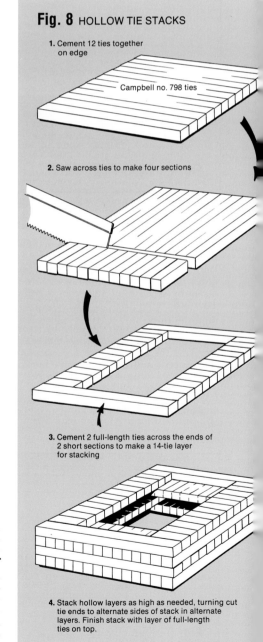

**Fig. 8** HOLLOW TIE STACKS

1. Cement 12 ties together on edge

Campbell no. 798 ties

2. Saw across ties to make four sections

3. Cement 2 full-length ties across the ends of 2 short sections to make a 14-tie layer for stacking

4. Stack hollow layers as high as needed, turning cut tie ends to alternate sides of stack in alternate layers. Finish stack with layer of full-length ties on top.

## An industry you can model

Following a prototype in Totowa, N. J., the author built this concrete plant from an HO kit introduced by Revell of Germany and later sold by IHC.

# Raia Industries cement works

## Kitbash an HO rail-serviced cement plant

### BY KARL ERK
### PHOTOS BY THE AUTHOR

JUST OFF New Jersey Rt. 80 on Minnisink Rd. in Totowa, N. J., is a concrete batch plant operated by Raia Industries. As it is brightly painted and of an interesting design, it quickly caught the attention of the local modelers. See figs. 1 and 2. Interest then waned until the release by Revell (of Germany), and then IHC, of a kit very similar to the Raia facility in Totowa.

The plant is about four years old and of German design. In this particular operation, all material is brought in by truck, with cement arriving in 18-wheel tank/hopper trucks. The aggregates, sand, and gravel come in dump-body semitrailers and are dumped close to their respective bins so a dragline bucket can reach them. See fig. 2. Any material that isn't close enough gets pushed in by a bucket front-end loader.

The bucket and dragline keep pushing and pulling the materials to the top of the piles to keep the mixing bins full. There's a large pipe under the high end of each pile to deliver the materials to the mixing bucket. See fig. 3a.

The dry aggregates are automatically measured into a 10-yard bucket at ground level. When this bucket is filled with the predetermined amount, it's hoisted up to the mixing drum that straddles the cement truck loading area. In fig. 4 the drum is inside the enclosure just above the concrete delivery truck. As the dry material is mixed, cement, other compounds, and water are added, and when ready it's dumped into the waiting cement truck below to be delivered to a happy customer.

### BUILDING THE MODEL

My model is a free-lance version. I've used the prototype to understand how the plant functions and to duplicate the paint scheme. I started with an IHC kit and altered the model so cement will be brought in by rail.

Following the kit instructions, assemble the kit into five subassemblies. For the first assembly, put the two base pieces together, the three walls and door that go next to the half-circle storage bins, and later the two supports for the stairs.

The next subassembly is the top mixing/loading building, stairs, and building supports. Don't attach this to the base yet. Construct the silos next,

**Fig. 1.** The HO scale model closely follows the arrangement of this Raia Industries concrete batch plant, even to the signs on the end silos.

followed by the related plumbing and the building it rests on. You can assemble the plumbing and silos as one item to check alignment, but don't permanently secure the parts of this subassembly until after painting. When you attach the heavy pipes from the silos to the mixing building, I suggest a flexible glue such as Walthers Goo for ease of repeated assembly and disassembly.

The kit designers were not overly safety conscious, so I added safety

railings around the tops of the silos. See figs. 5, 6, and 7. These were made out of .020″-diameter brass wire formed to shape and Athearn diesel handrail stanchions that I straightened out for the posts. You could even get fancier by putting a cage around the ladder, but I chose not to.

Next, assemble the crane, leaving the roof off so you can install glass after painting. In addition, leave off the rear top cover with the hole so you can later

adjust the thread (cable) for the bucket. See fig. 4b.

Now dry assemble (i.e. no glue) the walls for the aggregates bins and the other subassemblies so as to get a feel of the complete complex. Cut a piece of 1″-thick foam board for the base of the complex, and start to lay out where your other structures and details are to go. My piece is 1″ x 29″ x 30″, but you can cut yours to fit your own requirements.

### ADDITIONAL STRUCTURES

One structure I added is a single-level office made from an old container. My model has a new foundation, along with a Pikestuff door and window. The office can be seen on the near left side of the silos in fig. 4. I constructed the foundation using Vollmer brick material, making it six courses high. Another building is an Atlas trackside shanty used for the gatekeeper. Similar models can be substituted here.

### PAINTING

When all your buildings are finished, it's time to paint them in the company colors. Raia Industries painted everything except the cement trucks in a light blue. My blue started out as about one-third of a bottle of Floquil Reefer White with a small amount of Conrail Blue mixed in. Spray everything with a coat of gray Primer. Next, everything except the walls of the aggregates bins and the roof of the Atlas shanty is painted blue.

**Fig. 2.** Sand and gravel aggregates are brought into the plant by 18-wheel trucks with dump-body semitrailers. Vehicles of this type are necessary parts of the model project, too.

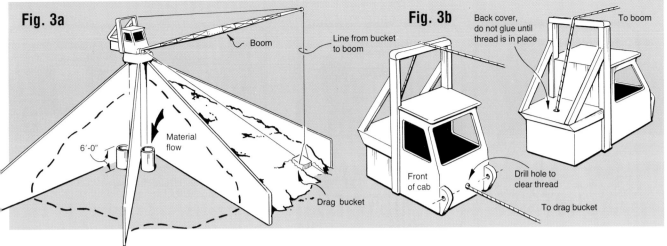

**Fig. 3a** Boom · Line from bucket to boom · Material flow · 6'-0" · Drag bucket

**Fig. 3b** Back cover, do not glue until thread is in place · To boom · Front of cab · Drill hole to clear thread · To drag bucket

Raia Industries was kind enough to provide me with some company labels with their logo in blue. I cut these out and cemented them to the end silos. Copies are provided here for O, S, HO, and N scales.

When everything has dried, install all the glazing in the buildings and the crane cab. You can now cement the roof on the crane, but don't glue the back cover on yet. Put the crane aside.

Now cement the subassemblies together, including the bin walls. When these have dried, glue in some tapered, wedge-shaped extruded foam fillers. The idea is to fill up the space in the bins so as not to use up lots of expensive ballast and such. See fig. 4. Fill the gaps along the walls with some white glue and facial tissue.

You can carve the foam tops with a knife, but I used Testor's liquid plastic cement to soften the foam and make ruts to represent tracks left by the dragline bucket. The brush in the bottle is fine for this work. When dry, tilt the assembly, one bin at a time, so the foam filler top is level.

Mix batches of tan or gray paint using brown or black acrylic tube color and white latex paint to match each aggregate material you'll use, and apply heavy coats to the extruded fillers. I used a coarse gray/blue ballast, fine gray, black, and fine tan aggregate materials. Pour a layer of the model aggregate into each over the heavy coat of paint. See figs. 5 and 6. For fine sand I used a window screen to sift material sold for sandboxes.

## MOUNTING THE STRUCTURES

Use white glue to mount the structures on the foam base. Mix earth-colored latex paint (brown tube color and white latex paint) with a soupy batch of plaster for earth. Pour this mess into every nook and cranny, but not over the concrete pad under the main building. Work outside on a nice day so the mix that runs off the sides goes on the ground. After this paint/plaster mix has dried, mix another soupy batch of dark gray. Use this to represent blacktop aprons to the main building.

## FENCING

While the plaster dries, make the chain link fence. I used window screen cut into 1½"-wide strips with the wires on a 45-degree angle. For the posts I used .040"-diameter wire, making about half of them 1½" high to match the fencing. The other posts were cut 2" long so I could stick the fence in the ground.

I used Walthers Goo to attach the screen to the posts, with the posts

**Fig. 4.** This photo shows the extruded foam used under the material piles to limit the amount of gravel and sanded needed. Ruts were cut into the foam by applying Testor's liquid cement to the surfaces and letting it erode the foam. The safety railings are .020"-diameter brass wire with Athearn diesel handrail stanchions.

INCORPORATED ®

INCORPORATED ®

S scale

O scale

INCORPORATED ®

INCORPORATED ®

HO scale

RAIA INDUSTRIES
INCORPORATED ®

RAIA INDUSTRIES
INCORPORATED ®

N scale

## Bill of materials

**Athearn**
340019 diesel handrails

**Atlas**
702 trackside shanty

**Con-Cor**
8300 undecorated container

**Floquil paint**
110009 Primer
110011 Reefer White
110058 Conrail Blue

**International Hobby Corp.**
5007 concrete plant (Revell 2016)

**Kibri**
10208, 10294, 10340 front loader

**Micro Engineering**
10106 code 70 flextrack

**Pikestuff**
1103 door
2101 window

**Precision Scale**
3870 .020"-diameter brass wire
4975 .040"-diameter brass wire

**Sequoia**
2001 track bumper

**Vollmer**
6028 brick

**Miscellaneous**
ballast
black acrylic tube paint
brown acrylic tube paint
cement trucks (use any type)
   EKO: 2103, 2104
   Kibri: 10042, 10044, 10254
   Roco: 1541
   Wiking: 682
dump trucks (use any type)
   Alloy Forms: 3140, 7012, 7024
   Con-Cor: 7001, 7024
   Kibri: 10416
extruded foam, 36" x 36" x 1"
ground foam, green and light brown
plaster
sand
white latex paint
window screen

spaced approximately 1¾" apart. Assemble the material so it matches the particular piece of model real estate you're working with (lengths, ground irregularities, and the like). You need to have a long post at each end of fence and at each corner. In between alternate long and short posts. If you want better detailed and more expensive fence, use Alloy Forms' kit no. 2009.

### RAILROAD SPUR AND SCENICKING

When the ground has dried, glue down a piece of weathered code 70 flextrack with some white glue. Next, brush grass-green latex paint around the perimeter of the whole diorama, and then sprinkle on some ground foam grass and weeds. Finish up by applying the ballast of your choice to the track. Wet this down with a spray of rubbing alcohol and then apply some diluted white glue.

Don't forget to ballast between the tracks and the building with the silos. As this is where the cement hoppers are unloaded, sprinkle some raw plaster around the area to represent spilled cement. Finally, add a Sequoia bumper to the end of the track.

### WEATHERING

A structure such as this gets dirty fast. Mix up two batches of light and dark gray latex paint. With several sizes of brushes and a cup of water, start streaking colors down the silos and the buildings. Get different shades by mixing the two colors together. This is what will really set these structures off. Give the Raia signs a light coat of grime too.

Back on the ground at the outer edges of the aggregates bins, build up some piles of stone from coarse sand. Make it look like one of the trucks is dumping the material. Glue some sand in the dump body, and wet these piles down with alcohol and soak with white glue. Let a little material spill around as it would in real life. Spray some more with the alcohol, and apply the glue as needed.

At the bins, make up real thin plaster mixes using a much darker color of whatever you used for the ground, and pour these around the bottoms of the piles out in an odd direction or two. This will look like wet ground caused by the workers spraying the areas with water to keep down the dust. Run some of your model trucks though this to simulate tracks. When dry, put on some gloss varnish for that real wet look. Drybrush tire marks on the blacktop and concrete aprons both around and under the plant itself, and also from the bins out in the yard to the driveway. Refer to the photos as a guide.

### DETAILS AND FINISHING TOUCHES

Finish detailing the scene by adding appropriate items such as trash cans, shovels, a soda machine, a scale, and so forth around the area. I painted some figures in a company uniform of light blue shirt, dark blue pants, black boots, and yellow hard hats. You'll need some cars for the employees, cement trucks, and a truck or two delivering some kind of gravel.

My main group of cement trucks came from Hot Wheels, which had the largest amount of any one kind of truck with the same colors. EKO, Kibri, Roco, and Wiking have concrete trucks too. Alloy Forms, Con-Cor, and Kibri offer the big 18-wheeler dump trucks. You'll also need a front-end loader. Mine is a Zylmex toy to which I added a cab. Then I weathered it and ran it through the mud while it was still wet. Kibri has two such vehicles: nos. 10208 yellow and 10294 red, along with a different type, no. 10340.

Now's the time to add the crane. Cement the boom to the cab at about 25 degrees to the horizontal, centered over one of the bins. Drill holes in the cab front and the back cover panel, and attach black thread to the bucket and run to the boom and cab as shown in fig. 3b. I positioned the bucket about midway up the slope, added the appropriate material in the bucket, wet this with alcohol and white glue, and let it set. You want to make this look like the bucket is actually pulling material up the slope. When the bucket and material are firm, draw the thread cables taut, glue them into place inside the cab, and secure the back cover.

At last you can add the chain link fence and vehicles and then set the diorama in place on your layout. Once you've hooked up the siding to the main line, you're ready to go. Appropriate

**Fig. 5.** The Con-Cor container in the foreground was converted into an office with the addition of a Pikestuff door and window. A diesel switcher delivers cement in covered hopper cars.

freight cars for this service include all the short covered hoppers that are now on the market. Equipment from Model Die Casting and Eastern Car Works, the ACF car from Front Range or Ramax, and the old AHM/Con-Cor PS-2 will be just fine. Don't forget to weather these cars.

Besides being an attractive industry, this model can provide some interesting operation for your railroad. In real life the plant would be switched at least once every 24 hours.

I'd like to thank Raia Industries for letting me tour their plant in Totowa and for providing the logo, and my friend Wayne Peterson for the vehicles used in this project. Happy modeling. ✿

**Fig. 6.** The street-side view of the author's Raia concrete plant reveals lots of activity. A semi-trailer truck has just finished dumping a load of aggregate, the dragline is pulling the fresh load up to the delivery intake, and the front-end loader is pushing more stone onto one of the piles.

**Above:** The Davies Steel coke plant occupies a long rectangular site with the raw coal receiving track running behind the bank of ovens.

**Fig. 1. Right:** Coal processing begins at the far right and procee[ds] through the coke ovens, to the concrete quench tower at the far l[eft].

# The Davies Steel coke plant: Part 1

## Modeling a major-size railroad customer

**BY DEAN FREYTAG**
**PHOTOS BY THE AUTHOR**

COAL IS ONE of the most important commodities hauled by North American railroads. Millions of tons move via rail to America's power plants, industries, and export docks. Miniature coal mines have been popular layout additions for many years, and power plants now appear regularly on model railroads. Yet few modelers attempt to build the industrial portion of the coal marketing cycle.

Heavy industry uses coal in great quantity, both as a fuel and as an ingredient. Coal is especially important in the iron and steel industry, where it serves as a major raw material. For this use, coal is converted to coke by baking it in huge ovens to remove volatile gases and liquid substances, leaving an almost pure carbon structure.

In turn, coke is used in blast furnaces and foundries as a reducing agent, along with the fluxing action of limestone, to convert iron ore into metallic iron. Coke is also used with other materials in the production of steel.

My modeling has followed the steel industry for many years, so a coke plant seemed like a natural addition. Merchant coke plants sell to anyone, but they are generally located close to their largest customers. Coke plants also appear as part of the major facilities within most large steel plants. No matter where they are located, coke plants receive long strings of inbound coal hoppers, while the finished coke is shipped out in a wide variety of modified extra-capacity hoppers.

Prototype coke plants are huge industrial complexes that spread over far more territory than most modelers can ever devote to a single business. However, by carefully choosing and reproducing the major elements of the process, I was able to selectively compress the process into a manageable size. Now, before I get into the model

construction, let's take a look at the steps involved as the coal is "processed" through my HO scale Davies Steel Corp. coke plant (shown in fig. 1).

### THE BASIC PROCESS

The process begins with the arrival of raw coal in ordinary open hoppers. These inbound carloads are pushed through the dumper to the end of track, leaving the last one in the concrete dump house. Workers in this small building open the hopper doors to dump the coal into an underground pit. From there, the coal is directed into a bucket conveyor and lifted to a holding bin built on top of the crusher house.

Next, the raw coal travels downward through a crusher, which breaks it into the appropriate sizes (1″ to 3″ in diameter) for the coke ovens. This uniform size coal is lifted by another conveyor to the transfer house and then moved via a belt conveyor into the coal dock for storage.

An electrically operated multiple-hopper charging "Larry" car is used to

handle the coal between the overhead coal dock and the coke ovens. A scale is built into the area beneath the coal dock to control the amount of coal loaded into the Larry. Then the Larry travels across the roof of the ovens until its outlets are positioned over the appropriate hatches. The oven hatches are opened, the Larry discharges its coal into the oven, and the hatches are closed.

A large yellow Wilputte pusher machine (fig. 2) moves back and forth on tracks along the rear bench of the coke ovens. It includes a leveling bar that works like a giant hoe to level the top of each charge of raw coal. Leveling removes the peaks under the charging holes, thereby making the baking process work more evenly and assuring an easier discharge of the hot coke.

The raw coal is then heated, in the absence of oxygen, so all of its volatile gases and liquids are driven out. These vaporized materials are collected and piped to a nearby by-product plant, where they are refined and used to

make many other industrial chemicals. The ovens bake the coal at temperatures between 1,600 and 2,000 degrees Fahrenheit for 12 to 18 hours.

The hot coke is then removed from the ovens. Once again the Wilputte machine goes to work, along with a door-removing machine and a coke guide on the opposite side. Both end doors are removed from the oven, the coke guide is positioned to direct the hot coke into the quench car, and the Wilputte machine's large pusher arm is aligned with the open door. The entire charge of white-hot coke is shoved through the oven and out the opposite side (fig. 3), where it falls into a special custom-built steel car.

The quench car is a heavy-duty gondola-like car that has a sharply sloping floor and rugged sides to handle the hot coke (fig. 4). A protected industrial locomotive slowly moves the car as the coke is delivered so it falls in a thin layer across the sloping floor. The hot coke is moved into the concrete quench tower, where a measured amount of water is

dumped into the car, creating clouds of steam. The amount used is sufficient to lower the temperature below the combustion point yet still leave the coke hot enough to dry almost immediately.

After the water drains off, the locomotive pulls the quench car to the coke wharf, where its doors are opened to discharge steaming hot coke. This wharf is a narrow sloping surface, paved with firebrick, where the coke may be held temporarily. Workers with water hoses take care of any hot spots as the coke cools. A conveyor along the lower edge moves the cooled coke through a final crushing and screening process to separate the fine dust from the usable pieces. The finished coke is then loaded into special high-capacity hoppers for movement to the blast furnaces.

The finished coke is seldom stockpiled in large tipples, as it's relatively fragile compared to raw coal. Each handling of the coke crushes some of it into fine dust, which is undesirable for steelmaking. By loading it into hopper

**Fig. 2.** The Wilputte machine moves along the rear of the coke ovens to level the fresh charge of raw coal, open the doors, and eject the hot coke at the end of the baking cycle.

cars, these losses can be minimized as the coke is moved directly to its final destination without further handling.

### SIZING THE MODEL

Coke ovens are a classic example of the old "form follows function" school of industrial design. The coal dock and ovens have to be located side by side so the Larry car can travel across the entire installation. However, everything else (especially the inbound coal handling) can be shifted almost anywhere around the plant by adjusting the length of the various conveyors, track positions, and access stairways.

As it is, my HO coke plant occupies a space roughly 18" wide and 54" long and visible from both sides. Figure 5 shows how the plant is oriented with the pusher side to the north so the coal dock is at the east end, the quench tower to the west, and the coke wharf on the south side. For a narrower space, I'd model only the discharge side of the oven complex.

The coke ovens I modeled have interior dimensions that are approximately a scale 30'-0" long, 14'-0" high, and 30" wide. Considering the leveling space above the coal, a prototype oven of this size provides around 800 cubic feet of coke-processing space. Quality metallurgical coal weighs roughly 50 pounds per cubic foot, so each oven could handle about 20 tons of coal per cycle, or "turn." With its 36 ovens working on a 12-hour cycle, the coke plant would require 1,440 tons of coal per day.

On the outbound side of things, a typical plant produces three-quarters of a ton of coke for each ton of raw coal consumed (about 75 percent). If each oven produces about 15 tons per turn, that works out to 1,080 tons of coke per day.

The challenge — and the fun — for an operator will be determining how these quantities of coal and coke are transported to and from the plant. A cubic foot of coke weighs approximately 25 pounds. Thus, a hopper capable of bringing in 50 tons of coal can take out only about 25 tons of coke.

From these estimates, we can rough out the daily work the railroad must provide for the plant. Keep in mind which era you're modeling. Fifty-ton cars were common in the 1940s and '50s; since then 70- and 100-ton hoppers have been put into service. Clearly, a mix of cars will be needed to bring in the coal; then, more empty cars will have to be spotted to haul away the coke.

As track space is limited, this would be a good place to use a small industrial switcher: a GE 44-ton unit, an older 0-4-0 or 0-6-0 steam switcher, or a secondhand Alco or EMD diesel switcher.

### CONSTRUCTION MATERIALS

The Davies Steel coke plant is a big project built mostly of such plastic materials as Evergreen sheet and strip styrene, Plastruct molded ABS structural shapes, and Holgate & Reynolds embossed plastic brick. Few hobby shops carry enough of these items to do this project, so special orders may be necessary.

(Catalogs may be obtained from Evergreen Scale Models, 12808 N. E. 125th Way, Seattle, WA 98034 [$1 postpaid] and Plastruct, 1020 S. Wallace Pl., City of Industry, CA 91748 [$5].)

The materials for my HO model are identified by the manufacturer's code number and their size, as that's the way they're sold. Modelers in other scales will have to make size adjustments accordingly. Plastruct structural items are numbered by size in thirty-seconds of an inch: for example, I beam no. B-8 is 8/32" or 1/4" high. The firm's other products follow the same numbering pattern with different prefix initials.

Most of the tools I used are common model building items. However, I now consider my NorthWest Short Line

**Fig. 3.** After both oven doors are removed the white-hot coke is discharged, in a spectacular display of fireworks, through a coke guide that directs it into a special quench car.

**Fig. 4.** The plant's specialized coke-handling equipment includes a coke guide, a door opener, the quench car, and a locomotive.

Chopper to be an essential tool, especially when many parts of uniform size have to be produced.

I used several different adhesives to bond the various materials. Tenax liquid plastic cement, applied with a small brush, was used for all plastic joints where capillary action carried the cement between the parts. Testor's cement worked well on plastic joints where it was applied before the parts were placed in contact with each other. Thick-body tube plastic cement produced strong inside joints where it could be applied in hidden locations.

In addition, I used cyanoacrylate adhesive (CA) for metal-to-metal joints and to secure metal parts mounted in holes drilled in the styrene. I used Hotstuff CA to secure the large assemblies during final assembly and Walthers Goo to hold the running rails in place around the foundation.

**COMMON DETAILS**

In designing and building this freelance installation, I used a standard

**Fig. 5.** This north-side view of the plant shows the raw coal processing area at the left end, with the quench tower to the right.

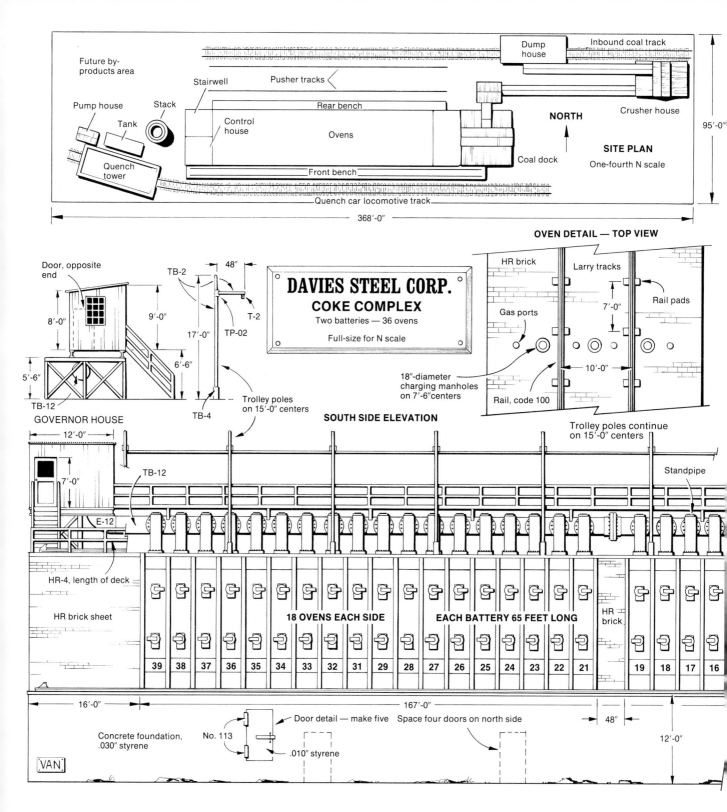

Future by-products area

Pump house

Stack

Tank

Quench tower

Stairwell

Pusher tracks

Control house

Rear bench

Ovens

Front bench

Dump house

Inbound coal track

Crusher house

NORTH

Coal dock

SITE PLAN
One-fourth N scale

Quench car locomotive track

95'-0"

368'-0"

Door, opposite end

8'-0"

5'-6"

TB-12

GOVERNOR HOUSE

TB-2

48"

9'-0"

17'-0"

6'-6"

T-2

TP-02

Trolley poles on 15'-0" centers

TB-4

**DAVIES STEEL CORP.**
**COKE COMPLEX**
Two batteries — 36 ovens

Full-size for N scale

OVEN DETAIL — TOP VIEW

HR brick

Larry tracks

Rail pads

Gas ports

7'-0"

10'-0"

18"-diameter charging manholes on 7'-6" centers

Rail, code 100

SOUTH SIDE ELEVATION

Trolley poles continue on 15'-0" centers

12'-0"

7'-0"

TB-12

E-12

Standpipe

HR-4, length of deck

HR brick sheet

18 OVENS EACH SIDE

EACH BATTERY 65 FEET LONG

HR brick

| 39 | 38 | 37 | 36 | 35 | 34 | 33 | 32 | 31 | 29 | 28 | 27 | 26 | 25 | 24 | 23 | 22 | 21 | | 19 | 18 | 17 | 16 |

16'-0"

167'-0"

48"

12'-0"

Concrete foundation, .030" styrene

No. 113

Door detail — make five  Space four doors on north side

.010" styrene

VAN

45-degree angle for all rooflines, conveyors, and stairways. This is an easy angle to work with, and it makes efficient use of material. Whenever an angled piece must be cut, the cutoff has a corresponding angle that's also usable. In addition, the repetitive angles help unify the appearance of the completed structure.

This plant has a lot of stairways and overhead access walkways that give it much of its visual impact. In the interests of uniformity, I made these items from Plastruct's molded HO scale stair and railing components. These parts make stair building easy. I cut an appropriate length of stairway and fit it to each location. Then I cut and fit the railings for each side and cement them in place to finish the job.

Heavy industry uses many shaded light fixtures to illuminate doorways, stairs, and other key locations. I use Plastruct LF-3 shades, mounted on pieces of .020" brass wire, to simulate these fixtures. My freestanding light standards are bent 180 degrees around a ¼" rod to obtain a uniform curvature, while the building installations are done similarly with 90-degree bends.

I also use a lot of round hatches and access doors in this type of project. They are easy to make using various sizes of round paper punches purchased in an office supply store. I have several sizes, which include ⅛" (scale 9"), ³⁄₁₆" (scale 15"), and ¼" (scale 21") diameters.

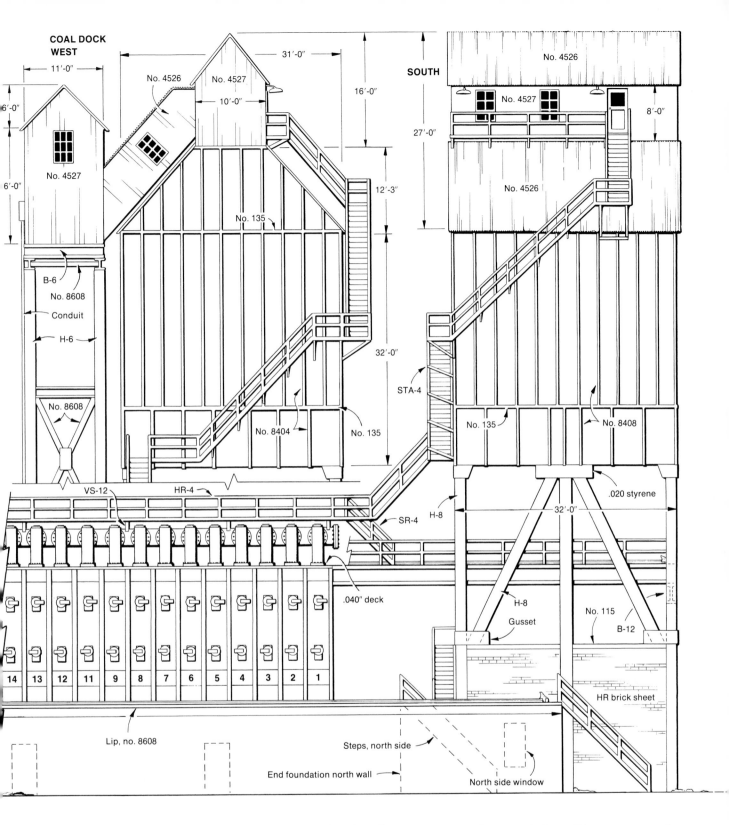

Just punch the desired size from a sheet of thin styrene and cement it in place.

### OVEN FOUNDATION

The concrete foundation for the coke ovens is made of .030″ styrene, cut into strips a scale 12 feet high. I cut one piece 135 feet long for the north wall and another 167 feet long for the south wall. Next, I cut four pieces 12 feet high and 45 feet long to make the end walls and interior cross pieces. I also

cut a handful of scale 6-foot squares, which I cut in half at a 45-degree angle for corner braces.

I used a pencil to mark the length of the north wall on the back of the south wall. The two interior walls are set in about 30 feet from either end, so I also marked these locations. Then I cemented the foundation together with the short walls inside the long ones, taking care to make the corners even and square. I added interior gussets in

each corner to keep things square and strengthen the assembly (fig. 6).

The lip that runs around the top of the foundation is made from lengths of Evergreen no. 8608 (scale 6″ x 8″) styrene strip. I cut and cemented these strips with their 8″ dimension against the walls. The top of the strip should be flush with the top of each wall.

Bench decks came next, and they are made from .040″ sheet styrene. The south side bench is 12′-0″ wide and

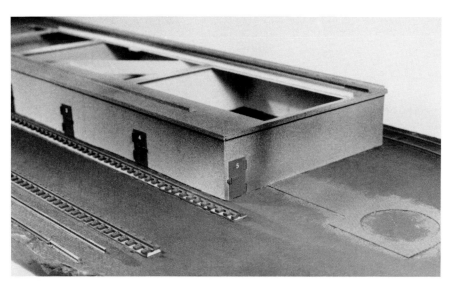

**Fig. 6.** The oven foundation is heavily cross-braced for added strength and to keep it square. All of the steel access doors are numbered in typical heavy-industry fashion.

168'-6" long (so there is a slight overhang at each end), while the north side bench is 8'-0" wide and 136'-6" long. I cemented these bench decks to the tops of the walls. I used pieces of Evergreen no. 147 (.040" x ⁵⁄₃₂") strip to make fillers for the gaps between the bench decks and cemented them to the tops of the end walls.

With the bench decks in place, I turned the assembly over on a flat surface and cemented bits and pieces of scrap styrene inside the foundation at each location that needed extra reinforcement. Next, I smoothed the visible joints with 200- and then 400-grit sandpaper to remove any rough spots.

The running rails for the oven service equipment must be installed next. I used code 100 rail for this, though code 83 or code 70 might look better. This area receives a lot of dirt and spillage, so the large rail is pretty well hidden. On the south bench, I marked a line a scale 9" from the outer edge and cemented the first rail just inside the line. A second rail was then positioned with standard HO track gauges and cemented in place. In each case, I tried to keep the rails as straight as possible even though the prototypes take a terrible beating.

A third line, spaced 10'-3" from the front edge of the south bench, was marked for the length of the ovens. I cemented an Evergreen no. 175 (.100" x .100") styrene strip inside this line to serve as a bottom brace for the ovens. This dimension is critical as it provides only a scale 3" to 6" of clearance between the rear of the coke guide and the front of the ovens.

Moving to the pusher side, I marked another line a scale 5 feet from the edge of the north bench and made sure this line remained parallel with the inside (oven) line on the south bench. Everything checked out, so I went ahead and cemented a no. 175 strip of styrene

along the inside of this line to support the north oven wall.

Further observation of the prototype convinced me to separate the east end coal dock a bit from the ovens. To do this, I wound up cutting additional pieces of .030" sheet styrene 12 feet high and making another section of foundation a scale 16 feet wide and 32 feet long. The top deck was made of .040" sheet styrene. After all the joints had dried, I smoothed the rough edges and spray-painted the foundation assemblies with a dark gray concrete color.

**OVEN FABRICATION**

The main coke ovens are rectangular in shape, with a series of uniform-size doors down both long sides. I made the sides from .030" sheet styrene cut to be a scale 18 feet high and 140 feet long (final trimming will be done later). Next, I set up the Chopper and cut 76 pieces of Evergreen no. 8608 and 76 pieces of no. 115 (.015" x .100") strip styrene for the 18-foot-high vertical stays between the individual ovens.

My Chopper also came in handy to cut the many pieces of styrene I laminated to represent the different thicknesses in the oven doors. See fig. 7. Each of the 72 doors is a scale 36" wide, with a single overlay added for the top 18" and two more overlays appearing 48" and 24" from the bottom. I cut numerous strips of .020" sheet styrene a scale 36" wide and chopped them up into 72 pieces a scale 18" long, 72 pieces 48" long, and 72 pieces 24" long. Accuracy is important here to keep the door wall assemblies square and uniform in appearance.

I began assembling the oven doors by cementing one of the Evergreen 8608 strips (with the 6" width against the surface) flush with left end of the side wall. This piece was checked with a square and allowed to set hard before I

continued. Then I added the .020" pieces by cementing one of the scale 18" pieces flush with the top of the oven and a 48" piece flush with the bottom edge. As soon as the cement set, I laminated a 24" piece on top of the 48" piece so it was also flush with the bottom of the wall. This completed one door.

Another 8608 strip was cemented in place, and this procedure was repeated until the first group of 18 doors was done on each side. After finishing up with another 8608 strip, the completed door assembly came out to be approximately 65 scale feet long.

(For a larger coke plant, add the ovens in multiples of three. Each group of doors will lengthen this assembly by about 10 feet, so a corresponding addition will be required in the foundation.)

I cut a supply of Evergreen no. 115 strips to a scale 18-foot length. I cemented one of these strips to the scale 6" face of the vertical 8608 strips so they were centered, forming a small flange on each side.

I repeated the door assembly procedure until I had 4 sidewalls completed, with 18 oven doors on each one. Then it was time to add the door latch details.

I added the door latches while I could still work on the flat walls. They consist of scale 24" lengths of Plastruct C-4 channel, with a scale 15"-diameter disk of .010" styrene and a 24" length of Evergreen no. 113 (.015" x .060") strip (figs. 7 and 8). These latches need to be accurately spaced a scale 36" down from the top of the oven door and 72" up

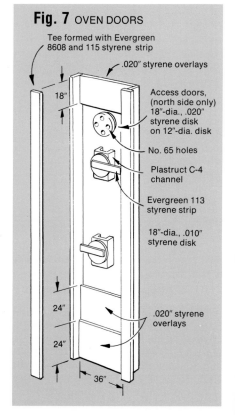

**Fig. 7** OVEN DOORS

Tee formed with Evergreen 8608 and 115 styrene strip

.020" styrene overlays

18"

Access doors, (north side only) 18"-dia., .020" styrene disk on 12"-dia. disk

No. 65 holes

Plastruct C-4 channel

Evergreen 113 styrene strip

18"-dia., .010" styrene disk

24"

.020" styrene overlays

24"

36"

from the bottom (I made a simple jig to do this). The disks are positioned a scale 3″ down from the tops of the channels. Then I fitted the top horizontal latch bar beneath the flange on the vertical strip to the right and the lower latch under the flange to the left.

The north side oven doors also have small access doors (called "choke" doors) that admit the coal leveling bar on the Wilputte machine. I simulated these doors with 21″-diameter disks of .015″ styrene cemented on top of 15″ disks. See fig. 8. These doors were assembled first and then cemented in place on the north doors. After the cement set hard, I went back and drilled four no. 65 holes in each access door to simulate the engagement holes used by the power door opener.

Figure 8 also shows the scale 48″-wide brick wall that separates the two batteries of ovens in my plant. I simulated this space on one front and one rear oven door assembly with small sections of Holgate & Reynolds embossed brick cemented alongside the last oven door.

Next, I used a steel straightedge and a triangle to square up the brick ends of the oven door assemblies. I cemented the two halves of each wall together, backing up the joints with pieces of .020″ sheet styrene.

While both sets of sidewalls were drying, I cut a supply of triangular gussets for use as corner reinforcements. I cut scale 12-foot squares of .040″ styrene (making sure I had 90-degree corners) and then cut each square diagonally.

My oven end walls are made of .030″ styrene that are cut a scale 18′-0″ high and 31′-6″ long. I cemented two of the gussets to each end of the short wall, flush with the edge of the part. Once these had set, I positioned the end wall against the sidewall and cemented the two together. I repeated this step for the opposite end.

I set the entire assembly on the foundation, snug against the edges. Using the foundation as a guide, I cemented the rear wall to the end walls and gussets. After the cement set, I smoothed the visible end joints and cemented the whole assembly to the foundation. Additional interior bracing followed until the structure began to gain some rigidity.

I added an overlay of Holgate & Reynolds brick to cover both ends of the ovens. Then I cemented a strip of Evergreen no. 8610 (scale 6″ x 10″) along the top interior walls on both sides and both ends to help support the roof.

My roof is made of .040″ sheet styrene that is a scale 32 feet wide and long enough to cover both sets of ovens. This roof must be set in from the south side about .040″, while the opposite side should be flush with the north side of the ovens. The roof should also be set in .040″ from each end to leave a ledge that will be used to support the end decks.

**Fig. 8.** North door details include a circular access hatch, a pair of horizontal latch bars, and oven numbers. (Note that zeros are not used, as the ovens are built in groups of three.)

## OVEN DETAILING

Three scale 18″-diameter charging holes are needed over each oven (7′-6″ centers between ovens). The top of my ovens is covered with Holgate & Reynolds brick sheet. I cut the sheet into strips wide enough to cover two ovens and punched six scale 18″-diameter holes through it. A six-hole jig helped space these holes uniformly (fig. 9). I laminated the brick sheet to the oven tops, taking care to get everything aligned with the tall doors on each side.

The covers for the charging holes are disks of .020″ styrene with scale 6″-long handles made of Evergreen no. 100 (.010″ x .020″) strip. These covers are cemented into the openings so they're recessed into the brick surface. It's easier to cement the covers on top of the brick sheet, but that won't suggest as much depth to these details.

Gas inspection ports also belong on the top of the ovens (fig. 9). Mine are scale 6″ disks of .010″ styrene cemented to the brick sheet, in rows of four, centered over the space between ovens.

Figure 9 also shows the pair of rails mounted across the length of the ovens for the charging car to ride on. Mine are pieces of code 100 rail mounted on scale 24″ pads of Evergreen no. 8212 (scale 2″ x 12″) strip. The rail was mounted on the styrene pads with CA, then the pads were cemented to the tops of the ovens so the rails are gauged a scale 7′-3″ apart. ⚙

**Fig. 9.** The oven topside details include a firebrick deck, three rows of round charging hatches, four rows of gas inspection ports, and a pair of running rails for the charging Larry.

As the Davies Steel coke plant shows, part of the fun of modeling heavy industry comes from simulating different materials, the variety of roof angles, and the special equipment.

# The Davies Steel coke plant: Part 2

## Modeling the supporting structures

**BY DEAN FREYTAG**
**PHOTOS BY THE AUTHOR**

IN THE April MODEL RAILROADER, I introduced the HO scale Davies Steel coke plant and explained how coal is processed into coke. Then I described building the ovens in the main structure. This time I'll tell you about the supporting structures and how to model them. You may find it helpful to refer to the drawings in the first part.

### EXHAUST GAS SYSTEM

Building the exhaust gas system wasn't difficult. Figure 1 shows how I made these pieces from Plastruct parts. The bodies of my standpipes consist of five pieces: a scale 60″ length of TB-8 (1/4″) tubing; .020″ styrene disks a scale 21″, 24″, and 17″ in diameter; and a handle made of Evergreen no. 100 strip.

I cemented the 17″ disk to the bottom of the pipe and added the 24″ and 21″ disks to the top. Next, I rounded and tapered the handle a bit before cementing it to the top of the small disk. This procedure was repeated until I had a stand-

pipe assembly for each oven. Then I cemented a Plastruct TPS-8 stub-in tee to the side of each standpipe, spaced about a scale 3″ down from the top and at right angles to the operating handle.

The main collector pipe that runs along the top of the ovens is made of Plastruct TB-12 (3/8″) tubing. I made this in two pieces so the assemblies

would be easier to handle. For the connections into the collector main, I used Plastruct TPS-12 stub-in tees with the male ends removed and filed flat. Using the ovens as a gauge, I cemented the first tee in place and let it set hard. Then I secured the remaining tees and pressed the entire assembly on a flat surface to get perfect alignment between them.

**Fig. 1** STANDPIPE ASSEMBLY (all Plastruct items)

No scale

- Walkway
- VS-12
- TPS-12
- TB-12
- TB-12
- TPS-8
- 60″

**Fig. 2**

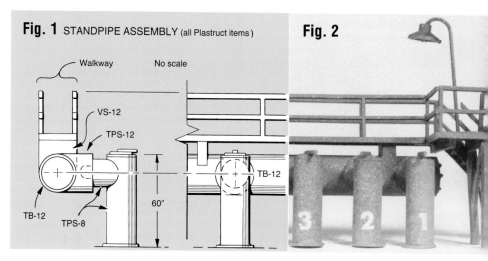

Once the collector assembly had set hard, I slipped the standpipe ends into the open ends of the collector tees, squared everything, and cemented them in position (fig. 2). A Plastruct F-4 breakout flange serves as the connection between my collector mains (fig. 3). A piece of .020″ sheet closes off the open end of the pipe. I used Plastruct VS-12 vessel saddles, spaced a scale 15 feet apart, to support the walkway that runs across the top of the collector main.

### GOVERNOR HOUSE

The gas collector main passes through a governor house at the west end of the ovens (fig. 4). This small building sits on an elevated platform of .030″ styrene that's a scale 8 feet deep and 12 feet wide. Two Plastruct B-6 (³⁄₁₆″) I beams support the long sides of the floor to strengthen the assembly. The elevated base of my structure was made from pieces of a Vollmer footbridge kit, but you could use Plastruct structural shapes.

I used a Plastruct E-12 elbow to bring the west end of the collector main up into the governor house, cutting a hole in the floor to accept it. An E-8 elbow and a short length of TB-12 tubing were used to simulate the outbound pipe on the north side that will eventually connect to a by-products plant. I made the bolting flange for the end of this pipe from a disk of .010″ styrene with eight no. 60 holes drilled around its circumference (fig. 5).

### WEST END CONTROL BUILDING

The control building is a simple two-story brick and concrete structure with a flat concrete roof. A stairway attached to one side provides access to the charging deck of the ovens, so I built this as a single assembly as shown in fig. 6.

The structure, including the roof, is made of Evergreen no. 4527 corrugated siding, using the dimensions shown in the coke oven plan. When I cut out the parts for the building, I made sure the east end door was positioned to provide

Fig. 4. Above: The collector main passes through the governor house mounted on the northwest corner of the charging deck. It is supported on a structural steel platform and detailed with an access stairway, a gutter strip above the doorway, and a light fixture to illuminate the area.

Fig. 5. Left: The collector main's connection to a future by-products plant is simulated with a Plastruct elbow, a short length of tubing, and a styrene bolting flange. This large pipe comes out of the floor beneath the governor house and is routed at a right angle to the collector main.

access to the catwalk on top of the collector main. The south side has a single doorway; the west end has a window.

The brick building is a scale 15 feet square, and it's made of .030″ sheet styrene. I made the .040″ styrene roof large enough to cover the top of the building as well as the stairwell area (including a .040″ overhang that fits into the notch on top of the west end of the oven wall). I covered the walls with Holgate & Reynolds brick and trimmed out the window areas. I made the ground-floor door from .010″ styrene trimmed with hinges and a latch. This door is flush-mounted on top of the brick with enough space beneath it to provide ground clearance.

I used Plastruct H-4 (¹⁄₈″) column for the vertical corner support and the horizontal beams under the top deck. The horizontal ties between the column and the building are pieces of Plastruct B-4

(¹⁄₈″) I beam (fig. 7). I added flange plates of .020″ styrene and nut-bolt-washers to simulate where they are bolted into the brick structure's wall. I cut an opening into the top deck near the oven wall and fitted the stairway as explained before.

Since this is a free-lanced building, a simpler solution would be to enlarge the control building so it runs completely across the end of the ovens. Then a small housing, with an angled roof, could be installed on the top deck to shelter the entrance to an internal stairway. If you do this, don't forget to add an exit door in the same corner at ground level.

### DUMP HOUSE

The dump house is a flat-roofed structure that covers the receiving end of the raw coal conveyor. I constructed mine over a cutout in the layout that simulates the receiving hopper (fig. 8). This

Fig. 3. A breakout flange and inverted pipe saddles are used to detail the collector pipe.

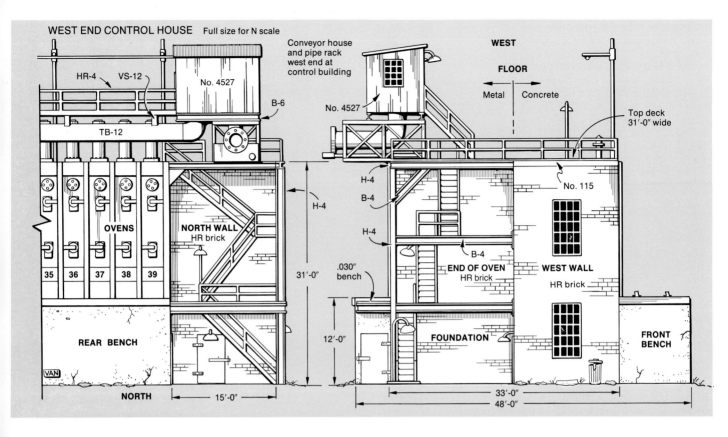

WEST END CONTROL HOUSE  Full size for N scale

HR-4    VS-12

No. 4527

B-6

TB-12

OVENS

NORTH WALL
HR brick

35  36  37  38  39

REAR BENCH

VAN

NORTH    |— 15'-0" —|

Conveyor house
and pipe rack
west end at
control building

No. 4527

WEST

FLOOR

Metal | Concrete

Top deck
31'-0" wide

H-4

H-4
B-4

H-4

No. 115

.030"
bench

B-4

END OF OVEN
HR brick

WEST WALL

HR brick

FOUNDATION

FRONT
BENCH

31'-0"

12'-0"

|— 33'-0" —|
|—— 48'-0" ——|

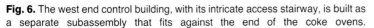

37  38  39

**Fig. 6.** The west end control building, with its intricate access stairway, is built as a separate subassembly that fits against the end of the coke ovens.

**Fig. 7.** Mounting flanges and nut-bolt-washer details are used to simulate joints between steelwork and masonry.

simple building is a scale 40 feet long, 16 feet wide, and 18 feet high, with end doorways 15 feet high and 12 feet wide. See fig. 9.

I used Evergreen no. 115 (.015" x .100") strip to form a slight lip around the edges of the roof and as lintels over the doorways. The balance of the structure was covered with Holgate & Reynolds brick sheet inside and out. A piece of Evergreen no. 118 (.015" x .188") strip was added around the base to simulate a concrete foundation. The flat concrete roof is scribed at 10-foot intervals, and the ventilators are made of plastic scraps and brass studs from a craft shop.

**CRUSHER HOUSE**

As the coal moves into the plant, it's conveyed into a 78-foot-high bunker. This structure, which is shown in fig. 10,

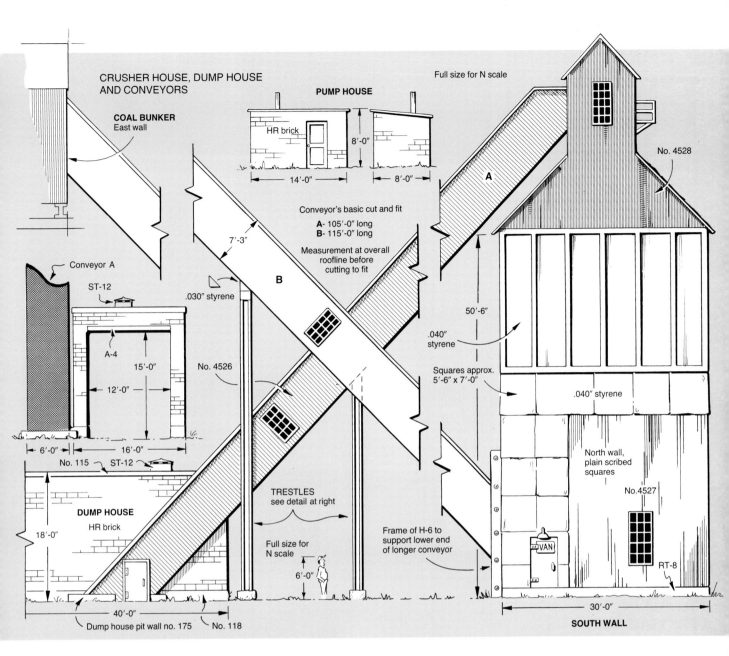

CRUSHER HOUSE, DUMP HOUSE
AND CONVEYORS

**COAL BUNKER**
East wall

Conveyor A

ST-12

A-4

15'-0"

12'-0"

6'-0" — 16'-0"

No. 115   ST-12

**DUMP HOUSE**
HR brick

18'-0"

40'-0"

Dump house pit wall no. 175   No. 118

**PUMP HOUSE**

HR brick

8'-0"

14'-0" — 8'-0"

Conveyor's basic cut and fit
**A**- 105'-0" long
**B**- 115'-0" long

Measurement at overall
roofline before
cutting to fit

7'-3"

B

.030" styrene

No. 4526

TRESTLES
see detail at right

Full size for
N scale

6'-0"

Frame of H-6 to
support lower end
of longer conveyor

Full size for N scale

A

No. 4528

50'-6"

.040"
styrene

Squares approx.
5'-6" x 7'-0"

.040" styrene

North wall,
plain scribed
squares

No. 4527

VAN

RT-8

30'-0"

**SOUTH WALL**

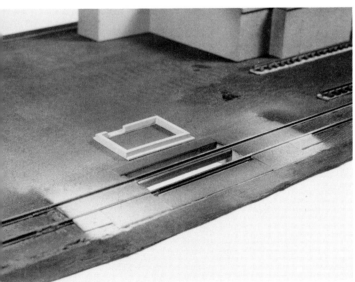

**Fig. 8.** A hole cut into the layout simulates the dump house pit. The rails are carried over the opening on paired lengths of I beam.

**Fig. 9.** The dump house is a simple masonry structure designed to cover the receiving end of the conveyor and help control coal dust.

103

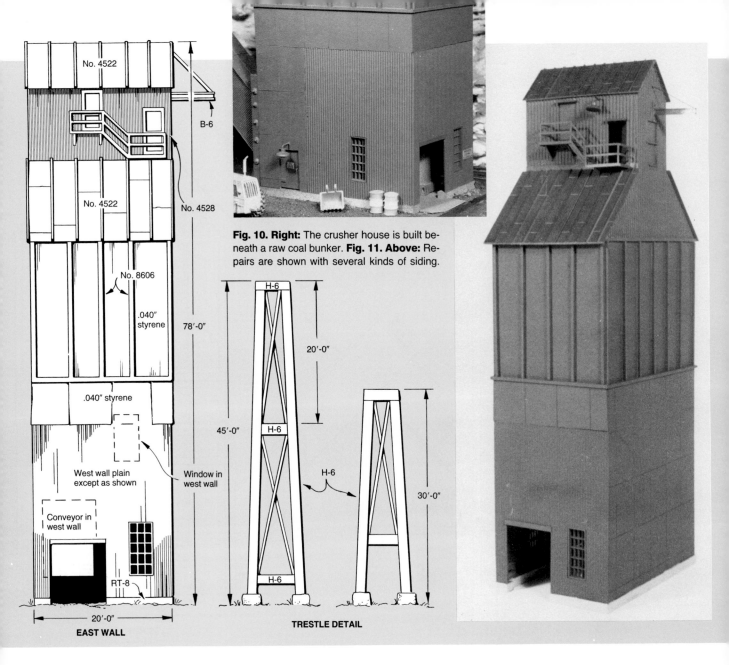

Fig. 10. Right: The crusher house is built beneath a raw coal bunker. Fig. 11. Above: Repairs are shown with several kinds of siding.

**EAST WALL**

No. 4522

B-6

No. 4522

No. 4528

No. 8606

.040″ styrene

78′-0″

.040″ styrene

West wall plain except as shown

Window in west wall

Conveyor in west wall

RT-8

20′-0″

**TRESTLE DETAIL**

H-6

20′-0″

H-6

45′-0″

H-6

H-6

30′-0″

H-6

is 20 feet wide and 30 feet long, with an enclosed base that helps contain the noise and protects the crushing machinery from the elements.

Most of this structure is made of .040″ sheet styrene, with the lower east end and 20 feet of the south wall being no. 4527 corrugated siding (fig. 11). These corrugated areas aren't necessary, but the different surface treatment suggests recent structural repairs.

The heavily reinforced coal bunker adds 20 feet to the height of the structure. In this case, I extended the side panels so they overlapped the ends by about a foot. I reinforced these joints with large strips of styrene cemented inside each corner. On the outside, I used Evergreen no. 8606 (scale 6″ x 6″) strips to simulate the vertical supports and capped them with no. 8608 (scale 6″ x 8″) strips to produce a shallow tee shape.

All the sidewalls in the top housing were cut from Evergreen no. 4528 metal siding. I cut the roofs at a 45-degree angle to conserve material. The cupola is a scale 10 feet wide; its roof peak is 26 feet above the top of the coal bunker. The location of the access doors and windows is arbitrary — just keep in mind where maintenance work must be performed.

You should include an access door with a small length of a B-6 I beam mounted over it. Such installations, common in heavy industry, enable replacement motors or other equipment to be lifted into position without a crane.

### CONVEYORS

Figure 12 shows the enclosed bucket conveyors, which are easy to construct. I made the sidewalls from Evergreen no. 4526 corrugated sheet cut into strips a scale 7′-3″ wide. (This height is the same width as my scale rule.) It's also a good idea to determine window locations and cut them in before the conveyor is assembled.

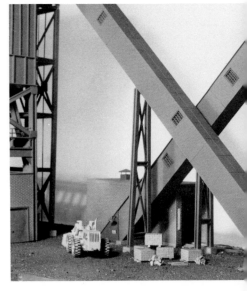

Fig. 12. Both angled conveyors have been fabricated from corrugated sheet styrene.

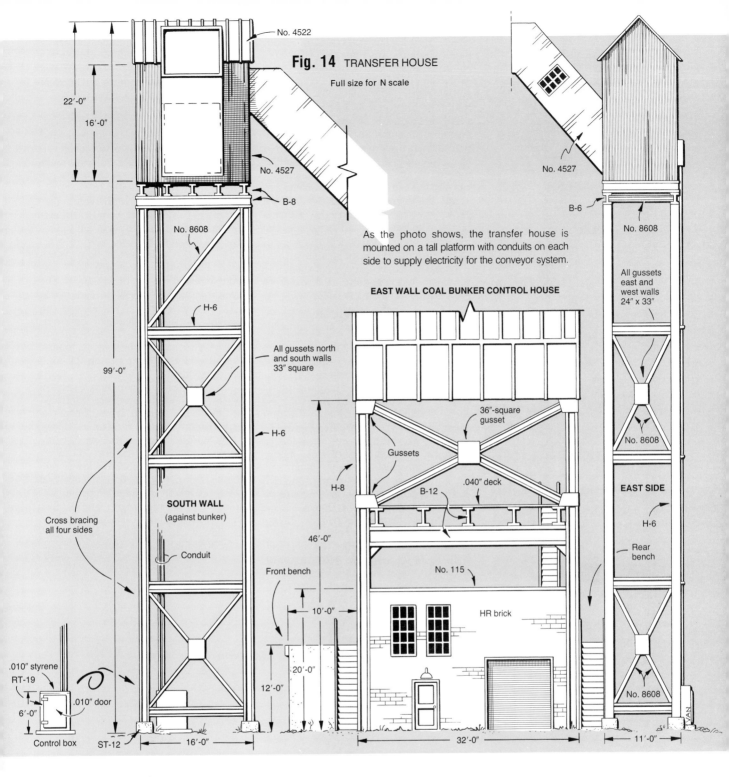

**Fig. 14** TRANSFER HOUSE

Full size for N scale

No. 4522

22'-0"

16'-0"

No. 4527

B-8

No. 8608

99'-0"

H-6

H-6

All gussets north and south walls 33" square

SOUTH WALL
(against bunker)

Cross bracing all four sides

Conduit

.010" styrene
RT-19

6'-0"

.010" door

Control box

ST-12

16'-0"

As the photo shows, the transfer house is mounted on a tall platform with conduits on each side to supply electricity for the conveyor system.

**EAST WALL COAL BUNKER CONTROL HOUSE**

36"-square gusset

Gussets

H-8

B-12

.040" deck

No. 115

HR brick

Front bench

46'-0"

10'-0"

20'-0"

12'-0"

32'-0"

No. 4527

B-6

No. 8608

All gussets east and west walls 24" x 33"

No. 8608

**EAST SIDE**

H-6

Rear bench

No. 8608

11'-0"

VAN

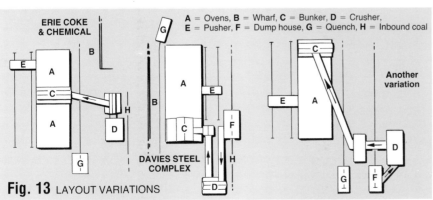

**ERIE COKE & CHEMICAL**

A = Ovens, **B** = Wharf, **C** = Bunker, **D** = Crusher,
**E** = Pusher, **F** = Dump house, **G** = Quench, **H** = Inbound coal

**DAVIES STEEL COMPLEX**

**Another variation**

**Fig. 13** LAYOUT VARIATIONS

I made the conveyor floors from .040" styrene cut to a 5'-6" width. The floor of the dump house to the crusher conveyor is 90 feet long, while that from the crusher to the storage conveyor is 115 feet long. In the process, I cut many 45-degree gussets to reinforce the walls.

My conveyor assembly began by cementing the floor inside one wall and then reinforcing it with a gusset applied every few inches. I cemented the second wall in place and reinforced it with gussets in contact with the first ones.

The roof of each conveyor was made of .015" sheet styrene scribed to simulate

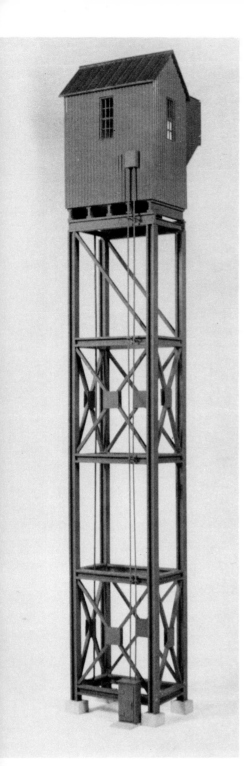

sheet metal. The intermediate conveyor supports are Plastruct H-6 (³/₁₆″) columns, with braces made of Evergreen no. 134 (.030″ x .080″) strip. My short trestle is a scale 30 feet tall, while the big one is 45 feet high.

All the top ends of my conveyors are anchored in holes cut into the building walls. Then I add a styrene strip across the underside of the conveyor near the top end to act as a keeper. That way I can slip the conveyor into the opening at about 90 degrees and bring it down gently to the proper angle. At this point, the keeper strip is inside the building, where it contacts the edge of the opening to retain the conveyor.

I detailed the bottom end of the lower conveyor with a simulated concrete foundation and an access door.

### TRANSFER HOUSE

A transfer house, at the top of the long conveyor, changes the direction of the coal transfer and guides it into the east end coal bunker via another short conveyor. In my installation, this point is next to the bunker, but this may be shifted around in almost any direction depending on the plant site. Figure 13 shows other arrangements. If a longer conveyor is used, the transfer house could be some distance from the bunker. It's a matter of form following function, so the supporting structures should be in logical and convenient places.

As fig. 14 shows, the transfer house consists of four walls made of Evergreen no. 4527 corrugated styrene, with roofs of their no. 4521 standing seam roofing. Both end walls are a scale 10′-6″ wide and 17′-0″ tall at the peak; the sidewalls are 17′-0″ tall and 16′-0″ wide. I put windows in the west and north walls, as the other two walls are occupied by the conveyors.

I built the tower with H-6 (³/₁₆″) columns for both the vertical supports and the horizontal bracing. The corner columns are a scale 70′-9″ tall, with crossbeams 13′-3″ wide on the sides and 7′-6″ wide across the ends. In effect the tower is four stories high, with cross bracing set into the first and third stories (a scale 16 feet apart). The cross bracing is Evergreen no. 8608 (6″ x 8″) strip — the 8″ dimension runs vertically. The center plates are .015″ styrene. I added single diagonals in the top story angling toward the conveyors.

Two Plastruct B-8 (¼″) I beams run the long way across the top of the tower. Five more pieces of the same beam run crosswise to support the transfer house. The base of the tower sits on 24″-high concrete pads.

Electrical conduits run up two sides of the tower to supply power for the transfer house machinery. I simulated the larger conduit, which runs up inside the tower, with a length of ³/₆₄″ wire, while the two outside conduits are .033″ wire. A bottom electrical control box was fabricated from a scale 6-foot section of Plastruct RT-19 rectangular tubing detailed with doors, hinges, and latches made of .010″ styrene. The entry box on the side of the transfer house is a scale 24″ x 30″ block of .060″ styrene. ⌀

This reinforced concrete quench tower extinguishes the fire as the final step in converting coal into coke at the HO scale Davies Steel coke plant.

# The Davies Steel coke plant: 3

## Modeling the east coal bunker and quench tower

### BY DEAN FREYTAG
#### PHOTOS BY THE AUTHOR

IN THE April and June issues of MODEL RAILROADER, I introduced the HO scale Davies Steel coke plant, explained the coke making process, and described how to build the ovens and some of the supporting structures. This time, I'll explain how to model the large coal bunker and the quench tower. You may find it helpful to refer to the drawings in the first part.

#### EAST COAL BUNKER

The large bunker at the east end of the facility stores prepared coal until it's needed to charge the ovens. Because of its size, this structure was built in two assemblies: the bunker (fig. 1) and supporting structure (fig. 2).

The bunker ends and sides are made of .030″ sheet styrene. Its shape is shown

in the coke oven drawing with rectangular sides a scale 30 x 32 feet. After cutting out the pieces, I used a hard pencil to mark the centers of the outside bracing on each panel. I cemented large reinforcing angles flush with the 30-foot edges of each side wall and added the ends that overlap the sides. After the assembly had set hard, I smoothed the corner joints with a flat file.

The outside bracing came next. I cemented in place the horizontal strip, made of Evergreen no. 135 (.030″ x .100″) styrene, that's 8 scale feet up from the bottom of the bunker. While it set, I cut 36 pieces of Evergreen no. 8408 (scale 4″ x 8″) strip for the vertical braces. I cemented them over the previously drawn center lines, taking care to keep them straight and square (the 4″ dimension is the cementing edge). I capped the lower braces with another horizontal strip of Evergreen no. 135. I repeated the procedure using strips of Evergreen

no. 8406 (scale 4″ x 6″), cut to fit the upper ends of the bin, and no. 8408 around the lower panel.

I measured the overall length and width of the bunker (including the side bracing) to determine the size of the floor. My floor extends beyond the sides of the bunker just enough to form the bottom flange around the bunker. The floor was made from .030″ sheet styrene and cemented in place.

Evergreen no. 4526 corrugated sheet was my choice for roofing on this bunker. I used no. 4527 corrugated sheet as sheathing for the clerestory housing. Its north wall is blank, but I did add windows and an access door to the south wall. An access door and small crane rail would be appropriate in the east wall. The corner trim pieces were Evergreen no. 8106 (scale 1″ x 6″) strip.

Installing the steps took a lot of cutting and fitting, but I like the result. (Less ambitious souls can provide access

**Fig. 1.** The east coal bunker was constructed as a subassembly that fits on top of the steel supporting structure built into one end of the ovens.

**Fig. 2.** A brick maintenance shop as well as a deck extension for the larry car were built into the supporting structure for the east coal bunker.

**Fig. 3. Upper right:** By building in subassemblies, it is much easier to add small details, like the stairways and railings, to very large models

**Fig. 4. Lower right:** Prepainting the small detail parts and brick panels makes it relatively easy to keep the prototype's neat appearance

with vertical safety-caged ladders.) I began by fitting only the platforms and stairs. A scale 36″-wide access platform on the side of the clerestory came first, and I worked down from there.

I held a section of Plastruct STA-4 stair in position and marked the length needed to reach the edge of the roof. Then I cut the stairway to size, filed the end smooth, and cemented its lower end to a scale 36″ x 66″ platform cut from .020″ styrene. This stair/landing assembly was then used to locate and add suitable bracing at the roof edge.

I anchored the stairway with lengths of Plastruct H-3 (³/₃₂″) column. A scale 10-foot length was mounted horizontally on the bunker wall 24″ below the roof edge. I also used two 5-foot columns to make the vertical supports and two pieces of no. 8406 (scale 4″ x 6″) for the outer angled braces. Then I mounted the stair assembly with a fast-setting CA (cyanoacrylate adhesive) to hold it until the cement had set. Last, I installed the stair and platform railings down to the lower landing.

I followed the same procedure to install the next stairway. Since it runs down along the bunker side, I used triangular brackets (attached to the vertical braces) to support the stairway and the corner landing. The last section brings the stairs to the bottom of the bunker (fig. 3). My bottom landing was then cut to fit whatever space remained to reach the corner.

The bunker is supported by six pieces of Plastruct H-8 (¹/₄″) column that measure a scale 45 feet long. This length provides a scale 15-foot clearance between the oven deck level and the bottom of the bunker for the charging car. I decided to include a brick structure beneath the bunker that would serve as a combination office, shop, and storage building (figs. 3 and 4).

I made the four side walls from .030″ styrene panels a scale 20′-0″ high and 14′-3″ wide. The two panels on the south side are plain; one on the north side has a window. These panels were cemented to the inside surfaces of the outer flanges with CA and allowed to set.

The east and west walls were also fabricated from .030″ styrene panels, though they are a scale 20 feet high and 28 feet long. The west wall is plain, while my east wall has two windows, a personnel door, and a 10 x 10-foot roll-up door (fig. 4). The roof is .030″ styrene scribed to represent reinforced concrete panels. I trimmed the roof edges with Evergreen no. 115 (.015″ x .100″) strip to give the roof a finished look.

Three pieces of Plastruct B-12 (³/₈″) I beam run across the space above the building to support the charging deck, as shown in fig. 4. I cut these parts to size, but didn't cement them to the vertical beams until I could make sure the deck height matched the oven deck (this dimension worked out to be a scale 4′-9″ above the roof on my model).

Five scale 49-foot lengths of B-12 I beam support the 28-foot-wide charging deck (made of .040″ sheet styrene). The beams were butted against the side of the coke oven assembly, then I measured the length of the deck required, including the extended lip that fits onto the small ledge at the top corner of the oven. The deck plate was trimmed to size.

Once the thickness of the deck assembly was known, I went back, positioned the supporting beams against the vertical columns, and cemented them in place. While the cement set, I cut .040″ gusset plates to fit beneath the beams as additional support. These triangular gussets are a scale 30″ on a side, with a 45-degree angle.

I fitted pieces of H-8 (¹/₄″) column to produce the long angle braces on each side and added .020″ gusset plates to secure them. The cross bracing on the end was B-6 (³/₁₆″) I beam, with gussets of .020″ styrene (fig. 5). I also added .020″ caps (scale 36″ square on the single beams, and 3 x 8 feet long at the center) to the tops of the vertical supports.

After cementing the bin in position, I

**Fig. 5. Above:** The large I beams that carry the charging deck are supported by crossbeams with triangular gusset plates at each leg.

**Fig. 6.** After mounting the subassemblies, the author fitted the intermediate access stair between the walkway and the bunker landing.

**Fig. 7.** The quench tower is made of heavily reinforced concrete to withstand the stresses created by the sudden temperature changes that occur when the hot coke is doused with water.

fitted the bottom stairway between the bunker and the walkway on top of the gas collector main. Figure 6 shows this stair assembly in position.

I decided to spray-paint the steelwork Pullman Green and the roof with a concrete color. Then I fitted Holgate & Reynolds brick sheet to the side panels of the lower building, spray-painted them with a dark-red brick color, and cemented them in place. I did the final cuts for the window and door openings after the brickwork was installed.

### QUENCH TOWER

Any coke plant requires a quench tower to douse the burning coke with a measured amount of water. This quick shower puts out the fire, but leaves the coke hot enough to dry itself out in a few minutes. Figure 7 shows my quench tower, which is an accurate replica of one built in 1925 for the Erie Coke & Chemical Co. of Fairport Harbor, Ohio.

The prototype quench tower is a poured concrete structure with fairly heavy reinforced walls to stand the

weight and temperature stresses. I fabricated the side walls from .030″ sheet styrene that I cut a scale 50 feet high and 47 feet long. The ends are also .030″ styrene, cut a scale 17 feet wide and 50 feet high. I cut the bottom 17 feet off each end and saved the cutoffs.

To thicken the end walls, I cemented pieces of no. 8608 (scale 6″ x 8″) strip as spacers (8″ side against the walls) at each side as well as in the center of the 17-foot-square cutoffs. These parts were cemented to the 30 x 50-foot end panels so the top and side edges lined up nice and square. This makes a wall that's a scale 15″ thick. I added a trim strip of Evergreen no. 147 (.040″ x .156″) flush with the bottom of the 17-foot panel and another across the bottom to produce a scale 6″ ledge (fig. 8).

I cemented the end walls inside the side walls, so the extra thickness was at the top, and made sure the corners were properly aligned. Scale 36″ triangular gussets were added immediately below the ledges to strengthen the corners.

After the joints had hardened, I cut

ten pieces of no. 8608 (scale 6″ x 8″) strip to a scale 17-foot length. One piece was added (8″ side against the side wall) to strengthen each corner. Then I added the remaining spacers, three to a side, spaced at even intervals. The inside walls were made of .030″ styrene, cut a scale 17 feet high, with the length carefully trimmed for a good fit. Additional strips of no. 147 (.040″ x .156″) styrene were used for trim at the bottom of the upper inside walls, thereby matching the ends.

Once the core had set hard, I laminated additional layers of .020″ styrene onto the outside surfaces to represent the different concrete thicknesses. This should be done one layer at a time.

Next, I cut the top strips a scale 36″ and 42″ wide with a little extra length. To install the 42″ trim, I aligned and cemented the first horizontal strip in place at a left-hand corner so it was overhanging to the right. The next wall's trim strip was cemented in place flush against the back of the overhang. I repeated this procedure all the way around the building. After the cement had hardened, I trimmed the overhangs flush to get smooth corner joints.

My end laminations were done next, with two vertical strips (a scale 24″ wide) cemented flush with the corners. The horizontal door lintels were also fitted and cemented on at this time.

Moving back to the sides, I cut the bottom lamination strips a scale 48″, 42″, and 36″ wide. The 48″ width was applied to both sides, overlapping the ends for later trimming. While the cement hardened, I cut a pair of scale 30″ strips and a pair of 24″ strips for the side wall verticals. These strips were fitted between the horizontals and cemented in place on both sides.

Then I added the balance of the trim strips, working one layer at a time and cleaning up the corner joints as I progressed. I found the corner strips had to

---

**Fig. 8** CONSTRUCTION

**ADD THICKNESS TO SIDE AND END WALLS**

Scale 15″ thick

6 x 8s

Top is open and vents steam when coke is quenched

Side of tower

Wooden suppress rests on this edge

Evergreen no. 147 trim strips

**Fig. 9.** A measured amount of water is pumped into the tank between cycles so that it can quench the next batch of coke.

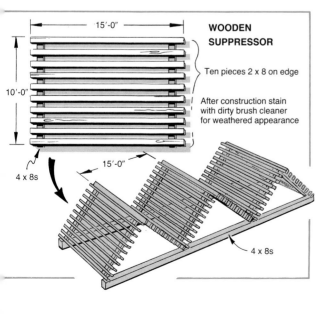

**WOODEN SUPPRESSOR**

15'-0"

10'-0"

Ten pieces 2 x 8 on edge

After construction stain with dirty brush cleaner for weathered appearance

4 x 8s

15'-0"

4 x 8s

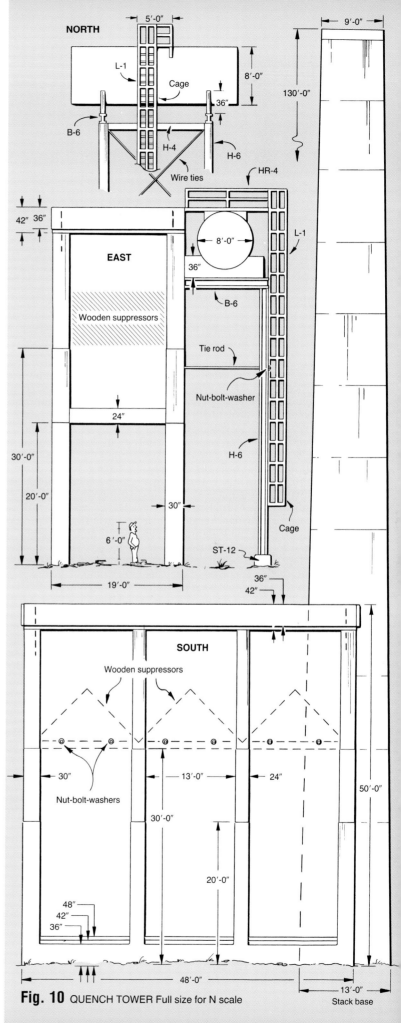

**NORTH**

5'-0"

L-1

Cage

8'-0"

36"

B-6

H-4

H-6

Wire ties

**EAST**

42" 36"

Wooden suppressors

24"

30'-0"

20'-0"

6'-0"

30"

19'-0"

HR-4

8'-0"

36"

L-1

B-6

Tie rod

Nut-bolt-washer

H-6

Cage

ST-12

36"
42"

9'-0"

130'-0"

**SOUTH**

Wooden suppressors

30"

13'-0"

24"

Nut-bolt-washers

30'-0"

50'-0"

20'-0"

48"
42"
36"

48'-0"

13'-0"

Stack base

**Fig. 10** QUENCH TOWER Full size for N scale

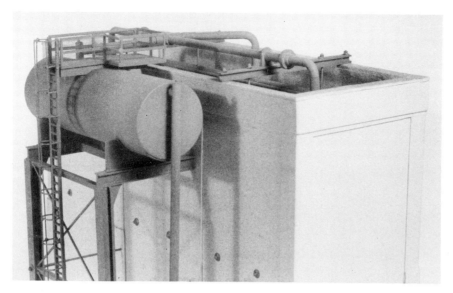

**Fig. 11.** The multiple pipe spray rack is made of a combination of Plastruct piping parts, styrene tubing, and plastic sprues supported by rods hung from beams running across the top of the tower.

be widened to get the proper fit as the trim thickness builds. Figure 9 shows the layers I added. My last step (after all the joints had hardened) was to fill any remaining cracks with body putty, let it set hard, and sand smooth. While sanding I softened the corners of the trim to look more like poured concrete.

I finished the top of the walls with a scale 18″-wide coping made of .040″ styrene. This was cemented in place so there was an approximate scale inch or so of overhang all the way around the building. The last step for this assembly was a spray coat of concrete paint.

A set of wooden suppressors occupies the top of the tower to capture most of the moisture and particulates (crud) from the cloud of steam emitted during quenching. I simulated these with three tent-shaped basswood grids.

I made six identical 10 x 15-foot grids from scale stripwood (fig. 10). Each grid required 12 slats fabricated from 2″ x 8″ (a scale 15 feet long) that are held together with a 10-foot-long 4″ x 8″ support mounted about a foot in from each end. I pinned masking tape, face up, on a board to hold the slats on edge. Then I applied wood glue along the wide side of each support, set them in place, and put a weight on top of the assembly to hold everything while the glue set.

As the grids dried, I cut two 45-foot pieces of 4″ x 8″ stripwood to use as mounting surfaces. I then cemented each pair of grids in place on 15-foot centers so they looked like a row of tightly spaced pup tents. I stained this woodwork with my dirty brush cleaner to get a weathered appearance.

Next, I added a row of six large nut-bolt-washer castings, painted a rust color, across each side of the tower a scale 32 feet from the bottom. I used these castings to simulate the mounting bolts that support the prototype suppressors. I dropped the suppressors in place and secured them to the ledges with CA.

The horizontal water tank, shown in fig. 9, is a scale 8 feet in diameter. Plastruct TB-32 (1″ diameter) tubing was used for the tank, with the ends and saddles of .030″ styrene. I made the 38-foot-tall uprights from H-6 (3/16″) column. These were spaced to match the middle concrete columns on the side of the tower. I made the horizontal spacers from Plastruct T-3 tees (trimmed to fit inside the flanges of the columns). The cross bracing is .033″ brass wire or Evergreen no. 220 .035″ styrene rod.

Both supporting beams are 12-foot

lengths of B-6 (3/16″) I beam. The top platform is a scale 60″ square butted against a 30″ x 72″ extension (to reach the ladder). I made my platform railing from Plastruct handrail parts; the scale 24″-high footings were Plastruct ST-12 square tubing that had .010″ styrene caps.

The spray rack in the top of the tower is free-lanced from lengths of plastic sprue hung from a pair of H-4 (1/8″) columns (figs. 11 and 12). It took only a few moments to find a convenient size and length of sprue with sufficient connecting "pipes" to simulate the prototype connections down into the spray heads. I trimmed and filed the extra nubs. To suspend the spray bars, I drilled matching mounting holes into the pipes and columns so the spray units could be suspended on .035″-diameter rods. I used large nut-bolt-washer castings to cover the holes through the beams so the whole assembly looks like it's been bolted together.

A small pump house sits alongside the tower to replenish the water between quench cycles. Shown in fig. 7, it's 12 feet long and 8 feet wide, with an 8-foot-high front wall and a 7-foot-high rear wall. An access door in the front wall is the only opening. I built the pump house of .040″ styrene covered with Holgate & Reynolds brick sheet. The roof is leftover corrugated siding.

I free-lanced the water piping, using Plastruct TB-4 (1/8″ diameter) tubing, E-4 90-degree elbows, and EL-4 45-degree elbows. The most visible vertical pipe leaves the pump house and runs along the end of the tank, where it terminates in a 90-degree elbow.

One short pipe connects the bottom center of the tank with the middle panel of the tower just below the tank. Another pipe leaves the top of the tank and runs across the top of the tower, where it joins a lengthwise distribution pipe. Beyond the pipe junction, the crosswise pipe turns 45 degrees to the right and then 90 degrees down to reach another lengthwise distribution pipe. I used breakout flanges to simulate joints in the pipes and large nut-bolt-washer assemblies to close the open ends of the pipe tees.

The scale 130-foot-tall concrete stack is a block of hardwood turned on a lathe. I marked it at 10-foot intervals to represent form joints and added plastic laminations at the top and bottom to dress it up. The stack is mounted on the layout with a 2½″-long wood screw to prevent it from wobbling.

### CONCLUSION

This completes the steel mill structure itself. Part 4 of the series, dealing with the rolling stock that serves the complex, was published in the October 1994 issue of MODEL RAILROADER Magazine. ⚙

**Fig. 12.** Wooden baffles help separate dirt from the steam that rises off the hot coke.

# H. M. Young fruit-packing shed

During the peak of the Tokay grape shipping season in the 1940s and 1950s, the H. M. Young shed accommodated five 40-foot refrigerator cars at a time.

## This narrow structure was once used for transferring boxes of grapes to railroad cars

**BY EUGENE S. MARTIN**
**PHOTOS BY THE AUTHOR**

IN 1971 I measured and photographed a structure in Lodi, Calif., that makes an excellent lineside structure for a model railroad. The long narrow proportions (216 x 16 feet) make it ideal for the many narrow confines found on most layouts. Even as a condensed-length model, such as the one I built in HO scale, the structure retains the characteristics of the real building.

The shed was built in 1941 by Harl M. Young, a local grape grower, as a shipping center. It was one of more than a dozen such sheds in the area. The land around Lodi is ideal for growing Tokay grapes, and 90 percent of the Tokays grown in the United States come from this central-California town. At one time the area shipped more than 6000 carloads every year.

At the beginning of the grape season the first few carloads were sent via REA (Railway Express Agency) reefers in the Southern Pacific *San Joaquin Daylight* passenger trains, headed for premium eastern markets.

At the peak of the season, 160 refrigerator cars a day would be shipped from the area. The Southern Pacific railroad handled cars for H. M. Young and adjacent firms, while the Central California Traction crews worked other area spurs. A company such as H. M. Young might move out five to ten cars a day. The boxes of grapes were brought in from the vineyards by truck to be shipped by rail. The truck side of the platform has 6 x 8 bumpers to protect the structure. At one end of the building there were office areas and a lavatory facility.

During the grape season there would be two crews busy at the shed. One crew unloaded boxes of grapes from the trucks and loaded them into waiting refrigerator cars. The second crew assembled boxes which were sent back to the vineyards in the same trucks that delivered the grapes.

The structure has timber construction, is composed of 24-foot-long bays, and is covered with corrugated sheet metal.

The H. M. Young grape-loading facility, as seen here in 1971 when Eugene Martin photographed it, obviously had not been used for some time since the doors are boarded up and some of the windows are broken. Also, a Firestone store occupies part of the space that had been the truck unloading area. A model scene simulating this condition could be used on a contemporary model railroad.

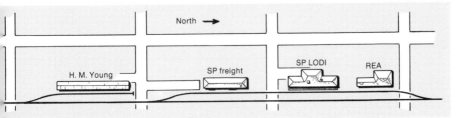

113

Both the enclosed and open areas of the HO model have been shortened. This side, and the open end of the dock, have 6 x 8 timber bumpers to keep trucks from damaging the structure. Eugene applied scale-size corrugated metal sheet material to the roof and the enclosed shed area.

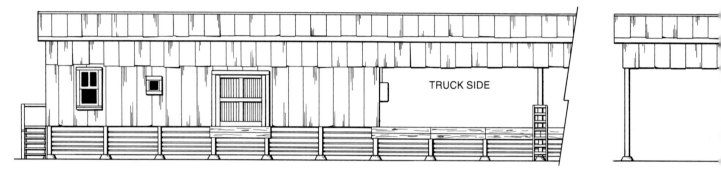

TRUCK SIDE

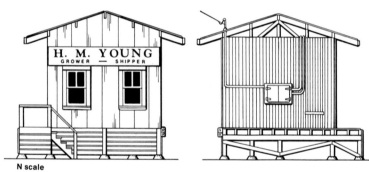

N scale

## MODELING NOTES

For my HO layout, which is modeled after the SP in Lodi, I made the open length of the structure shorter by two 24″ bays and cut the closed area in half. My model was constructed with Northeastern scale lumber, including a board-by-board 2 x 6 floor. First I constructed 6 roof and floor support sections and 8 intermediate floor supports (6 x 6 posts and 6 x 10 beams). Next, I joined these assemblies with 3 x 8 roof beams and 2 x 10 floor joists. The deck, 1 x 6 horizontal planks, and other wood details were added to this unit.

I used Campbell corrugated metal material for the sides and roof, painted a bluish gray to simulate the weathered look of the real shed. The roof sheets scale 2 x 12 feet, and the sides sheets are 2 x 4 and 2 x 9 feet. These pieces are overlapped and applied in the same arrangement as the real material.

Four Alexander Scale Models no. 2515 windows, one no. 2513 transom window, and one no. 2405 door were required for the condensed version. I prepainted these parts brown before installing them. I stained the wood portions weathered gray and added a few touches of rust-colored paint here and there to the corrugated material as a highlight.

The model siding will handle three 40-foot or two 50-foot refrigerator cars at a time. Simulate a pile of dirt at the end of the spur for a car stop.

You can also model this structure as a contemporary small industry. Many older structures have

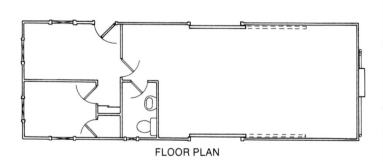

FLOOR PLAN

been taken over by a more modern concern, or even two. Often original old signs, such as the one on the end of the structure, can still be seen, even if in greatly weathered condition and sometimes half covered with the present establishment's sign. ۵

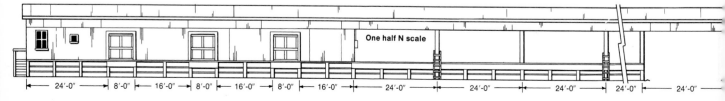

One half N scale

|←— 24'-0" —→|← 8'-0" →|←— 16'-0" —→|← 8'-0" →|←— 16'-0" —→|← 8'-0" →|←— 16'-0" —→|←— 24'-0" —→|←— 24'-0" —→|←— 24'-0" —→|← 24'-0" →|←— 24'-0" —→|

The track side of Eugene Martin's model shows some broken horizontal planks under the deck, a condition that exists on all sides of the real H. M. Young structure. While the length is condensed, the model structure follows the cross section construction features of the real building.

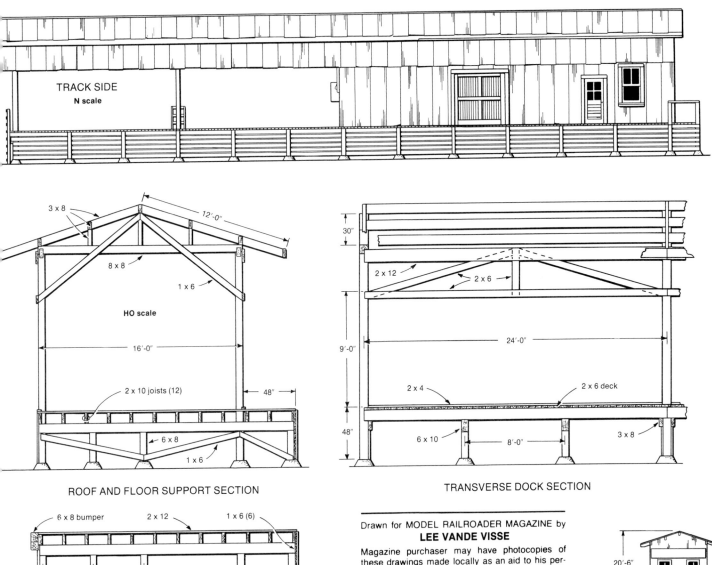

TRACK SIDE
**N scale**

**3 x 8**
**12'-0"**
**8 x 8**
**1 x 6**
**HO scale**
**16'-0"**
**2 x 10 joists (12)**
**48"**
**6 x 8**
**1 x 6**

ROOF AND FLOOR SUPPORT SECTION

**30"**
**2 x 12**
**2 x 6**
**9'-0"**
**24'-0"**
**2 x 4**
**2 x 6 deck**
**48"**
**6 x 10**
**8'-0"**
**3 x 8**

TRANSVERSE DOCK SECTION

**6 x 8 bumper**   **2 x 12**   **1 x 6 (6)**
**48"**  **48"**   **6 x 6**

INTERMEDIATE FLOOR SUPPORT SECTION

Drawn for MODEL RAILROADER MAGAZINE by
**LEE VANDE VISSE**

Magazine purchaser may have photocopies of these drawings made locally as an aid to his personal or commercial modelmaking or tool designing, but purchaser does not have the right to distribute copies of the drawings to others.

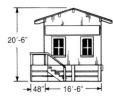

**20'-6"**
**48"** **16'-6"**

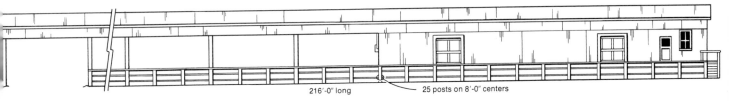

216'-0" long    25 posts on 8'-0" centers

Paul A. Erler

# Dolese Sand & Gravel

This basic industry can be made to fit almost any layout

## BY GORDON ODEGARD
### PHOTOS BY THE AUTHOR

THE Dolese Sand & Gravel at Crusher, Okla., is a vast complex. If you tried to model it full scale it would occupy most of the space Andy Sperandeo used for the first stage of the Washita & Santa Fe layout. With some selective compression and attention to detail and character, we can make a facsimile that will be as impressive as the real complex. See The Washita & Santa Fe Ry., Part 1, page 91, in the January 1982 MODEL RAILROADER for a photo of the DS&G installation.

In spite of the fact that there is a 28"-wide area for the crusher on the W&SF, the elements require some careful fitting. In planning I had to allow for the Arbuckle Mountains along the backdrop and two mainline tracks in the foreground. I made a full-size drawing of the area on paper and sketched in the plan of the model crusher, adjusting the size to fit the space. Then I developed rough elevation drawings. The resulting model complex is shown at the start of this article and on the cover. Refer to these two photos for the shape and position of the parts frequently during the construction.

Don't be too concerned with following my dimensions exactly. I use a lot of *just about* this size, and *cut and fit* when I build large model buildings. The important thing is that the proportions are good and that the general character of the real structure is evident in the finished model. I think I achieved that end.

### GETTING STARTED

I used styrene to construct the HO scale buildings for the Dolese Sand & Gravel, along with some cast plastic parts, and pieces from plastic structure kits. The crusher is covered with Campbell no. 803 corrugated aluminum siding. Evergreen Scale Models makes styrene corrugated siding, and you might want to consider using it in place of plain sheet styrene with the metal overlay. Both materials have good and bad points. The foil aluminum siding has the best appearance, but getting it to stick to styrene isn't easy. The corrugated styrene is easier to use, but it's harder to get a realistic finish.

Figure 1 shows the dimensions of my model, along with an exploded view of the crusher house. Remember to allow for the thickness of the material where necessary. The length of the east wall, for instance, is a scale 55 feet minus twice the material thickness. I used .060" sheet styrene. Commercially available sheets are 6" x 10½", and these have to be spliced together to make the full-size walls. Apply a ½"- to 1"-wide splice to the inside of the junction of the two

pieces. For large models such as this one, I purchase 4 x 8-foot sheets of styrene from a local plastics purveyor. I can lay out all the elements full size without splices. Unfortunately large sheets of styrene are generally available only in large metropolitan areas. Some purveyors will not sell retail, but give it a try.

Lay out all the pieces, including the window and door openings, with a 12" combination square, a 24"-long straight-edge, and a soft (no. 2) pencil. Get a supply of sharp knife blades and single-edge razor blades. Change blades often and throw the dull ones into the trash barrel where they belong. A dull cutting edge will cause the blade to wander as you score the material and will make a high raised groove on each side of the score or cut.

Start out by scoring the outlines of the pieces with a knife. Position a score line over the edge of the workbench and briskly snap the piece off. Smooth the edges with a sharp 10" mill file and square the edges at the corners.

At this point I assemble all of the main pieces with masking tape to be sure they fit. See fig. 2. It's common to find a piece that's too long or too short, or a joint that doesn't quite fit the way you had planned. No problem. Simply alter as necessary, trimming or adding filler as needed. Styrene is a versatile material, and patches

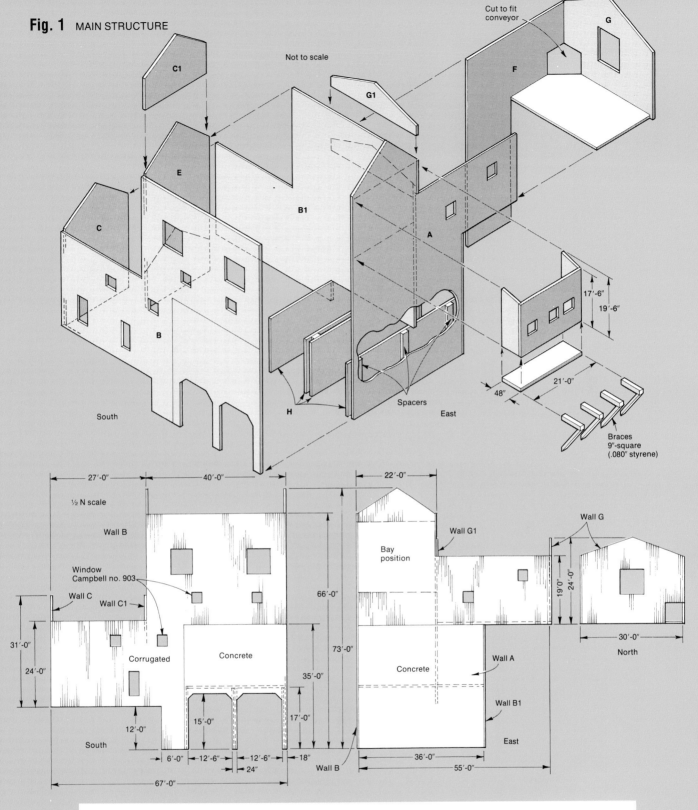

**Fig. 1** MAIN STRUCTURE

Not to scale

Cut to fit conveyor

G

F

G1

C1

E

B1

A

C

B

South

H

Spacers

East

Braces
9"-square
(.080" styrene)

17'-6"

19'-6"

48"

21'-0"

½ N scale

27'-0"

40'-0"

22'-0"

Wall G

Wall B

Bay
position

Window
Campbell no. 903

Wall C

Wall C1

66'-0"

Wall G1

24'-0"

19'-0"

30'-0"

North

31'-0"

24'-0"

Corrugated

Concrete

73'-0"

Concrete

Wall A

35'-0"

Wall B1

12'-0"

15'-0"

17'-0"

South

6'-0"

12'-6"

12'-6"

18"

Wall B

36'-0"

East

24"

55'-0"

67'-0"

**Bill of materials**

**Campbell Scale Models**
2 no. 255 lampshades (pkg.)
6 no. 803 corrugated
aluminum (pkg.)
3 no. 903 windows (pkg.)
1 no. 924 smoke jack

**Grandt Line**
1 no. 5021 door
1 no. 5031 windows (pkg.)

**Evergreen Scale Models**
1 no. 164 .080" x .080" strip
1 no. 186 .125" x .125" strip
1 no. 4061 siding
1 no. 9020 .020" sheet
3 no. 9040 .040" sheets
6 no. 9060 .060" sheets

**Miscellaneous**
1 K&S Engineering no. 137 $^{7}/_{16}$"
brass tube
1 Kibri no. 9950 cement plant kit
2 Faller no. B-2151 N scale
overpass kits
1 Plastruct no. 103 $^{3}/_{32}$"
plastic tube
2 Vollmer no. 5211 bridge kits
6" .030" wire (lampshade staffs)

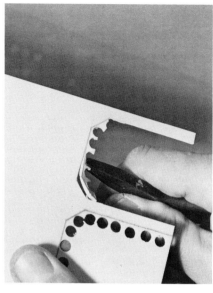

**Fig. 2.** Test fit all of the crusher walls, and then check alignment before cementing them together.

**Fig. 3.** Score the openings, drill holes around inside edges, and break off the excess with a pliers.

**Fig. 4.** Assemble the crusher on a piece of plate glass and use machinist's squares to align parts.

and mistakes can be easily covered up.

Score all the openings and drill holes in the areas to be removed. I use a flat-nose pliers to break off the excess material. See fig. 3. File the open edges smooth and square where necessary. Openings for window and door castings can be a little irregular, as long as the castings completely cover the openings. Fit the window castings, but do not install them yet. I'm sure the back sides of the real structures have windows and doors, but since none of these can be seen when the model is installed on the layout, I didn't make any.

## WALL ASSEMBLY

Assemble the main walls on a flat surface. I use a piece of plate glass and combination squares. See fig. 4. You can use one such square and draftsman's triangles or blocks of wood with one square (90 degree) corner. I like to use several combination squares as shown, since they are heavy enough to hold the pieces in place until the cement dries. I use Testor's Cement where I need a little time to position the parts and Tenax 7R where I want a faster bond. When the assembly is dry, scrape and file panel junctions smooth.

The lower portions of the crusher are concrete. See fig. 1. To simulate a rough concrete finish such as is found on structures of this type, I first roughened the areas with coarse sandpaper. I then applied a coating of Testor's Cement to the surfaces, allowed it to dry slightly, and then went over the areas with a wire brush. These surfaces will be painted later on.

Make roof panels from .040"-thick styrene sheet. They should have a scale 9" overhang all around. I haven't provided any exact dimensions. It's better that you cut and fit these pieces to suit your

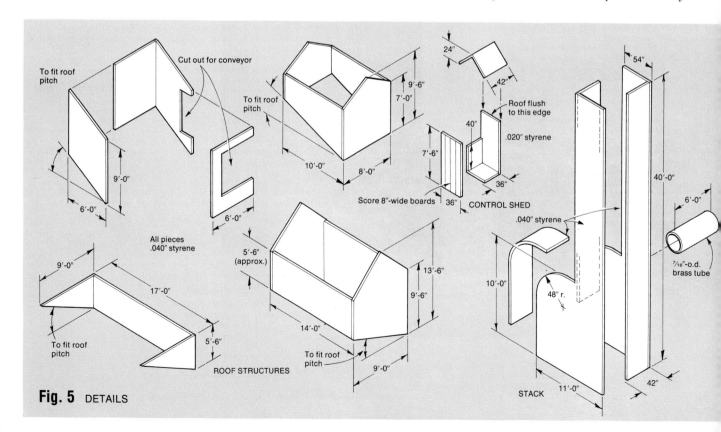

**Fig. 5** DETAILS

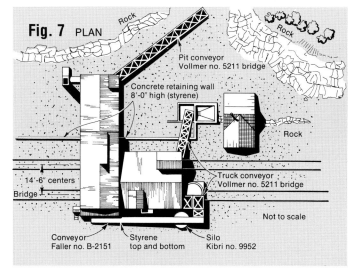

**Fig. 6.** The storage bin is made out parts from a Kibri no. 9950 Cement Plant kit.

model. Bevel the edges at the center junction of the peaked roof pieces. I suggest you laminate a .060″-thick piece to the underside of all the large roof panels for added strength. Even a thick styrene sheet can warp and give the structure a Chinese pagoda look. These reinforcing panels should be narrow enough to fit inside the walls. Attach the roof panels to the walls.

### ROOF STRUCTURES, CONTROL SHACK, AND STACK

There are four small structures on the crusher roofs. See fig. 5. I used .060″-thick styrene for the walls and .040″ for the roofs. Custom-fit these pieces to the roof pitches and affix these elements to the main roof panels.

I used .040″ styrene for the stack. It rests on the south end of the crusher. Do not attach the stack as yet. The control shed is made from .020″-thick styrene. Do not attach it to the crusher either.

### STORAGE BINS AND CONVEYORS

Make the storage-bin complex a separate assembly to fit under the end of the crusher. See fig. 6. The two large circular bins on the north end of the crusher are about 14 feet in diameter and 12 feet high. You can make these bins and the supporting structure, or you can use parts from a Kibri plastic no. 9950 Cement Company kit as I did. This kit has enough material for the two large bins, the small tank, the supporting structures, and some steps and ladders. The top of the Kibri cement plant silo (part no. F 107) is the bottom piece on the crusher bin. There is only one of these in the kit, so use it on the most northerly bin where it will show.

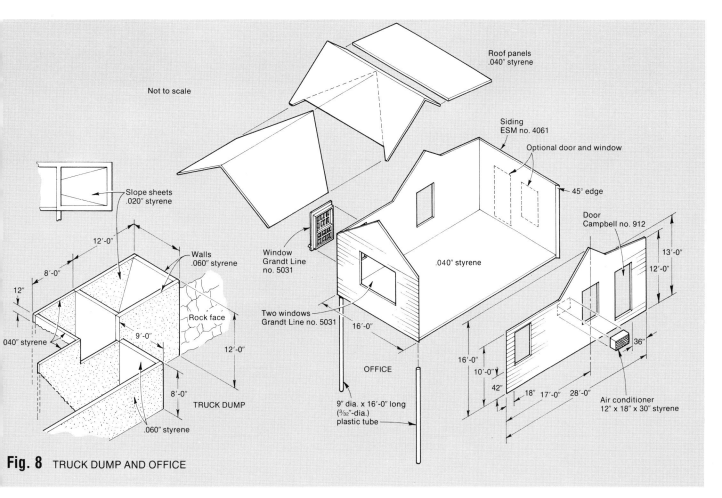

**Fig. 8** TRUCK DUMP AND OFFICE

The platform under the tanks is cut from .060″-thick styrene.

The supporting structure corner braces are X-braces from the Kibri kit with one leg cut off. The step assembly is from the Kibri kit also. The conveyors across the top of the tanks and out to the main elevator are made from a Vollmer no. 5211 bridge kit. Conveyors can be made using plastic or metal structural shapes if you feel ambitious. The two beams supporting the overhanging portion of the one conveyor are scale 8 x 8 styrene.

The long slanting conveyor on the east wall is made from a Faller B-2151 Pedestrian Overpass kit. The top and bottom are .040″ styrene sheet. It is 3 feet wide and 4′-3″ high. The triangular elevator supports are to be added later. They are cut from parts in the Faller kit.

The smaller tank is Kibri part no. F 103. It is 8 feet in diameter and 12 feet high, and rests on a .020″-thick by a scale 10-foot-square piece of styrene. The piping is made from casting sprues.

The rear portion of the crusher plant is a scale 12 feet above grade. I used Styrofoam sheet to provide a subgrade. Position the crusher in its setting and mark the location of the truck hopper and the pit conveyor. See fig. 7. Determine the length of the pit and truck conveyors. None of the element positions are critical. The conveyors are made from Vollmer no. 5211 Bridge kits. Cut openings in the crusher structure as necessary. See figs. 1 and 7.

### CORRUGATED SIDING

I applied Campbell no. 803 corrugated aluminum siding to the crusher walls and roofs. I used rubber cement to laminate the aluminum to the various panels. Apply a thin coat to the exposed side of the wall or roof panel and to one side of the aluminum. When the cement is almost dry, press the pieces together. Walthers Goo or a two-part epoxy are other adhesives that can be used. Unfortunately all the adhesives I've found are just adequate for joining these two materials.

Real corrugated siding is applied in overlay sections that are 4 feet wide and from 8 to 24 feet long. You can follow this procedure, or you can apply as large a sheet as you can get. I used the later technique. Start applying the aluminum at the bottom edge of each wall or roof panel. Overlap the rows about 6 scale inches. Allow the material to overhang sides and top, then trim it flush to the roof all around.

Cut scale 12″-wide cap pieces, score them lengthwise down the middle, and apply them to the peaks of the roofs. Allow the panels to be a little bit battered and beat-up looking. Most structures of this type show the effects of time and use and are pretty well battered. Apply the siding right over all openings. I cut these out with a *sharp* knife after all the siding had been applied and the adhesive was dry.

The sliding doors in the north and south walls are just rectangular pieces of aluminum siding cemented to the walls. The overhead tracks are .030″-square styrene. Cement the Campbell no. 902 windows in place.

### CRUSHER ASSEMBLY

Now is the time to attach the main elevator and the storage bins to the crusher. Refer to the photos of the finished crusher plant and figs. 6 and 7. Cement the storage bins in place under the north end of the crusher. Cut three triangular braces (from Faller B-2151 kit) to support the slanting elevator and cement this assembly in place. Cut two delivery chutes a scale 11″ square (.125″ x .125″ styrene) and attach them from the east wall to the main conveyor. Also attach the vertical elevator from the Kibri cement plant kit and connect it to the crusher roof with a scale 11″-square styrene piece.

Attach the control shed to the south wall of the crusher, with the floor about 7 feet off the ground, and fit a set of steps (about 10 treads' worth) from the pieces in the Kibri no. 9950 kit. There will be a rise in the ballast grade to meet the bottom step when the model is in place.

### PAINTING

I sprayed the concrete portions of the crusher with my own special Floquil paint mix. It has 6 parts no. 11 Reefer White, 2 parts no. 85 Antique White, and 1 part no. 82 Concrete. I also applied a light irregular coat of Floquil no. 144 Platinum to the corrugated siding. I left the storage bins and conveyor pieces the color they were cast in. Paint the styrene top and bottom to the slanted elevator black to match the color of the cast sides. Paint the stack Floquil Rust outside and Grimy Black inside the top.

### OFFICE AND TRUCK HOPPER

The dimensions and materials for the office and the truck hopper are shown in fig. 8. I used Evergreen Scale Models no. 4061 styrene siding for the walls of the office and .020″-thick styrene for the roof. The roof panels should overhang the walls about a scale 9″. The roof is masking tape, applied in scale 36″-wide strips. I found a source of black masking tape, and it is superior to the common tan masking tape, which often doesn't take paint too well. Paint the walls Antique White. The truck hopper is painted concrete color. Add some Cambell no. 255 light shades at various places around the crusher. Paint the inside of the reflector white, and the outside green.

### DETAILS AND INSTALLATION

Before the crusher plant elements are all set in place, everything should be weathered. Add a few rust spots to the corrugated material with paint or powdered chalk, and a few spots of thinned Grimy Black around the conveyor and elevator machinery. Finally, dust the entire model with Floquil Antique White.

Figure 9 shows the pieces in place on the layout. I used white glue to fasten them to the layout. The Arbuckle Mountains don't show in this photo, but they should be added, and the background scenery finished before the crusher plant is secured in position.

Construct an 8-foot-high retaining wall as shown in figs. 7 and 9. I used .060″-thick styrene. Paint it concrete color and weather it with Antique White. I used Highball Limestone ballast around the crusher, affixed with matte medium.

All that needs to be added now are a small four-wheel mechanical switching locomotive, dump trucks, a crane, figures, and some litter in the form of broken machinery parts and boards. The complex can be made to fit most model railroads by altering the size and locations of the elements. ⊙

**Fig. 9.** Add an 8-foot-high retaining wall after the building elements are in place. In addition to weathering the model with some rust and grease spots, coat everything off-white to represent rock dust.